Treating Transgender Children and Adolescents

Extremely gender variant children and adolescents (minors), increasingly referred to as 'trans' or 'transgender children', are small in number. In recent years, their situation has become highly sensationalized, whilst the matter of how to best treat them remains an area of controversy. A growing body of research supports emerging treatment approaches, but more research is still needed to answer a host of questions: Do trans minors have a psychiatric disorder or a normal variation of gender presentation? Should treatment be aimed at helping them accept the bodies into which they were born or should parents, clinicians and schools accommodate their wishes of transition? At what age should transition begin? What are the implications – physical, psychological, social and ethical – of various treatment approaches?

The first part of this volume explores different clinical approaches to transgender minors in the USA and abroad. The second part contains responses to these approaches by commentators from various fields including biology, child psychiatry, civil rights activism, ethics, law, gender studies, queer theory and psychoanalysis. The work will be an invaluable source for parents and families looking at how to proceed with a trans child, as well as clinicians seeking to make appropriate referrals.

This book was originally published as a special issue of the *Journal of Homosexuality*.

Jack Drescher, MD, is Clinical Associate Professor at New York Medical College, USA. He is President of the Group for Advancement of Psychiatry and a member of DSM-5 Workgroup on Sexual and Gender Identity Disorders, and the WHO Working Group on (ICD) Classification of Sexual Disorders and Sexual Health. Previous publications include *Psychoanalytic Therapy and the Gay Man* (1998). He is Emeritus Editor of the *Journal of Gay and Lesbian Mental Health*.

William Byne, MD, PhD is Associate Professor at Mount Sinai School of Medicine, USA. He is Director of the Laboratory of Neuroanatomy and Morphometrics, and Chair of the American Psychiatric Association Task Force on Treatment of Gender Identity Disorder.

Treating Transgender Children and Adolescents

An Interdisciplinary Discussion

Edited by

Jack Drescher and William Byne

Routledge
Taylor & Francis Group

LONDON AND NEW YORK

First published 2013
by Routledge
2 Park Square, Milton Park, Abingdon, Oxfordshire OX14 4RN

Simultaneously published in the USA and Canada
by Routledge
711 Third Avenue, New York, NY 10017
First issued in paperback 2014

Routledge is an imprint of the Taylor and Francis Group, an informa business

British Library Cataloguing in Publication Data
A catalogue record for this book is available from the British Library

ISBN 978-0-415-63482-3 (hbk)
ISBN 978-1-138-84477-3 (pbk)

Typeset in Times New Roman
by Taylor & Francis Books

Publisher's Note

The publisher would like to make readers aware that the chapters in this book may be referred to as articles as they are identical to the articles published in the special issue. The publisher accepts responsibility for any inconsistencies that may have arisen in the course of preparing this volume for print.

Contents

CONTENTS

Citation Information

The chapters in this book were originally published in the *Journal of Homosexuality*, volume 59, issue 3 (March 2012). When citing this material, please use the original page numbering for each article, as follows:

Chapter 1
Introduction: The Treatment of Gender Dysphoric/Gender Variant Children and Adolescents
Jack Drescher and William Byne
Journal of Homosexuality, volume 59, issue 3 (March 2012) pp. 295-300

Chapter 2
Clinical Management of Gender Dysphoria in Children and Adolescents: The Dutch Approach
Annelou L. C. de Vries and Peggy T. Cohen-Kettenis
Journal of Homosexuality, volume 59, issue 3 (March 2012) pp. 301-320

Chapter 3
Psychological Evaluation and Medical Treatment of Transgender Youth in an Interdisciplinary "Gender Management Service" (GeMS) in a Major Pediatric Center
Laura Edwards-Leeper and Norman P. Spack
Journal of Homosexuality, volume 59, issue 3 (March 2012) pp. 321-336

Chapter 4
From Gender Identity Disorder to Gender Identity Creativity: True Gender Self Child Therapy
Diane Ehrensaft
Journal of Homosexuality, volume 59, issue 3 (March 2012) pp. 337-356

Chapter 5
A Comprehensive Program for Children with Gender Variant Behaviors and Gender Identity Disorders
Edgardo Menvielle
Journal of Homosexuality, volume 59, issue 3 (March 2012) pp. 357-368

Chapter 6
A Developmental, Biopsychosocial Model for the Treatment of Children with Gender Identity Disorder
Kenneth J. Zucker, Hayley Wood, Devita Singh, and Susan J. Bradley
Journal of Homosexuality, volume 59, issue 3 (March 2012) pp. 369-397

Notes on Contributors

Clinical Contributors

Susan J. Bradley, MD founded the Gender Identity Service for children and adolescents at the Centre for Addiction and Mental Health in Toronto in 1975. She was the Chair of the Subcommittee on Gender Identity Disorders for DSM-IV.

Peggy T. Cohen-Kettenis, PhD is Professor of Medical Psychology and Director of the Center of Expertise on Gender Dysphoria, at the VU University Medical Center, Amsterdam, the Netherlands. She is a registered clinical psychologist and psychotherapist who, from 1987 to 2002, initiated at the Department of Child and Adolescent Psychiatry of the University Medical Center Utrecht the first outpatient clinic for children and adolescents with gender problems and intersex conditions in Europe. She is the chair of the APA DSM-5 subworkgroup on GID.

Laura Edwards-Leeper, PhD is an Assistant in Psychology at Children's Hospital Boston and an Instructor in Psychology at Harvard Medical School, USA. She is the clinical psychologist on the Gender Management Service (GeMS) at Children's Hospital where she completes comprehensive psychological evaluations with transgender patients to help determine whether a medical intervention is in their best interest. She is also involved with various GeMS research endeavors.

Diane Ehrensaft, PhD is a developmental and clinical psychologist in the San Francisco Bay Area who specializes in assessment, consultation and psychotherapy with gender nonconforming children and their families. She serves on the faculty of the Psychoanalytic Institute of Northern California and is a steering committee member of an emergent Northern California pediatric gender clinic without walls. She is also a board member of Gender Spectrum.

Edgardo Menvielle, MD, MSHS is Associate Professor of Psychiatry at George Washington University, USA, and staff Psychiatrist at Children's National Medical Center in Washington DC where he is the director of the Gender and Sexuality Development Program which provides clinical services and training for child psychiatry and psychology trainees and students. Since 1998, he has focused on childhood and adolescent gender and sexuality issues, has authored several articles on topics related to childhood gender variance and is conducting research on the experience of families with a child with gender variance.

Devita Singh, MA is a doctoral candidate in clinical child psychology at the University of Toronto, Canada. Her doctoral dissertation pertains to a long-term follow-up study of boys with gender identity disorder (co-authored with Zucker et al).

Norman P. Spack, MD is an Associate in Endocrinology at Children's Hospital Boston and Assistant Professor of Pediatrics at Harvard Medical School, USA. In 2007 he co-founded Children's Hospital's unique 'Gender Management Service', an interdisciplinary clinic for Disorders of Sex Development and Transgenderism. He was a member of the Endocrine Society's international task force that published 'Clinical Guidelines for Endocrine Treatment of Transsexual Persons' in September 2009.

Annelou L. C. de Vries, MD is a child and adolescent psychiatrist working at the VU University Medical Center in Amsterdam, the Netherlands. She works as a consultation-liaison psychiatrist in the Pediatrics department, focusing on sick children with mental health problems. In addition she does clinical work with gender dysphoric adolescents and is also engaged in a PhD study evaluating their psychological functioning and the long term outcome of GnRH analogue treatment.

Hayley Wood, PhD, C.Psych. is a psychologist in the Gender Identity Service at the Centre for Addiction and Mental Health in Toronto, Canada. She is currently conducting empirical research on the relationship between gender identity disorder and autism-spectrum disorders (co-authored with Zucker et al).

Kenneth J. Zucker, PhD, is the Head of the Gender Identity Service, Child, Youth, and Family Program at the Centre for Addiction and Mental Health in Toronto, and Professor, Department of Psychiatry, University of Toronto, Canada. He is the Chair of the DSM-5 Workgroup on Sexual and Gender Identity Disorders. Since 2002, he has been the Editor of *Archives of Sexual Behavior*.

Discussants

Anne Fausto-Sterling, PhD is the Nancy Duke Lewis Professor of Biology and Gender Studies in the Department of Molecular Biology, Cell Biology and Biochemistry, Brown University, Providence, Rhode Island, USA. She is the author of *Sexing the Body: Gender Politics and the Construction of Sexuality* (2000) and *Myths of Gender: Biological Theories about Women and Men* (1987).

Shannon Price Minter, JD is Legal Director of the National Center for Lesbian Rights, an advocacy organization for lesbian, gay, bisexual, and transgender people. He is a founding board member of the Transgender Law and Policy Institute and has authored a number of books and articles about transgender issues, including *Transgender Rights* (2006) and *Family Law for Lesbian, Gay, Bisexual and Transgender People* (2010).

D. Townsend Reiner, MA is a private Research Consultant with a background in philosophy, the sciences, and mathematics from St. Johns College in Annapolis, Maryland, USA, and a Master's of Arts from Boston College in Political Science and Philosophy. He has consulted in the pediatric world for the Child Research Section of the National Center for Disaster Mental Health Research as well as for the Psychosexual Development Clinic of the University of Oklahoma Health Sciences Center in Oklahoma City, Oklahoma, USA.

William G. Reiner, MD is Professor of Pediatric Urology and Child and Adolescent Psychiatry, University of Oklahoma Health Sciences Center, USA. He has 18 years of experience in pediatric urological surgery and 15 years experience in clinical and research child and adolescent psychiatry. In both careers he has had extensive experience working with children with disorders of sex development and, in child psychiatry, with gender dysphoric children as well.

David C. Rettew, MD is Associate Professor of Psychiatry and Pediatrics at the University of Vermont College of Medicine, USA, where he is the Training Director of the Child Psychiatry Fellowship Program. His main research interest is in the area of child temperament and its interface with psychiatric disorders across development.

David Schwartz, PhD is a psychoanalyst in private practice in Westchester and Manhattan. He serves on the editorial boards of the *Journal of Gay and Lesbian Mental Health* and *Psychoanalysis, Culture and Society.*

Edward Stein PhD, JD, is Vice Dean, Professor of Law, and Director of the Program in Family, Law, Policy, and Bioethics at Cardozo School of Law in New York City, USA. He is the author of *The Mismeasure of Desire: The Science, Theory and Ethics of Sexual Orientation* (1999) and *Without Good Reason: The Rationality Debate in Philosophy and Cognitive Science* (1997) and has written dozens of law and philosophy articles and chapters relating to sexual orientation, gender, family law, science, and ethics. He is an Adjunct Professor of Law at New York University, USA.

Introduction

The Treatment of Gender Dysphoric/ Gender Variant Children and Adolescents

JACK DRESCHER, MD
New York Medical College, New York, New York, USA

WILLIAM BYNE, MD, PhD
Mount Sinai School of Medicine, New York, New York, USA

We were both honored and intrigued when John Elia invited us to guest edit an issue of the *Journal of Homosexuality* on any subject of our choice. We decided to invite contributions from diverse clinicians who describe their approach to gender dysphoric/gender variant children and adolescents as well as several discussants to comment on those clinical approaches with a focus on the philosophical and ethical issues they raise.

One of us (Drescher) has been serving for several years as a member of the DSM-5 Work Group on Sexual and Gender Identity Disorders (WGSGID) and was recently appointed to serve on the World Health Organization's Working Group on the Classification of Sexual Disorders and Sexual Health for the ICD-11. The other (Byne) recently chaired an American Psychiatric Association (APA) Task Force on the Treatment of Gender Identity Disorder whose charge was to perform a critical review of the literature on the treatment of Gender Identity Disorder (GID) at different ages and to present a report to APA's board of trustees. The report would include an opinion as to whether or not there is sufficient credible literature to take the next step and develop treatment recommendations. This report (Byne et al., in press) was approved by the APA's board of trustees in September 2011 and will be published in the *Archives of Sexual Behavior* and available through the APA's Web site.

We were not entirely surprised by the task force's findings. Although the current state of research is sufficient to support evidence-based psychiatric guidelines for the treatment of gender dysphoric/gender variant (GID/GV) in adults, and while the task force noted several areas of clinical consensus regarding the treatment of GID/GV in children and adolescents, there is clearly a current lack of consensus regarding fundamental issues in treating these age groups. These issues include realistic and ethical treatment goals as well as questions regarding effective and ethical methods of treatment to achieve them.[1]

As Drescher (2010) previously noted, the APA's 2008 announcement of the appointment of the DSM-5 WGSGID generated several controversies in the lesbian, gay, bisexual, and transgender (LGBT) community (Chibbaro, 2008; Osborne, 2008) and, shortly afterward, these controversies were taken up by the mainstream media as well (Carey, 2008). One contentious issue, that "clinical efforts with gender variant children aimed at getting them to reject their felt gender identity and to accept their natal sex were unscientific, unethical, and misguided" (Drescher, 2010, p. 428), was only briefly mentioned in Drescher's otherwise exhaustive review. However, the following questions were left unanswered, hopefully to be addressed in future discussion:

- Are all presentations of gender variance in children nonpathological?
- Is the psychological distress associated with gender incongruence in children the result of internal processes or unaccepting social responses?
- Is it possible to clinically distinguish a pathological gender identity disorder of childhood (GIDC) from normative gender atypical behavior of children who may or may not grow up to be gay or transgender?
- Given that most cases of childhood gender incongruence do not persist into adulthood, are there subtypes of GIDC? If so, can they be distinguished from each other?
- Does empirical research support the claim that clinical interventions with gender variant children can prevent persistence of gender incongruence into adolescence and adulthood? If so, is it advisable or ethical to treat children in order to prevent adult transsexualism?
- To whom does it matter if a child grows up either gay or transgender?
- Does the current state of empirical research support treating prepubescent children with hormone blockers to prevent the onset of puberty and the facilitation of transition in later life? Does such treatment in and of itself increase the likelihood of persistence?
- What of the gender variant child whose social environment both accepts and encourages an early transition but may be unaware that the child, unwilling to disappoint, has had a change of heart (P. T. Cohen-Kettenis, personal communication)?
- Who should be designated as the best advocates for gender variant children? Parents? Teachers? Government agencies? Mental health professionals? Adult transgender activists? Queer theorists?
- These and many other questions are not easily answered and all will require further study as well as thoughtful analysis and discussion (Drescher, 2010, p. 454).

With APA revising the *Diagnostic and Statistical Manual of Mental Disorders* (4th ed., text rev; *DSM-IV-TR*; APA, 2000) and considering the possibility of drafting treatment recommendations, and with the World Health Organization in the midst of revising the International Classification of Diseases (ICD), we, as guest editors, decided to venture on a scholarly exploration of some of the clinical controversies surrounding the assessment and treatment of children and younger adolescents with gender dysphoria (GD) as well as of children referred by their caregivers due to perceived gender variance (GV). While adults with GD/GV can make decisions on their own behalf, we see a lack of consensus among clinicians regarding the most basic issues of treatment goals and approaches to treatment of children that can pose a difficult dilemma for parents seeking to make the best decisions for their children. One goal of this issue is to assist caregivers who face this dilemma by providing authoritative detailed descriptions of the various treatment goals and approaches to treatment of children together with several scholarly comparative analyses of these various approaches.

Finally, why the use of the "GD/GV" terminology? As Meyer-Bahlburg (2010) notes, "The nomenclature in the area of gender variations continues to be in flux, in regard to both the descriptive terms used by professionals, and, even more so, the identity terms adopted by persons with GIV [Gender-Identity-Variants]" (p. 461). For example, the DSM-5 WGSGID initially proposed that the designation "GID" be replaced in the *DSM-5* by "Gender Incongruence" but currently proposes that it be replaced by "Gender Dysphoria." In order to give our contributors free rein, we placed no restrictions on their use of terminology and only asked that they be clear and consistent in defining their usage.

THE 5 CLINICAL ARTICLES

In putting together this special issue of the *Journal of Homosexuality,* we invited several clinicians who are currently working directly with children and younger adolescents to draw on their own clinical experience and to present their clinical and theoretical points of view, providing illustrative examples where possible. Citation of published data to support the clinicians' perspective was encouraged; however, given the limits of empirical research in this area, this was not always possible.

The clinical articles, in alphabetical order by first author, are as follows:

- "Clinical Management of Gender Dysphoria in Children and Adolescents: The Dutch Approach," by Annelou L. C. de Vries and Peggy T. Cohen-Kettenis
- "Psychological Evaluation and Medical Treatment of Transgender Youth in an Interdisciplinary 'Gender Management Service' (GeMS) in a

Major Pediatric Center," by Laura Edwards-Leeper and Norman P. Spack

- "From Gender Identity Disorder to Gender Identity Creativity: True Gender Self Child Therapy," by Diane Ehrensaft
- "A Comprehensive Program for Children with Gender Variant Behaviors and Gender Identity Disorders," by Edgardo Menvielle
- "A Developmental, Biopsychosocial Model for the Treatment of Children with Gender Identity Disorder," by Kenneth J. Zucker, Hayley Wood, Devita Singh, and Susan J. Bradley

We asked the clinical contributors to consider the following specific issues as they pertain to GD/GV in children and younger adolescents. However, this was not presented as a rigid guideline and all of the contributors were told they could organize their remarks in any way they deemed appropriate.

- What constitutes an assessment?
- On what basis is it decided that treatment is indicated?
- What is the disposition of referred cases for which no clinically significant GD/GV is observed?
- When treatment is indicated, what are the rationale and goals for treatment, and, as specifically as possible, how does treatment proceed?
- How are the relative risks and benefits of treatment as well as the impact of treatment on outcome explained to caregivers?
- Is prevention of adult transsexualism a reasonable treatment goal, and given the low frequency with which GID persists into adulthood, how is it possible to determine the efficacy of treatment in attaining that goal?
- What are the risks and benefits for using hormonal blockers to delay the onset of puberty in GD/GV children or to block the progression of puberty in adolescents? What is the rationale for offering or withholding such treatment?
- To what extent should clinicians engage in modifying the social environment of GD/GV children, and what are appropriate interventions with parents, schools, and communities?
- What constitutes a successful outcome? What constitutes a treatment failure?
- Further, in reviewing the clinical articles, the issue was raised regarding lack of insurance coverage for GID diagnoses as well as the obstacles this creates for providing children and adolescents with appropriate treatment.

We were aware from our own reading and professional experience that there are philosophical disagreements among contemporary clinicians who treat GD/GV children. We asked that such disagreements not be part of the clinical articles as we wished to leave the argument to the discussants (see below). The clinical contributors were simply asked to make an affirmative case for their own approach without arguing with any approaches with which they disagreed. While this instruction proved difficult to follow, as editors, we did not allow any reference to disagreements of one clinician with another to make its way into the issue you are reading.

THE DISCUSSANTS

Our goal was to invite discussants who had no prior history of writing in the area of GD/GV per se, but who might hopefully bring a range of expertise as well as fresh insights to issues pertaining to gender, research and bioethics. We asked a number of colleagues whose training and professional interests cover a wide range of disciplines (child and adolescent psychiatry, ethics, gender studies, law, LGBT civil rights, molecular biology, pedagogy, pediatric urology, pediatrics, philosophy, psychology, and psychoanalysis) to contribute a discussion of the clinical articles. Six were able to provide discussions within our publication timeframe:

- "The Dynamic Development of Gender Variability," by Anne Fausto-Sterling
- "Supporting Transgender Children: New Legal, Social, and Medical Approaches," by Shannon Price Minter
- "Thoughts on the Nature of Identity: How Disorders of Sex Development Inform Clinical Research about Gender Identity Disorders," by William G. Reiner and D. Townsend Reiner
- "Apples to Committee Consensus: The Challenge of Gender Identity Classification," by David C. Rettew
- "Listening to Children Imagining Gender: Observing the Inflation of an Idea," by David Schwartz
- "Commentary on the Treatment of Gender Variant and Gender Dysphoric Children and Adolescents: Common Themes and Ethical Reflections," by Edward Stein

This issue concludes with summaries of what we believe is known and what we have yet to learn about minors with GD/GV, their families, their treatment, and their surrounding cultures. It is our hope that this issue will not only fill in a much-needed gap in thoughtful discussions of a complex issue, but that it will also serve as a springboard for future discussions aimed at improving the quality of care and wellbeing of gender variant individuals. We sincerely wish to thank all of our contributors, both the clinicians and the discussants, for the generosity they have exhibited in sharing their clinical expertise and thoughtful commentaries. We hope, by participating in this project, that they have learned something as well.

NOTE

1. Nevertheless, the task force concluded that sufficient clinical consensus exists for the development of consensus psychiatric recommendations for the treatment of GD/GV in children and adolescents.

REFERENCES

American Psychiatric Association. (2000). *Diagnostic and statistical manual of mental disorders* (4th ed., text rev.). Washington, DC: Author.

Byne, W., Bradley, S., Green, R., Coleman, E., Eyler, A. E., Menvielle, E., Meyer-Bahlburg, H. F. L., Pleak, R. R., & Tompkins, D. A. (in press). Report of the American Psychiatric Association task force on treatment of gender identity disorder. *Archives of Sexual Behavior*.

Carey, B. (2008, December 18). Psychiatrists revising the book of human troubles. *New York Times*, pp. A1, A20.

Chibbaro, L. (2008, May 30). Activists alarmed over APA: Head of psychiatry panel favors "change" therapy for some trans teens. *Washington Blade*. Retrieved from Washingtonblade.com http://www.washingtonblade.com/2008/5-30/news/national/12682.cfm

Drescher, J. (2010). Queer diagnoses: Parallels and contrasts in the history of homosexuality, gender variance, and the *Diagnostic and Statistical Manual* (*DSM*). *Archives of Sexual Behavior*, *39*, 427–460.

Meyer-Bahlburg, H. F. (2010). From mental disorder to iatrogenic hypogonadism: Dilemmas in conceptualizing gender identity variants as psychiatric conditions. *Archives of Sexual Behavior*, *39*, 461–476.

Osborne, D. (2008, May 15). Flap flares over gender diagnosis. *Gay City News*. Retrieved from *Gay City News* http://gaycitynews.com/site/news.cfm?newsid=19693908&BRD=2729&PAG=461&dept_id=568864&rfi=6

Clinical Management of Gender Dysphoria in Children and Adolescents: The Dutch Approach

ANNELOU L. C. DE VRIES, MD, PhD and
PEGGY T. COHEN-KETTENIS, PhD

VU University Medical Center, Amsterdam, the Netherlands

The Dutch approach on clinical management of both prepubertal children under the age of 12 and adolescents starting at age 12 with gender dysphoria, starts with a thorough assessment of any vulnerable aspects of the youth's functioning or circumstances and, when necessary, appropriate intervention. In children with gender dysphoria only, the general recommendation is watchful waiting and carefully observing how gender dysphoria develops in the first stages of puberty. Gender dysphoric adolescents can be considered eligible for puberty suppression and subsequent cross-sex hormones when they reach the age of 16 years. Currently, withholding physical medical interventions in these cases seems more harmful to wellbeing in both adolescence and adulthood when compared to cases where physical medical interventions were provided.

The first specialized gender identity clinic for children and adolescents in the Netherlands opened its doors at the Utrecht University Medical Center in 1987. The number of applicants was initially low: No more than a few children and adolescents were referred to the clinic annually. In 2002, the clinic moved to the VU University Medical Center in Amsterdam and is now

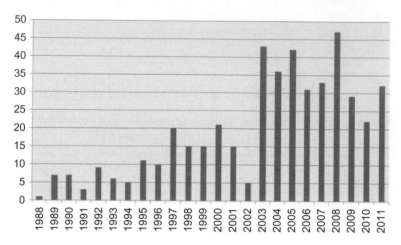

FIGURE 1 Referred children, Dutch Gender Identity Clinic, 1987–2011.

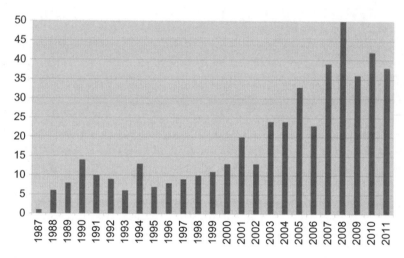

FIGURE 2 Referred adolescents, Dutch Gender Identity Clinic, 1987–2011.

part of the Center of Expertise on Gender Dysphoria. Compared to the early years, the number of referrals increased considerably. To date, more than 400 children and an almost equal number of adolescents have attended the gender identity clinic (see Figures 1 and 2).

Between 2004 and 2009, an average of 40 children and 40 adolescents registered per year for the first time at the clinic with a mean age of 8.0 and 14.3 years, respectively. In the past decade, 12- to 18-year-old adolescents have been attending the clinic in ever greater numbers and at ever younger ages (see Figures 2 and 3).

When the gender identity clinic for children and adolescents first opened, there were no diagnostic guidelines, no Dutch language screening instruments, and no guideline or protocol for dealing with gender

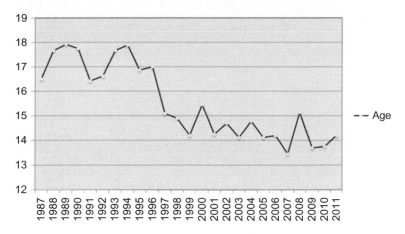

FIGURE 3 Mean age of referred adolescents, 1987–2011.

dysphoria at an early age. A great deal has been accomplished in this field in the past three decades. In addition to the increasing numbers of referrals, the care for these gender dysphoric children and adolescents has also experienced growth. Over the course of years, diagnostic protocols for children under 12 years, as well as adolescents from 12 to 18 years, of age have been constructed (Cohen-Kettenis & Pfäfflin, 2003; Delemarre-van de Waal & Cohen Kettenis, 2006), screening and diagnostic instruments have been developed, and there are now specific approaches for both age groups.

These are not isolated developments: Outside of the Netherlands, even more experience has been gained and knowledge has expanded in the field of juvenile gender dysphoria. Various international treatment guidelines have been developed (de Vries, Cohen-Kettenis, & Delemarre-van de Waal, 2007; Di Ceglie, Sturge, & Sutton, 1998; Hembree et al., 2009; World Professional Association of Transgender Health, WPATH, 2011).

Especially with regard to the clinical management of gender dysphoria in adolescents, the Netherlands has pioneered and played a leading role internationally. The "Dutch protocol" has become proverbial in this field. Various publications have demonstrated the efficacy of parts of this approach (Cohen-Kettenis & van Goozen, 1997; de Vries, 2010; de Vries, Steensma, Doreleijers, & Cohen-Kettenis, 2010; Smith, van Goozen, & Cohen-Kettenis, 2001), although the protocol has also been subject to criticism (Korte et al., 2008).

As a likely result of the professional and media attention to the Dutch approach, there is an increasing clinical interest in the rationale and description of the ways gender dysphoria in children and adolescents is managed in the Netherlands (Kreukels & Cohen-Kettenis, 2011). However, to date such a description did not exist. In this article, we will, therefore, give an account of our diagnostic and treatment protocols, which differ for children and adolescents. Before proceeding, we will dwell shortly on the context of views on etiology and gender development that have contributed to developing the Dutch approach. This discussion of the context is by no means complete.

CONTEXT

Etiology

No unequivocal etiological factor determining atypical gender development has been found to date. The most extreme form of gender dysphoria, Gender Identity Disorder (GID) in the current *Diagnostic and Statistical Manual of Mental Disorders* (American Psychiatric Association, 2000) is most likely a multifactorial condition in which psychosocial as well as biological aspects play some role. In recent years, a great deal of attention has been paid to biological theories (for an overview, see Meyer-Bahlburg, 2010), whereas psychosocial factors used to be considered of primary importance in the past. For instance, it was once theorized that GID was a symptom of certain psychiatric disorders such as borderline personality (Lothstein, 1984) or psychosis (a Campo, Nijman, Merckelbach, & Evers, 2003). Current studies on psychopathology among adults with GID do not support either of these conclusions (e.g., Gomez-Gil, Vidal-Hagemeijer, & Salamero, 2008; Haraldsen & Dahl, 2000; Smith, van Goozen, Kuiper, & Cohen-Kettenis, 2005).

However, the relationship between certain forms of psychopathology and GID is still not entirely clear (Meyer-Bahlburg, 2010). In adults, elevated psychopathology has been found in some studies (e.g., Bodlund, Kullgren, Sundbom, & Hojerback, 1993; De Cuypere, Janes, & Rubens, 1995; Hepp, Kraemer, Schnyder, Miller, & Delsignore, 2005). Research among children and adolescents referred to gender identity clinics has demonstrated more frequent (internalizing) psychopathology than observed in their peers from the general population (Cohen-Kettenis, Owen, Kaijser, Bradley, & Zucker, 2003; de Vries, Doreleijers, Steensma, & Cohen-Kettenis, 2011; Di Ceglie, Freedman, McPherson, & Richardson, 2002; Wallien, Swaab, & Cohen-Kettenis, 2007; Zucker & Bradley, 1995; Zucker, Bradley, Owen-Anderson, et al., 2010; Zucker, Owen, Bradley, & Ameeriar, 2002). One theory about this relationship is that a predisposition to anxiety combined with parental psychopathology in gender variant children can lead to full-blown GID (Zucker & Bradley, 1995). Zucker and colleagues (Zucker, Bradley, Ben-Dat, et al., 2003; Zucker, Bradley, & Lowry Sullivan, 1996) have found among children referred to the Toronto gender identity clinic more separation anxiety in the boys and more psychopathology in their mothers than in the general population. At the Dutch gender identity clinic, some indications were found for a predisposition to anxiety among the referred children (Wallien, Swaab, et al., 2007; Wallien, van Goozen, & Cohen-Kettenis, 2007). However, parental psychopathology was not demonstrated (Wallien, 2008).

The increasing quantity of research on typical gender development demonstrates that a number of psychological and social factors play a role (for a review, see Ruble, Martin, & Berenbaum, 2006), in addition to biological factors. It remains to be seen whether and to what degree these same influences also influence gender dysphoric development. Biological factors do seem to be involved in the etiology of GID. For example, brain anatomy and brain activation patterns are reported to be different in adult transsexuals in comparison to non-gender dysphoric controls (Carrillo et al., 2010; Garcia-Falgueras & Swaab, 2008; Kruijver et al., 2000; Luders et al., 2009; Zhou, Hofman, Gooren, & Swaab, 1995; Berglund, Lindstrom, Dhejne-Helmy, & Savic, 2008; Gizewski et al., 2009; Schoning et al., 2010). Genetic factors are also likely to be important in the development of gender dysphoria (e.g., Coolidge, Thede, & Young, 2002; van Beijsterveldt, Hudziak, & Boomsma, 2006). However, this research is still very limited and the findings are sometimes inconsistent. It is unclear whether these findings are also applicable to less extreme forms of gender dysphoria.

With the current state of knowledge, it remains most plausible that a complex interaction between a biological predisposition in combination with intra- and interpersonal factors (Crouter, Whiteman, McHale, & Osgood, 2007; Maccoby, 1998; Zucker & Bradley, 1995) contribute to a development of gender dysphoria, which may come in different forms and intensities. Assuming, therefore, that gender dysphoria is most likely determined multifactorially, in clinical practice an extensive work-up weighing various symptoms and evaluating all kinds of potentially relevant factors seems indicated.

Perspective of Developmental Trajectories

In the diagnosis and treatment of gender dysphoric children and adolescents, one must take the perspective of development into account. Gender variant behavior and even the wish to be of the other gender can be either a phase or a normal developmental variant without any adverse consequences for a child's current functioning (e.g., Bartlett, Vasey, & Bukowski, 2000). Follow-up studies have demonstrated that only a small proportion of gender dysphoric children become transsexual at a later age, that a much larger proportion have a homosexual sexual orientation without any gender dysphoria, and that a small proportion of these children develop into heterosexual adults. The proportions of persistence found in the initial studies were below 10% (for a review of the literature, see Zucker & Bradley, 1995). More recent studies show a variation from 12 to 27% (Cohen-Kettenis, 2001; Drummond, Bradley, Peterson-Badali, & Zucker, 2008; Wallien & Cohen-Kettenis, 2008). It is important to note that these figures are for children attending a gender identity clinic; in a study on children from the general population, these numbers were different. Adults, whose parents had indicated that their children either showed gender variant behavior or expressed the wish to be of the other gender during childhood, more frequently indicated that they were either homosexual or bisexual, but none of them was transsexual (Steensma, van der Ende, Verhulst, & Cohen-Kettenis, in press). This implies that gender variant children, even those who meet the criteria for GID prior to puberty, for the most part are not gender dysphoric at a later age. To date, we do not yet know exactly when and how gender dysphoria disappears or desists. Clinical experience has shown that this most often takes place right before or right after the onset of puberty. This is also confirmed by youths in a qualitative study in whom the gender dysphoria disappeared after puberty (Steensma, Biemond, de Boer, & Cohen-Kettenis, 2011).

In contrast to what happens in children, gender dysphoria rarely changes or desists in adolescents who had been gender dysphoric since childhood and remained so after puberty (Cohen-Kettenis & Pfäfflin, 2003; Zucker, 2006). Youths who began the reversible treatment with puberty suppression at an average age of 14.75 years, to enable them to explore their gender dysphoria and treatment wish, were still gender dysphoric nearly two years later. All started with the first steps of their actual gender reassignment trajectory, the cross-sex hormones (de Vries, Steensma, Doreleijers, & Cohen-Kettenis, 2011).

CHILDREN

Diagnosis

In the Amsterdam gender identity clinic, several sessions spread out over a longer period of time are allotted to prepubertal children below age 12 for diagnosis. This is done to gain insight into how the gender dysphoria develops over time. The children and their parents are seen at least once together, each of the parents is interviewed individually, and the child is observed a number of times and subjected to an extensive psychodiagnostic assessment. The procedure is concluded with an advisory consultation.

One aim of the examination is to determine whether the criteria for a GID diagnosis have been met. This can be rather simple with children demonstrating an extreme degree of gender dysphoria or who are very explicit in their desire for gender reassignment. However, the clinical picture is not always that clear. Gender dysphoria is a dimensional phenomenon and can exist to a greater or lesser degree. This is something to be taken into greater account in *DSM-5* (APA, for proposed revision see www.dsm5.org) than is presently the case (Zucker, 2010). In addition, it can also manifest itself in various ways. One child with a strong gender dysphoric feeling may be very sensitive to his or her surroundings and only dares to come out at certain times and under certain circumstances. In another child, we can see very openly expressed gender dysphoria (Meyer-Bahlburg, 2002). In other cases, a child can show gender variant behavior without suffering from actual gender dysphoria. In those cases, the reason for referral usually lies more in the environment (e.g., parents struggling with their child's behavior) than in the child.

All kinds of aspects of the children's functioning are subsequently evaluated, such as their cognitive level, psychosocial functioning, and scholastic performance. For example, a boy may like playing with girls, not because he is unhappy being a boy, but because he has difficulty joining in with other boys of his age due to limited cognitive faculties and immaturity. Any other possible psychopathology is dealt with extensively (Wallien, Swaab, & Cohen-Kettenis, 2007). If any is found, the possible relationship between the gender dysphoria and other diagnoses is investigated. In this way, for example, one can investigate whether an autistic boy's fascination for fancy dresses and long hair is more part of his autism or whether his autism reinforces certain aspects of his gender dysphoria (de Vries, Noens, Cohen-Kettenis, van Berckelaer-Onnes, & Doreleijers, 2010). Some psychiatric diagnoses may be unrelated to the gender presentation but still need attention (e.g., tic disorders). There are also problems or psychiatric disorders that can arise as a consequence of the gender dysphoria (social anxiety, depression, oppositional defiant disorders).

Furthermore, a good assessment of family functioning as well as the role of the child's gender variant behavior on family functioning is useful in order to gain a complete clinical picture.

Treatment

The Dutch approach to clinical management of children with GID contains elements of a therapeutic approach but is not directed at the gender dysphoria itself. Instead, it focuses on its concomitant emotional and behavioral and family problems that may or may not have an impact on the child's gender dysphoria.

PARENT COUNSELING

After the evaluation described above, the results of the assessment and diagnostic procedure are discussed with the parents (and partially with the child) and an ensuing individual recommendation is given. For children in whom no concomitant problems have been observed, who have sensitive parents with an appropriate style of child rearing, advice aimed at dealing with the gender dysphoria is sufficient. This sometimes results in more counseling at a later point in time when the family again needs support or advice or finds it increasingly difficult to deal with the uncertainties with regard to the child's psychosexual outcome. Because most gender dysphoric children will not remain gender dysphoric through adolescence (Wallien & Cohen-Kettenis, 2008), we recommend that young children not yet make a complete social transition (different clothing, a different given name, referring to a boy as "her" instead of "him") before the very early stages of puberty. In making this recommendation, we aim to prevent youths with nonpersisting gender dysphoria from having to make a complex change back to the role of their natal gender (Steensma & Cohen-Kettenis, 2011). In a qualitative follow-up study, several youths indicated how difficult it was for them to realize that they no longer wanted to live in the role of the other gender and to make this clear to the people around them (Steensma, Biemond, et al., 2011). These children never even officially transitioned but just were considered by everyone around them as belonging to the other (non-natal) gender. One may wonder how difficult it would be for children living already for years in an environment where no one (except for the family) is aware of the child's natal sex to make a change back. Another reason we recommend against early transitions is that some children who have done so (sometimes as preschoolers) barely realize that they are of the other natal sex. They develop a sense of reality so different from their physical reality that acceptance of the multiple and protracted treatments they will later need is made unnecessarily difficult. Parents, too, who go along with this, often do not realize that they contribute to their child's lack of awareness of these consequences.

Parents are furthermore advised to encourage their child, if possible, to stay in contact with children and adult role models of their natal sex as well. Moreover, we advise them to encourage a wider range of interests in objects and activities that go with the natal sex. Gender variant behavior, however, is not prohibited. By informing parents about the various psychosexual trajectories, we want them to succeed in finding a sensible middle of the road approach between an accepting and supportive attitude toward their child's gender dysphoria, while at the same time protecting their child against any negative reactions from others and remaining realistic about the actual situation. If they speak about their natal son as being a girl with a penis, we stress that they have a male child who very much wants to be a girl, but will need an invasive treatment to align his body with his identity if this desire does not remit. Finding the right balance is essential for parents and clinicians because gender variant children are highly vulnerable to developing a negative sense of self (Yunger, Carver, & Perry, 2004). This goes especially for situations of social exclusion or teasing and bullying (Cohen-Kettenis, Owen, et al., 2003). Fortunately, social exclusion does not invariably take place, as can be seen from a recent study of gender dysphoric Dutch children (Wallien, Veenstra, Kreukels, & Cohen-Kettenis, 2010).

Parents can play a significant role in creating an environment in which their child can grow up safely and develop optimally. In this regard, it is also important that appropriate limit setting is part of the parent's style of raising their child. For example, if a young boy likes to wear dresses in a neighborhood in which aggression can be expected, they could come to an understanding with their son that he only wears dresses at home. In such a case, it is crucial that the parents give their child a clear explanation of why they have made their choices and that this does not mean that they themselves do not accept the cross-dressing. The child will, thus, sometimes be frustrated and learn that not all of one's desires will be met. The latter is an important lesson for any child, but even more so for children who will have a gender reassignment later in life. Although hormones and surgery effectively make the gender dysphoria disappear (Murad et al., 2010), someone's deepest desire or fantasy to have been born in the body of the other gender will never be completely fulfilled.

TREATMENT OF NON-GENDER DYSPHORIA RELATED PROBLEMS

If concomitant problems are observed (e.g., substantial problems with peers, psychiatric problems, or conflicts with parents or siblings), the child may be referred to a local mental health agency. The primary aim is for the child and, if necessary, the family to function better. If these problems have contributed to causing or keeping up some gender dysphoria, the dysphoria will likely disappear by tackling these other problems. Although there is little evidence that psychotherapeutic interventions can eliminate gender dysphoria in general, it is conceivable that in some cases gender variant behavior can change as a result of therapy. In our own practice, a reduction or disappearance of gender variant behavior seems to take place particularly when this behavior appeared to be a clear reaction to certain events or situations which in themselves are amenable to therapy (e.g., a boy suddenly dressing up and saying he wants to be a girl as an expression of extreme jealousy after the birth of a younger sister). There are, however, no controlled studies that have investigated psychological interventions aimed at influencing certain types of gender dysphoria. It remains for the most part unclear if "treated" children have been "cured" through interventions or just "grew out of" their gender variance. Yet, even if there is no change in the gender dysphoria, many children with gender dysphoria can benefit from psychotherapy or counseling aimed at securing a positive self-image or dealing with negative reactions from others. Without such support, these children run the risk of developing social relationship problems, emotional problems such as anxiety and depression, behavioral problems, or problems at school due to difficulties with concentration, or a low self-esteem.

PHYSICAL MEDICAL INTERVENTIONS

The Amsterdam gender identity clinic does not provide any physical medical interventions before puberty. Parents are advised to adopt an attitude of watchful waiting. Not until the child arrives at puberty and is still gender dysphoric will he or she be seen again in our gender identity clinic. Parents and child are informed about this possibility.

ADOLESCENTS

Diagnosis

In nearly all cases seen, adolescents age 12 and up come to the Amsterdam gender identity clinic with a desire for gender reassignment. While gender dysphoric feelings in younger children will usually remit, in adolescents this is rarely the case. Similar to the children, a diagnostic trajectory is initiated that is spread out over a longer period of time. Here, too, there is an intake session with the adolescents and their parents, followed by individual talks with the parents and the youths and a psychodiagnostic assessment. Shortly before the start of any physical medical treatment, adolescents will also have a child psychiatric examination by a member of the team other than the diagnostician and a medical screening by the pediatric endocrinologist. Finally, a recommendation concludes the procedure. When an adolescent is considered eligible for puberty suppression, the diagnostic trajectory is extended, as the puberty suppression phase is still considered diagnostic. This medical intervention puts a halt to the development of secondary sex characteristics. It has been used for over 20 years now in the treatment of precocious puberty and there is evidence that gonadal function is reactivated soon after cessation of treatment (Mul & Hughes, 2008).

The Amsterdam gender identity clinic follows the international Standards of Care of the World Professional Association for Transgender Health (WPATH, 2011), which advises that the decision to undergo gender reassignment be taken in several steps. In the *Standards of Care*, the diagnostic phase is followed by the real-life experience stage in which cross-sex hormones are prescribed and, eventually, the subject can undergo gender reassignment surgery.

In developing a rapport with adolescents and their parents, particular attention is paid to obtaining open and nonjudgmental contact with the youths and their parents. Many elements of this are recognizable as the developmental approach described by Di Ceglie (2009). In a number of sessions, the diagnostician tries to gain a picture of the youth's general and psychosexual development. Information is gathered about current functioning, individually, with peers and in the family. As to sexuality, the subjective meaning of dressing up or the type of clothing, sexual experience, sexual behavior and fantasies, sexual orientation and body perception are discussed.

Adolescents are considered eligible for puberty suppression when they are diagnosed with GID, live in a supportive environment and have no serious psychosocial problems interfering with the diagnostic assessment

16

or treatment (Cohen-Kettenis, Delemarre-van de Waal, & Gooren, 2008; Delemarre-van de Waal & Cohen-Kettenis, 2006). During the diagnostic trajectory, information is obtained from both the adolescents and their parents to assess whether the adolescents meet the eligibility criteria. Therefore, first it is ascertained whether adolescents are suffering from a very early onset gender dysphoria that has increased around puberty, or whether something else brought them to the clinic (e.g., confusion about homosexuality or transvestic fetishism). About one quarter of the referrals in Amsterdam do not fulfill diagnostic criteria for GID and most of them drop out early in the diagnostic procedure for this reason or because other problems are prominent (de Vries, et al., 2011). Second, the youth's further general and psychological functioning is assessed. Are there psychiatric problems or other issues that could hinder a correct assessment or future treatment compliance? Third, an assessment is made of the adolescent's social support. As puberty suppression and subsequent hormone treatment and surgery have far-reaching implications, an adolescent needs adequate support.

The diagnostic stage does not only focus on obtaining information. To prevent unrealistically high expectations from gender reassignment in the future, all the possibilities and impossibilities of the treatment are discussed extensively with the adolescent and the family. Giving such information starts early in the trajectory. Sometimes, the way in which the youth responds to this information is also diagnostically informative.

If the eligibility criteria are met, gonadotropin releasing hormone analogues (GnRHa) to suppress puberty are prescribed when the youth has reached Tanner stage 2–3 of puberty (Delemarre-van de Waal & Cohen-Kettenis, 2006); this means that puberty has just begun. The reason for this is that we assume that experiencing one's own puberty is diagnostically useful because right at the onset of puberty it becomes clear whether the gender dysphoria will desist or persist. Starting around Tanner stages 2–3, the very first physical changes are still reversible (Delemarre-van de Waal & Cohen-Kettenis, 2006). Because the protocol for young adolescents had started in a period when there were no studies on the effects of puberty suppression, the age limit was set at 12 years because some cognitive and emotional maturation is desirable when starting these physical medical interventions. Further, Dutch adolescents are legally partly competent to make a medical decision together with their parent´s consent at age 12. It is, however, conceivable that when more information about the safety of early hormone treatment becomes available, the age limit may be further adjusted (de Vries, 2010).

Treatment

When it appears from the advisory consultation that there are concomitant psychiatric or family problems, some form of psychological treatment will be sought. This treatment is usually given close to the youth's home rather than at our clinic. Certainly, when the problems are destabilizing and there is an insufficient guarantee that the youth is committed to the therapeutic relationship necessary for a physical medical intervention, the treatment will be postponed. In a study investigating the extent of psychiatric problems in gender dysphoric adolescents, it appeared that the diagnostic stage in some cases may take more than one and a half years before physical medical intervention actually can begin (de Vries, Doreleijers, et al., 2011). This was the case in about one third of the youths with a GID diagnosis. These youths more frequently suffered from an oppositional defiant behavioral disorder or more than three psychiatric diagnoses (in addition to the GID diagnosis) compared with adolescents who were considered immediately eligible. They also were less likely to live with both biological parents and on average had a lower intelligence. Furthermore, they were, on average, older at the time of referral (de Vries, Doreleijers, et al., 2011). Clearly, psychiatric problems were not the only factor influencing the delay in starting puberty suppression.

However, for many of the gender dysphoric youths, there are no psychological problems other than the gender dysphoria. Yet, these adolescents do need good counseling. Some themes need repeatedly to be touched upon, because they gain a new dimension as the adolescents grow older, for example, dating when you have a body that has not yet been operated on, or infertility. Regular contact with the psychologist is also necessary for adequate preparation for the next treatment steps. An increasing problem is that many adolescents do not realize that an unhealthy lifestyle (smoking, obesity) has a negative influence on the treatment, surgery in particular. In addition to a preparation for the future, some profit from a form of psychotherapy. This may be because they are anxious, need to become more assertive or feel insecure. For those who do not easily verbalize their concerns, psychomotor therapy can be helpful to let them feel more at ease with their bodies and to learn to talk more easily about their problems.

TRANSITIONING

Many gender dysphoric youths choose to begin living in the desired gender role simultaneously with the beginning of puberty suppression. The adolescents and their families are then supported in this process so that it can be achieved successfully. Many youths also obtain help from Transvisie, the only self-help organization working with trans youth in the Netherlands. It is, however, not a requirement to begin with the real life experience as long as cross-sex hormones are not taken.

PHYSICAL MEDICAL INTERVENTIONS

Physical medical interventions can be divided into completely reversible interventions (puberty suppressors such as GnRHa), partially reversible interventions (cross-sex hormones) and completely irreversible gender reassignment surgery (WPATH, 2011).

Completely reversible interventions. Puberty suppression has two aims. First and foremost, they offer the adolescent time to smoothly explore his or her gender identity and to find out if a gender reassignment trajectory is really what the youth wants. Moreover, the knowledge that their bodies in this stage will not continue to develop in the undesired direction often results in a vast reduction of the distress they have been suffering from since the onset of puberty. Second, stopping the development of secondary sex characteristics makes passing in the desired gender role easier than delaying treatment until adulthood. This entails advantages for functioning throughout one's life (Ross & Need, 1989). The team's view that puberty suppression does not automatically have to lead to actual treatment (gender reassignment) is explicitly discussed with the youths and their parents. While with some adolescents it is clear early on that there is only a very small chance that they will abandon this trajectory, they still have to see their psychologist or psychiatrist regularly in the years that they are on GnRHa or cross-sex hormones. Each adolescent is also regularly given consideration in the weekly multidisciplinary conferences in which the pediatric endocrinologist also participates. As soon as necessary, extra help is deployed or the trajectory is adjusted.

Youths with psychiatric or family problems can also become eligible for puberty suppression if the mental health treatment they receive is adequate enough to ensure that the diagnostic or treatment process is not unduly disturbed. To achieve this, good, regular contact with their external therapists or counselors is necessary. Special attention is given to gender dysphoric adolescents with an autism spectrum disorder. It is certainly the case for them that the treatment has to be introduced calmly and each step must take place in close consultation with the other mental health clinicians (de Vries, Noens, et al., 2010).

Partially irreversible interventions. Gender dysphoric adolescents are eligible for the first step of the actual gender reassignment when they have reached the age of 16. This age has been chosen because in the Netherlands (as well as in many other countries), young people are then considered to be able to make independent medical decisions. While their parents do not have to approve, the Amsterdam clinic prefers their approval, as most adolescents are still very much dependent on their caretakers. Furthermore, adolescents have to meet the same criteria as at the onset of puberty suppression (except for the Tanner stage criterion). Although most of the youths will have already made a social transition, this is now a requirement because sex characteristics of the desired gender will become visible to others.

Cross-sex hormones will result in a start of puberty of the desired gender. Male-to-females (MTF) or trans girls receive estrogens which result in breast growth and female fat distribution. Female-to-males (FTM) or trans boys receive androgens, and will become more muscular and develop a low voice and facial-and body hair growth (Delemarre-van de Waal & Cohen-Kettenis, 2006).

In addition, new themes will be brought up in sessions. In this stage, some of the youths will start going out with someone for the first time and they will be more consciously dealing with dating, romantic relationships, partner choice, careers, and having children. Because the operations suddenly seem to be close at hand, the possibilities and limitations of the gender reassignment surgery, about which they will gradually have to make choices (e.g., various types of metaidoioplasty or phalloplasty, or no genital surgery for trans boys), are once again discussed (Cohen-Kettenis, 2006).

Completely irreversible interventions. When the adolescent has come of age at 18 and still meets all the eligibility criteria, he or she can be eligible for the last step of the gender reassignment treatment trajectory, the gender reassignment surgeries. Trans boys may undergo several operations: (if they came relatively late to the clinic and already had some breast development) mastectomy, hysterectomy or oovariectomy, and, if desired, genital operations (metaidoioplasty or phalloplasty). Trans girls usually undergo vaginoplasty and, if necessary, at their own financial expense, augmentation mammoplasty. Trans girls who began puberty suppression at a young age often have insufficient penile skin for a classical vaginoplasty and need an adjusted surgical procedure using colon tissue.

Treatment evaluation

While there are still reservations about physical medical interventions in youths under the age of 18 (e.g., Korte et al., 2008; Meyenburg, 1999; Viner, Brain, Carmichael, & Di Ceglie, 2005), many clinicians are changing their views on this (Cohen-Kettenis, Delemarre-van de Waal, & Gooren, 2008). There are indications that starting cross-sex hormones early (under 18 but over 16 years of age) followed by gender reassignment surgery at 18 can be effective and positive for general and mental functioning (Cohen-Kettenis & van Goozen, 1997; Smith, van Goozen, & Cohen-Kettenis, 2001; Smith, van Goozen, Kuiper, & Cohen-Kettenis, 2005).

By now, two studies have been performed evaluating the effects of puberty suppression. Psychological functioning of the first 70 gender dysphoric adolescents eligible for puberty suppression was measured twice: at their attendance at the clinic and shortly before the start of cross-sex hormones. Their behavioral and emotional problems and depressive symptoms decreased, while general functioning as measured by the Global Assessment Scale (Shaffer et al., 1983) improved significantly during puberty suppression. No adolescent withdrew from puberty suppression and all started cross-sex hormone treatment, the first step of the actual gender reassignment (de Vries, Steensma, Doreleijers, et al., 2010). A second group, assessed postoperatively, appeared to be satisfied with their lives and no longer gender dysphoric (de Vries, 2010). Many studies in gender dysphoric adults have demonstrated that gender reassignment treatment is effective. These initial results demonstrate that this is also the case in young people who have received GnRHa to suppress puberty at an early age, followed by the actual gender reassignment (de Vries, 2010).

The concern that early physical medical intervention has unfavorable physical effects has to this date not been confirmed (Delemarre-van de Waal & Cohen-Kettenis, 2006). Initial studies on, for example, bone development and insulin sensitivity demonstrate favorable results (Schagen et al., in press; Vance, et al., in press).

SUMMARY AND CONCLUSIONS

At the Amsterdam gender identity clinic the clinical approach to prepubertal children under the age of 12 is different from the approach to adolescents starting at age 12. In children, the diagnosis is focused on elucidating all possible factors that could play a role in gender dysphoria, but the gender dysphoria itself is not actively dealt with in treatment. A general recommendation is given not to have transitioning take place too early, but to carefully observe how the gender dysphoria develops in the first stages of puberty. Parents and child are supported in tolerating the uncertainty about the outcome. Of special concern are concomitant problems and, whenever present, necessary help is actively sought so that the child can develop in an optimal way.

Gender dysphoric adolescents who have reached puberty also undergo meticulous diagnosis, but, in contrast to prepubertal children, they can be considered eligible for physical medical interventions under strict conditions. This does not, however, rule out parallel psychotherapy or other psychological interventions. Any vulnerable aspects of the youth's functioning or circumstances deserve thorough concern. These need not be contraindications to physical medical interventions, but they do need due attention. Using an approach that cares for every aspect of the adolescent´s psychosocial functioning and not only aims at eliminating the gender dysphoria, we try to provide the future young adult with the necessary resources for an optimal psychological development and a good quality of life. Despite the understandable concern about potential harm that could be done by early physical medical interventions, it seems currently that withholding intervention is even more harmful for the adolescents' wellbeing during adolescence and in adulthood. It is fortunate that nearly all diagnostic and treatment aspects, except for breast enlargement, are covered by insurance. Transgender individuals in the Netherlands do not need to suffer from incomplete or inadequate treatment because of financial problems.

REFERENCES

a Campo, J., Nijman, H., Merckelbach, H., & Evers, C. (2003). Psychiatric comorbidity of gender identity disorders: a survey among Dutch psychiatrists. *American Journal of Psychiatry, 160,* 1332–1336.

American Psychiatric Association. (2000). *Diagnostic and Statistical Manual of Mental Disorders, Fourth Edition, Text Revision.* Washington, DC: Author. www.dsm5.org

American Psychiatric Association. (in press). *Diagnostic and statistical manual of mental disorders* (5th ed.). Washington, DC: Author.

Bartlett, N. H., Vasey, P. L., & Bukowski, W. M. (2000). Is gender identity disorder in children a mental disorder? *Sex Roles, 43,* 753–785.

Berglund, H., Lindstrom, P., Dhejne-Helmy, C., & Savic, I. (2008). Male-to-female transsexuals show sex-atypical hypothalamus activation when smelling odorous steroids. *Cerebral Cortex, 18,* 1900–1908.

Bodlund, O., Kullgren, G., Sundbom, E., & Hojerback, T. (1993). Personality traits and disorders among transsexuals. *Acta Psychiatrica Scandinavica, 88*(5), 322–327.

Carrillo, B., Gomez-Gil, E., Rametti, G., Junque, C., Gomez, A., Karadi, K., et al. (2010) Cortical activation during mental rotation in male-to-female and female-to-male transsexuals under hormonal treatment. *Psychoneuroendocrinology, 35,* 1213–1222.

Cohen-Kettenis, P. T. (2001). Gender identity disorder in DSM? *Journal of the American Academy of Child and Adolescent Psychiatry, 40,* 391.

Cohen-Kettenis, P. T. (2006). Gender identity disorders. In C. Gillberg, R. Harrington, & H.-C. Steinhausen (Eds.), *A clinician's handbook of child and adolescent psychiatry* (pp. 695–725). New York, NY: Cambridge University Press.

Cohen-Kettenis, P. T., Delemarre-van de Waal, H. A., & Gooren, L. J. (2008). The treatment of adolescent transsexuals: changing insights. *Journal of Sexual Medicine, 5,* 1892–1897.

Cohen-Kettenis, P. T., Owen, A., Kaijser, V. G., Bradley, S. J., & Zucker, K. J. (2003). Demographic characteristics, social competence, and behavior problems in children with gender identity disorder: a cross-national, cross-clinic comparative analysis. *Journal of Abnormal Child Psychology, 31,* 41–53.

Cohen-Kettenis, P. T., & Pfäfflin, F. (2003). *Transgenderism and Intersexuality in Childhood and Adolescence* (Vol. 46). Thousand Oaks, CA: Sage.

Cohen-Kettenis, P. T., & van Goozen, S. H. (1997). Sex reassignment of adolescent transsexuals: a follow-up study. *Journal of the American Academy of Child and Adolescent Psychiatry, 36,* 263–271.

Coolidge, F. L., Thede, L. L., & Young, S. E. (2002). The heritability of gender identity disorder in a child and adolescent twin sample. *Behavior Genetics, 32,* 251–257.

Crouter, A. C., Whiteman, S. D., McHale, S. M., & Osgood, D. W. (2007). Development of gender attitude traditionality across middle childhood and adolescence. *Child Development, 78,* 911–926.

De Cuypere, G., Janes, C., & Rubens, R. (1995). Psychosocial functioning of transsexuals in Belgium. *Acta Psychiatrica Scandinavica, 91,* 180–184.

Delemarre-van de Waal, H. A., & Cohen-Kettenis, P. T. (2006). Clinical management of gender identity disorder in adolescents: a protocol on psychological and paediatric endocrinology aspects. *European Journal of Endocrinology/European Federation of Endocrine Societies*, *155*(Suppl. 1), 131–137.

de Vries, A. L. (2010). *Gender dysphoria in adolescents: Mental health and treatment evaluation*. Published PhD Dissertation. VU University Amsterdam.

de Vries, A. L., Cohen-Kettenis, P. T., & Delemarre-van de Waal, H. A. (2007). Clinical management of gender dysphoria in adolescents. *International Journal of Transgenderism*, *9*(3–4), 83–94.

de Vries, A. L., Doreleijers, T. A., Steensma, T. D., & Cohen-Kettenis, P. T. (2011). Psychiatric comorbidity in gender dysphoric adolescents. *Journal of Child Psychology and Psychiatry*, *52*(11), 1195–1202.

de Vries, A. L., Noens, I. L., Cohen-Kettenis, P. T., van Berckelaer-Onnes, I. A., & Doreleijers, T. A. (2010). Autism spectrum disorders in gender dysphoric children and adolescents. *Journal of Autism and Developmental Disorders*, *40*(8), 930–936.

de Vries, A. L., Steensma, T. D., Doreleijers, T. A., & Cohen-Kettenis, P. T. (2011). Puberty suppression in adolescents with gender identity disorder: A Prospective Follow-Up Study. *Journal of Sexual Medicine*, *8*(8), 2276–2283.

Di Ceglie, D. (2009). Engaging young people with atypical gender identity development in therapeutic work: A developmental approach. *Journal of Child Psychotherapy*, *35*, 3–12.

Di Ceglie, D., Freedman, D., McPherson, S., & Richardson, P. (2002). Children and adolescents referred to a specialist gender identity development service: Clinical features and demographic characteristics. *International Journal of Transgenderism*. Retrieved from www.symposion.com/ijt/ijtvo06no01_01.htm

Di Ceglie, D., Sturge, C., & Sutton, A. (1998). The Royal College of Psychiatrists: Gender identity disorders in children and adolescents: Guidance for management. *International Journal of Transgenderism*, *2*(2).

Drummond, K. D., Bradley, S. J., Peterson-Badali, M., & Zucker, K. J. (2008). A follow-up study of girls with gender identity disorder. *Developmental Psychology*, *44*, 34–45.

Garcia-Falgueras, A., & Swaab, D. F. (2008). A sex difference in the hypothalamic uncinate nucleus: relationship to gender identity. *Brain*, *131*(Pt. 12), 3132–3146.

Gizewski, E. R., Krause, E., Schlamann, M., Happich, F., Ladd, M. E., Forsting, M., et al. (2009). Specific cerebral activation due to visual erotic stimuli in male-to-female transsexuals compared with male and female controls: an fMRI study. *Journal of Sexual Medicine*, *6*, 440–448.

Gomez-Gil, E., Vidal-Hagemeijer, A., & Salamero, M. (2008). MMPI-2 characteristics of transsexuals requesting sex reassignment: comparison of patients in prehormonal and presurgical phases. *Journal of Personality Assessment*, *90*, 368–374.

Haraldsen, I. R., & Dahl, A. A. (2000). Symptom profiles of gender dysphoric patients of transsexual type compared to patients with personality disorders and healthy adults. *Acta Psychiatrica Scandinavica*, *102*, 276–281.

Hembree, W. C., Cohen-Kettenis, P., Delemarre-van de Waal, H. A., Gooren, L. J., Meyer, W. J., III, Spack, N. P., et al.. (2009). Endocrine treatment of transsexual persons: an Endocrine Society clinical practice guideline. *Journal of Clinical Endocrinology and Metabolism, 94,* 3132–3154.

Hepp, U., Kraemer, B., Schnyder, U., Miller, N., & Delsignore, A. (2005). Psychiatric comorbidity in gender identity disorder. *Journal of Psychosomatic Research, 58,* 259–261.

Korte, A., Lehmkuhl, U., Goecker, D., Beier, K. M., Krude, H., & Gruters-Kieslich, A. (2008). Gender identity disorders in childhood and adolescence: currently debated concepts and treatment strategies. *Deutsches Aerzteblatt International, 105*(48), 834–841.

Kreukels, B. P., & Cohen-Kettenis, P. T. (2011). Puberty suppression in gender identity disorder: The Amsterdam experience. *Nature Reviews Endocrinology, 7*(8), 466–472.

Kruijver, F. P., Zhou, J. N., Pool, C. W., Hofman, M. A., Gooren, L. J., & Swaab, D. F. (2000). Male-to-female transsexuals have female neuron numbers in a limbic nucleus. *Journal of Clinical Endocrinology and Metabolism, 85,* 2034–2041.

Lothstein, L. M. (1984). Psychological testing with transsexuals: a 30-year review. *Journal of Personality Assessment, 48,* 500–507.

Luders, E., Sanchez, F. J., Gaser, C., Toga, A. W., Narr, K. L., Hamilton, L. S., et al. (2009). Regional gray matter variation in male-to-female transsexualism. *Neuroimage, 46,* 904–907.

Maccoby, E. E. (1998). *The two sexes: Growing up apart, coming together. Family and public policy.* Cambridge, MA: Belknap Press/Harvard University Press.

Meyenburg, B. (1999). Gender identity disorder in adolescence: outcomes of psychotherapy. *Adolescence, 34*(134), 305–313.

Meyer-Bahlburg, H. F. (2010). From mental disorder to iatrogenic hypogonadism: dilemmas in conceptualizing gender identity variants as psychiatric conditions. *Archives of Sexual Behavior, 39,* 461–476.

Meyer-Bahlburg, H. F. L. (2002). Gender identity disorder in young boys: A parent- and peer-based treatment protocol. *Clinical Child Psychology and Psychiatry, 7,* 360–376.

Murad, M. H., Elamin, M. B., Garcia, M. Z., Mullan, R. J., Murad, A., Erwin, P. J., et al. (2010). Hormonal therapy and sex reassignment: A systematic review and meta-analysis of quality of life and psychosocial outcomes. *Clinical Endocrinology, 72*(2), 214–231.

Mul, D., & Hughes, I. A. (2008). The use of GnRH agonists in precocious puberty. *European Journal of Endocrinology/European Federation of Endocrine Societies, 159*(Suppl. 1), 3–8.

Ross, M. W., & Need, J. A. (1989). Effects of adequacy of gender reassignment surgery on psychological adjustment: a follow-up of fourteen male-to-female patients. *Archives of Sexual Behavior, 18,* 145–153.

Ruble, D. N., Martin, C. L., & Berenbaum, S. A. (2006). Gender development. In N. Eisenberg, W. Damon & R. M. Lerner (Eds.), *Handbook of child psychology: Vol. 3, Social, emotional, and personality development* (6th ed., pp. 858–932). Hoboken, NJ: Wiley.

Schagen, S. E. E., Cohen-Kettenis, P. T., van Coeverden-van den Heijkant, S. C. C. M., Knol, D. L., Gooren, L. J., & Delemarre-van de Waal, H. A. (in press). Bone mass development in transsexual adolescents receiving treatment with gonadotropin-releasing hormone analogues in combination with cross-sex hormones to induce cross-sex puberty. *Journal of Clinical Endocrinology and Metabolism.*

Schoning, S., Engelien, A., Bauer, C., Kugel, H., Kersting, A., Roestel, C., et al. (2010) Neuroimaging differences in spatial cognition between men and male-to-female transsexuals before and during hormone therapy. *Journal of Sexual Medicine, 7,* 1858–1867.

Shaffer, D., Gould, M. S., Brasic, J., Ambrosini, P., Fisher, P., Bird, H., et al. (1983). A children's global assessment scale (CGAS). *Archives of General Psychiatry, 40,* 1228–1231.

Smith, Y. L., van Goozen, S. H., & Cohen-Kettenis, P. T. (2001). Adolescents with gender identity disorder who were accepted or rejected for sex reassignment surgery: a prospective follow-up study. *Journal of the American Academy of Child and Adolescent Psychiatry, 40,* 472–481.

Smith, Y. L., van Goozen, S. H., Kuiper, A. J., & Cohen-Kettenis, P. T. (2005). Sex reassignment: outcomes and predictors of treatment for adolescent and adult transsexuals. *Psychological Medicine, 35,* 89–99.

Steensma, T. D., Biemond, R., de Boer, F., & Cohen-Kettenis, P. T. (2011). Desisting and persisting gender dysphoria after childhood: A qualitative follow-up study. *Clinical Child Psychology and Psychiatry, 16*(4), 499–516.

Steensma, T. D., & Cohen-Kettenis, P. T. (2011). Gender transitioning before puberty? *Archives of Sexual Behavior, 40*(4), 649–650.

Steensma, T. D., van der Ende, J., Verhulst, F. C., & Cohen-Kettenis, P. T. (in press). Childhood gender variance and adult sexual orientation: A 24-year prospective study. *Journal of Sexual Medicine.*

van Beijsterveldt, C. E., Hudziak, J. J., & Boomsma, D. I. (2006). Genetic and environmental influences on cross-gender behavior and relation to behavior problems: a study of Dutch twins at ages 7 and 10 years. *Archives of Sexual Behavior, 35,* 647–658.

Vance, S. R., Jr., Schagen, S. E. E., Gooren, L. J., Wouters, F. M., Knol, D. L., Cohen-Kettenis, P. T., et al. (in press). Insulin sensitivity in adolescents with gender identity disorder during puberty suppression with GnRH analogues.

Viner, R. M., Brain, C., Carmichael, P., & Di Ceglie, D. (2005). Sex on the brain: dillemmas in the endocrine management of children and adolescents with gender identity disorder. *Archives of Disease in Childhood, 90* (Suppl. 2), A78.

Wallien, M. S. (2008). *Gender dysphoria in children; Causes and consequences.* PhD Dissertation. VU University, Amsterdam.

Wallien, M. S., & Cohen-Kettenis, P. T. (2008). Psychosexual outcome of gender-dysphoric children. *Journal of the American Academy of Child and Adolescent Psychiatry, 47,* 1413–1423.

Wallien, M. S., Swaab, H., & Cohen-Kettenis, P. T. (2007). Psychiatric comorbidity among children with gender identity disorder. *Journal of the American Academy of Child and Adolescent Psychiatry, 46,* 1307–1314.

Wallien, M. S., van Goozen, S. H., & Cohen-Kettenis, P. T. (2007). Physiological correlates of anxiety in children with gender identity disorder. *European Child and Adolescent Psychiatry, 16,* 309–315.

Wallien, M. S., Veenstra, R., Kreukels, B. P., & Cohen-Kettenis, P. T. (2010). Peer group status of gender dysphoric children: a sociometric study. *Archives of Sexual Behavior*, *39*, 553–560.

World Professional Association of Transgender Health (WPATH). (2011). *Standards of care*. Seventh edition. Retrieved from http//www.wpath.org/

Yunger, J. L., Carver, P. R., & Perry, D. G. (2004). Does gender identity influence children's psychological well-being? *Developmental Psychology*, *40*, 572–582.

Zhou, J. N., Hofman, M. A., Gooren, L. J., & Swaab, D. F. (1995). A sex difference in the human brain and its relation to transsexuality. *Nature*, *378*(6552), 68–70.

Zucker, K. J. (2006). Gender Identity Disorder. In D. A. Wolfe & E. J. Mash (Eds.), *Behavioral and emotional disorders in adolescents: Nature, assessment, and treatment* (pp. 535–562). New York, NY: Guilford.

Zucker, K. J. (2010). The *DSM* diagnostic criteria for gender identity disorder in children. *Archives of Sexual Behavior*, *39*, 477–498.

Zucker, K. J., & Bradley, S. (1995). *Gender identity disorder and psychosexual problems in children and adolescents*. New York, NY: Guilford.

Zucker, K. J., Bradley, S. J., Ben-Dat, D. N., Ho, C., Johnson, L., & Owen, A. (2003). Psychopathology in the parents of boys with gender identity disorder. *Journal of the American Academy of Child and Adolescent Psychiatry*, *42*, 2–4.

Zucker, K. J., Bradley, S. J., & Lowry Sullivan, C. B. (1996). Traits of separation anxiety in boys with gender identity disorder. *Journal of the American Academy of Child and Adolescent Psychiatry*, *35*, 791–798.

Zucker, K., Bradley, S., Owen-Anderson, A., Singh, D., Blanchard, R., & Bain, J. (2010). Puberty-blocking hormonal therapy for adolescents with gender identity disorder: A descriptive clinical study. *Journal of Gay & Lesbian Mental Health*, *15*(1), 58–82.

Zucker, K. J., Owen, A., Bradley, S. J., & Ameeriar, L. (2002). Gender-dysphoric children and adolescents: A comparative analysis of demographic characteristics and behavioral problems. *Clinical Child Psychology and Psychiatry*. 7, 398–411.

Psychological Evaluation and Medical Treatment of Transgender Youth in an Interdisciplinary "Gender Management Service" (GeMS) in a Major Pediatric Center

LAURA EDWARDS-LEEPER, PhD and NORMAN P. SPACK, MD

Harvard Medical School, Boston, Massachusetts, USA

In 2007, an interdisciplinary clinic for children and adolescents with disorders of sex development (DSD) or gender identity disorder (GID) opened in a major pediatric center. Psychometric evaluation and endocrine treatment via pubertal suppressive therapy and administration of cross-sex steroid hormones was offered to carefully selected patients according to effective protocols used in Holland. Hembree et al.'s (2009) Guidelines for Endocrine Treatment of Transsexual Persons published by the Endocrine Society endorsed these methods. A description of the clinic's protocol and general patient demographics are provided, along with treatment philosophy and goals.

INTRODUCTION

We are in a transitional period regarding the treatment of transgender youth. Although gender variance is still a stigmatized condition, there is an increased, albeit gradual, acceptance of transgender people in American society. Individuals are also declaring their gender variance at younger ages, forcing those who care for these youth to reexamine the framework from which we understand Gender Identity Disorder (GID) as designated by the *Diagnostic and Statistical Manual of Mental Disorders* (4th ed., text rev; *DSM-IV-TR*; American Psychiatric Association, 2000). We have learned that delaying proper diagnosis can lead to significant psychological consequences. Moreover, the window of optimal psychological evaluation and endocrinologic management occurs during adolescence, yet few medical and mental health providers treating adolescents provide services to this population due to lack of knowledge, inadequate insurance coverage, and possibly their discomfort with transgender people. Here we describe our interdisciplinary approach to the psychological evaluation and medical treatment of transgender youth.

TERMINOLOGY

There is great variability among transgender individuals and healthcare providers regarding the most accurate definitions and preferred nomenclature. Below are the definitions of the terms used in this article. *Gender identity* also refers to one's identification as a boy/man or girl/woman, as opposed to one's anatomical sex at birth, referred to as *biological sex*. Gender identity includes the preferred gender role and behavior, and is the inherent sense of being male or female; it is not defined by one's genitalia. *Gender dysphoria* is discomfort with one's biological sex and/or the gender role assigned to it. *Gender variant* is a term used interchangeably with *gender nonconforming* and describes someone whose interests and behaviors fall outside the cultural norms for biological sex. *Transgender* is an umbrella term often used to describe gender-variant individuals and is not a formal diagnosis. It includes individuals whose gender identity is different from their biological sex and/or whose gender expression does not fall within the stereotypical definitions of masculinity and femininity. *Transsexual* refers to individuals who wish to live and be accepted as a member of the other gender and often includes a desire to make their anatomy congruent. *Male-to-female (MTF)* and *female-to-male (FTM)* are terms recently replaced by many in the transgender community by *affirmed female* or *trans-woman*, and *affirmed male* or *trans-man*. This shift in terminology reflects the increasingly common belief that a transgender individual's gender does not change, as his or her brain (or soul) has always been his or her affirmed gender. *Transphobia* refers to discrimination against transsexualism and transgender people, based on their internal gender identity. *Sexual orientation* is often confused with gender identity but is an entirely different construct, referring to the gender of individuals to whom one is sexually or romantically attracted, and includes the categories homosexual, heterosexual, and bisexual. To better distinguish between gender identity and sexual orientation, consider the biological male who affirms a female identity and is attracted to women. This individual would likely identify as lesbian.

GID AND LACK OF INSURANCE COVERAGE

Many, if not most, young adolescent American transgender patients who are deemed appropriate candidates for the recommended medical intervention described below are unable to obtain the treatment due to insurance denial. Denial is based on the premise that GID is a mental disorder, rather than a physical one and necessary medical and surgical evaluation and treatment is excluded. This leaves patients and families with an impossible dilemma, given the incredibly high cost of the recommended medication and surgeries. Consequently, we have witnessed a socioeconomic divide in regard to who is able to obtain treatment in our clinic. This insurance issue also makes it difficult for patients to find any non-mental health providers willing to treat them, due to a concern among providers about whether they will be reimbursed for their services.

DESCRIPTION OF THE GENDER MANAGEMENT SERVICE (GEMS) AT CHILDREN'S HOSPITAL BOSTON AND ITS PATIENT POPULATION

We believe that those working with transgender children, adolescents, and adults are faced with the responsibility to provide treatment that: a) respects and trusts every patient's self-affirmed gender identity while recognizing and accepting the fact that it may be fluid, particularly in children; b) adheres to standards of care that are empirically supported whenever possible; and c) abides by ethical principles which support interventions that do no harm to the patient.

Although many academic centers treat GID adults, few pediatric centers provide psychological *and* hormonal treatment for GID adolescents. Until the recent publication of the Endocrine Society guidelines (Hembree et al., 2009), there had never been a professional medical society's recommendation to medically treat GID in young adolescents. The Division of Endocrinology at Children's Hospital Boston has been evaluating and treating GID youth since 1998, including patients with a broad range of ages, pubertal status, mental health histories, and psychiatric diagnoses. In 2007, the Gender Management Service (GeMS), an interdisciplinary clinic initially created for pediatric patients with disorders of sex development (DSD), formerly referred to as *intersex conditions*, began to include patients with GID and became the only pediatric clinic of its kind in the Western Hemisphere.

The first contact patients, parents, schools, or referring providers have with the GeMS clinic is with the administrative assistant who obtains general information related to the referral. This information is then passed to the GeMS social worker who schedules an initial intake with the patient and/or parent. These are typically done over the phone to obtain basic demographic, psychosocial functioning, therapy status, and insurance information. The phone calls typically take 30–60 minutes to complete, but can easily require more time due to parental anxiety about their child's condition and urgency for medical intervention due to the onset of puberty and the resulting increased psychological distress.

Parents of prepubertal children are offered support during the intake call, but are ultimately referred to outside therapists for ongoing treatment and assessment. The GeMS social worker follows up with these individuals annually to document the persistence of gender dysphoria and to facilitate entrance into GeMS when deemed appropriate.

The primary goal of the GeMS clinic is to provide medical treatment to appropriately screen gender dysphoric adolescents, along with the comprehensive psychological evaluation recommended by the Adolescent Gender Identity Research Group (AGIR) and the Endocrine Society for making this clinical decision. The clinic does not currently provide ongoing mental health services to patients and families but assists families in finding appropriate mental health therapists in their communities. In addition, a Children's Hospital Boston staff psychiatrist, who specializes in gender identity and sexuality issues, is available to provide both psychotherapy and psychopharmacological treatment where needed.

A pubertal individual who meets the following five criteria may be seen by the GeMS team: 1) a triage history of behavior suggestive of gender dysphoria; 2) commencement of puberty by parental or primary physician report; 3) participation in counseling for at least 6 months at the time of the first GeMS appointment; 4) supportive parents; and 5) a letter of support from a mental health care professional, ideally with a background and experience working with transgender youth.[1]

During the initial GeMS appointment, patients see the team psychologist for a comprehensive evaluation, which assesses the following:

a. adolescent's current degree of gender dysphoria;
b. complete history of gender identity development;
c. psychosexual functioning;
d. body image concerns;
e. current wishes regarding medical interventions;
f. coexisting psychiatric conditions and overall psychological/emotional functioning;

g. information about the family system, psychiatric history, and support;
h. school and educational information; and
i. social history/peer relationships.

This information is gathered during a 4–5 hour appointment that includes a comprehensive interview with the patient and parents, along with a battery of psychosocial and gender-related measures. This psychometric testing battery was adapted from the protocol used by the Amsterdam Gender Clinic for Children and Adolescents and agreed on by the International Adolescent Gender Identity Research Group (AGIR; de Vries, Cohen-Kettenis, Delemarre-Van de Wall, Holman, & Goldberg, 2008). Following this evaluation, the results and recommendations are discussed at the weekly GeMS team meeting to determine whether the patient is appropriate for medical intervention.

The team generally agrees that a patient is a good candidate if the following criteria are met: a) the results of the comprehensive evaluation indicate strong and persistent gender dysphoria and a desire by the patient to receive a medical intervention; b) there is no evidence of severe (e.g., psychosis), untreated psychiatric conditions; c) the patient's parents (or legal guardians) are in support of the medical intervention; d) the patient has agreed to remain in ongoing mental health counseling during the course of treatment in the GeMS clinic. By the time most patients are seen in the GeMS clinic, they are unlikely to be denied treatment due to our triage system that determines whether the initial criteria are met. However, in some instances, a patient may be denied medical intervention after undergoing the psychological evaluation. This may occur when an outside mental health provider refers a patient prematurely or inappropriately (e.g., the patient's gender identity has not been consistent or persistent), or if the patient has a co-occurring autism-spectrum disorder and the team feels that it is in his or her best interest to undergo additional gender-clarifying work with the outside mental health provider before being further considered for a medical intervention.

When a decision has been made to proceed with medical treatment for GID adolescents, the treatment depends on their stage of pubertal development. The following briefly describes what medical treatment patients may be eligible to receive upon initial evaluation in the GeMS clinic. Additional information regarding the medical treatment will be discussed in a later section.

a. Those in early or mid puberty (Tanner 2–3; breast budding or testicular increase to 4-8 cc.) initially receive pubertal-suppressive medical therapy, either GnRH analog (preferred) or high-dose progestin.
b. At approximately age 16 years, if the patient is deemed psychologically ready, and the stature of the affirmed gender can be optimized, patients

are given the option to receive cross-sex hormones to develop desired secondary sexual features.

c. Those who present nearly or fully developed (Tanner 4–5) and are deemed psychologically ready may be immediate candidates to receive cross-sex hormones. For those deemed not ready, pubertal suppressive medical therapy may be used in conjunction with recommendations and guidance around making a social transition (i.e., "real life experience"), if the patient has not already done this. In these cases, ongoing counseling with the outside mental health provider, along with additional psychological evaluation, must occur before being reconsidered for cross-sex hormone treatment.

Approximately 50% of patients seen since 1998 have been Tanner 4 or 5 at initial presentation. Prior to each step in the medical treatment protocol (i.e., puberty blocking medication, cross-sex hormones, and eventually surgery), the patient must be reevaluated by the team psychologist to assess whether the patient: a) continues to experience severe and persistent gender dysphoria, b) is psychiatrically stable, c) is cognitively and emotionally mature enough to make the decision regarding moving forward medically, d) has followed the GeMS requirement to remain in supportive psychotherapy during the course of treatment, and e) has a family who continues to be supportive of the patient's affirmed gender and additional medical intervention.

During the course of treatment in the GeMS clinic, patients are seen every 3–6 months for medical and psychiatric followup but are expected to continue meeting with their outside mental health provider on a regular basis (typically weekly or biweekly). It is also often recommended that family members, parents, in particular, seek their own supportive counseling with a knowledgeable therapist to address the impact of their child's gender dysphoria on them.

PSYCHOLOGICAL CO-MORBIDITIES

Prior to receiving medical intervention, many gender dysphoric adolescents are considerably depressed, anxious, or both. Many engage in self-harming behavior and report suicidal ideation and attempts (Grossman & D'Augelli, 2007; Spack et al., 2012). They often exhibit low self-esteem and a lack of self-worth. These adolescents frequently report being socially isolated and rejected by peers and adults, describing numerous incidents of teasing and bullying. Wallien, Swaab, and Cohen-Kettenis (2007) found that more than half of the children diagnosed with GID held an additional psychiatric diagnosis. Similarly, a study examining Dutch and Canadian children with GID found that both groups exhibited problems with social competence and behavior problems (Cohen-Kettenis, Owen, Kaijser, Bradley, & Zucker, 2003). A recently published study by Spack et al. (2012) found that 44% of transgender youth presenting for medical intervention had been previously diagnosed with a psychiatric disorder, the most common being depression, anxiety, and bipolar disorder. Thirty-six percent of these patients had been prescribed psychotropic medications and 9% had been hospitalized psychiatrically in the past. These psychological problems often intensify when transgender children reach puberty when they cannot escape the harsh reality of their biological sex, which is at odds with their affirmed gender identity. Although there are certainly cases of co-occurring psychiatric disorders (e.g., depression, anxiety), in our clinical experience these symptoms in transgender adolescents are often the result of feeling uncomfortable in their body and the social stigma and rejection they experience for being different. It is not uncommon for these symptoms to decrease and even disappear once the adolescent begins a social and physical transition. The previous diagnoses of major psychiatric disorders, especially mood disorders (e.g., major depressive disorder, bipolar disorder) in these patients are often secondary to their gender identity issue and many patients are "cured" of these disorders through medical intervention for the gender issue. We are currently collecting data to assess the mental health status of our patients more carefully as they progress through our treatment protocol.

AGE AT PRESENTATION

The GeMS clinic at Children's Hospital Boston only treats individuals who are on the cusp of puberty, determined by Tanner stage 2–3, and older. The youngest patients are approximately 10 years for girls and 12 years for boys due to sex differences in timing of physical maturation; however, the average age for patients seen in our clinic is a mid-teenager. Interestingly, biological boys are presenting earlier than biological girls, despite the fact that the initiation of male puberty is typically later than for females. One possible explanation for this statistically significant gender difference is our culture's greater acceptance of gender nonconforming females than males; thus, girls may be able to get by longer with a more androgynous or tomboy presentation without much social rejection and harassment. Furthermore, the need for a medical intervention may feel less pressing for biological females and their parents than for males due to the greater ease with which the former are able to pass without medical intervention. Aside from having a shorter than average stature for a male, biological females are able to bind their chests, and menstruation occurs without others' awareness. Biological males who affirm a female identity, on the other hand, are plagued with growth spurt, facial and body hair growth, Adam's apple development, facial bone structure changes, and lowering of the voice, all of which are very difficult to hide and either extremely costly or impossible to change once puberty is complete.

RECOMMENDED MEDICAL TREATMENT

The Endocrine Society recently approved guidelines for medically treating transgender adolescents (Hembree, et al., 2009). These recommendations are followed by the GeMS clinic and are described below.

A principle of the puberty blocking intervention is to buy time for the early pubertal patient to be evaluated without the stress of developing permanent physical characteristics of the biological sex and to delay initiation of permanent characteristics of the affirmed gender. Puberty is suppressed in young adolescents, and the use of cross-sex steroids and surgeries deferred until later adolescence when the patient is old enough to fully understand the implications of these treatments, including infertility.

Ideal treatment involves the use of pubertal suppression via GnRH analog at Tanner 2 genital development in biological males (doubling or tripling gonadal size to 4–8 cm without phallic or other evidence of testosterone effects) and at Tanner 2 bilateral breast budding in biological females. The physical benefits gained may include:

a. preventing a need for mammoplasties in biological females,
b. preventing menarche/menses which are psychologically traumatic,
c. allowing for a longer period of growth in biological females via delayed epiphyseal closure,
d. preventing skeletal changes, especially in facial bones, in biological males that accentuate brow, zygoma, mandible, and to prevent development of an Adam's apple,
e. preventing unwanted phallic growth and psychologically disturbing spontaneous erections,
f. preventing permanent male voice and virilized facial and scalp hair patterns, including temporal balding,[2]
g. GnRH-induced pubertal suppression is reversible, with retained ovulatory function and sperm production in patients who discontinue their gender transition.

Around the age of 16, following repeat intensive psychometric evaluation, appropriate candidates may begin to take cross-sex steroids to develop the secondary sexual characteristics of the affirmed gender. Patients who have continued to strongly and consistently identify with the other gender during the course of GnRH-analog treatment and who continue to meet the initial criteria for beginning a medical treatment, as described previously, are considered good candidates for the next step in treatment. This decision is made with additional psychometric testing, followed by a discussion of the results along with the patient's treatment progress, by the GeMS interdisciplinary team. Ideally, the steroids (parenteral testosterone, oral or patch estrogen) would be gradually introduced while the GnRH analog is continued until gonadectomies to restrain the endogenous gonads. In the United States, the above-mentioned lack of insurance coverage for medical and surgical therapy for GID often compromises the ability to provide ideal GnRH analog therapy for those dependent on insurance to cover their medical expenses, and less effective agents with more side effects, such as high dose estrogen must often be used.

Biological female patients age 16 years or over may be considered for virilizing mammoplasty, with further evaluation by the GeMS psychologist, and letters of support from their outside mental health professional and prescribing physician. Female-to-male transgender individuals rarely seek genitoplasty or phalloplasty because the final surgical product lacks functionality and has a limited cosmetic result. Bilateral oophorectomy and hysterectomy are increasingly being sought and any castrating procedure, including feminizing genitoplasty, is deferred in the United States until age 18, the age of majority, and only with strong letters of support.

For all patients considering any medical intervention, the risks and benefits are described, including probable infertility, in order for patients (and parents of minors), to give informed assent or consent.

PSYCHOLOGICAL BENEFITS OF PUBERTAL SUPPRESSION

There are numerous psychological benefits of suppressing puberty for transgender adolescents. First, this reversible intervention can prevent needless emotional and psychological suffering, which can be severe for some adolescents (e.g., self-harming behaviors and suicidality; Grossman & D'Augelli, 2007; Spack et al., 2012). Second, it buys time for the adolescent to continue meeting with a psychotherapist in an effort to determine whether the cross-gender identity is persistent and whether a full physical transition is ultimately in his or her best interest. Self-exploration without the intense distress caused by the physical effects of puberty may allow an adolescent more time to develop greater clarity and certainty. Third, this intervention allows the clinician to assess how the adolescent functions when unwanted secondary sex characteristics are suppressed. If prior psychological distress decreases, it is assumed that the source of the distress was related to the gender dysphoria. Finally, preventing puberty allows for a much easier full transition to the other gender at a later time because the individual's body remains a neutral, early pubertal state. The difficult-to-reverse physical effects of puberty are a source of much psychological distress for adult transsexuals wishing to pass as the other gender. Therefore, it is our clinical impression that preventing these unwanted secondary sex characteristics with puberty blocking medical intervention allows for better long-term quality of life for transgender youth than their experience without this intervention. This has been the clinical experience of those working in the Amsterdam Gender Clinic as well. The Amsterdam Clinic has treated and systematically followed over 100 adolescent patients with puberty blocking medication, and has found the physical and psychological outcomes to be excellent. These data will likely be published soon (P. Cohen-Kettenis, personal communication, October 2010). In addition, a large-scale prospective study of pubertal suppression will soon to be initiated in the GeMS clinic which will shed additional light on this topic.

GENDER VARIANCE IN CHILDREN

Although the GeMS clinic at Children's Hospital Boston does not treat gender variant children, we do receive numerous calls from parents, schools, medical providers, and mental health therapists seeking advice and guidance regarding how to address gender variance in children, and the numerous issues that accompany this condition.

Our team has a philosophical belief regarding how these children should be treated, informed by our experience working with adolescent patients who were either previously not treated or treated with a range of psychotherapeutic approaches. The lessons we have learned from these patients support the use of early individual and family therapy that encourages acceptance of the child's budding gender development while simultaneously emphasizing the importance of remaining open to the fluidity of his or her gender identity and sexual orientation. Issues related to homophobia and transphobia among family members, schools, and the broader communities (neighbors, religious affiliations) should be addressed during this time as well.

Also critical in supporting gender dysphoric children is the thoughtful decision regarding when and if a child should socially transition to his or her affirmed gender, and several factors should be considered in making this determination. First, the child's wishes and desires should be carefully considered, as the degree to which each child wishes to present as the other gender varies greatly. For example, some children may choose to remain in the gender that is congruent with their biological sex at school in order to avoid teasing and ridicule, but may wish to live in their affirmed gender at home and in other safe environments. Other children may become extremely depressed and even suicidal if not permitted to live in their affirmed gender in all areas of their lives. In these circumstances, our clinical recommendation is that every effort be made to support the child by allowing them to live in their affirmed gender to the extent that it is deemed safe.

Although we believe following the child's lead is paramount, certain precautions must be considered. First, the impact of the social transition on the child's siblings should be taken into consideration. Often, we find that siblings are the most supportive members in the family of the gender dysphoric child, often coming to accept the social transition quickly and becoming a primary ally when their gender dysphoric sibling is teased by peers. However, in other cases, the social implications of having a severely gender dysphoric brother or sister can be devastating.

Another issue relates to the broader community and school system in which a child lives. Although we have heard exceptions where rural schools and communities are surprisingly supportive of gender dysphoric youth, this is not always the case and often the opposite is true. Thus, the extent to which a child is permitted to socially transition must be done with consideration for the safety of the child and other family members, largely influenced by the degree to which one's community is accepting of diversity.

The decision to support an early social transition brings an understandable concern that the child will not feel free to switch back to the gender assigned to his or her biological sex if he or she so desires in the future. Some parents are uncomfortable with the ambiguity of the situation and the possibility of continued gender fluidity in their child. They may make it more difficult for younger children in particular to freely transition back to their birth-assigned gender. Every parent with whom we address this issue claims that they would be relieved if their child eventually accepted their gender assigned at birth for the obvious reasons that it would make their child's life less difficult and would not result in body-altering medical interventions. Nevertheless, we recognize that ambiguity around their child's gender identity can be uncomfortable for parents. Consequently, we believe it is critical to continually emphasize the importance of remaining open to the possibility of the child's gender shifting back at some point. We further cite research indicating that most gender dysphoric children will not, in fact, grow up to be transgender (Bradley & Zucker, 1997; Wallien & Cohen-Kettenis, 2008; Zucker & Bradley, 1995).

Finally, for those who do decide to transition back to their birth-assigned gender at a later time, a recent qualitative study of Dutch patients by Steensma, Biemond, de Boer, & Cohen-Kettenis (2011) found a retrospectively reported increase in psychological distress for a subset of biological females who lived as boys during childhood and then switched back to live as females in adolescence. Although this study raises an important issue that should be seriously considered when discussing the pros and cons of allowing young children to socially transition with parents, we have not seen any detrimental effects of early social transitioning in our patient population when done in a thoughtful way, taking into consideration all of the factors outlined above. In fact, we have only had one patient in our clinic who socially transitioned prior to puberty, was then approved for puberty blocking medication at the appropriate stage, and then one year later decided to switch back to the gender congruent with her biological sex. Inconsistent with the study described above, our clinical observations with this patient did not identify any indicators of psychological distress as a result of this decision, and, in fact, both she and her mother reported that it was only due to the freedom to experience living as a male and the availability of the puberty blocking medical intervention that she was able to make an informed decision regarding her gender identity. Without this opportunity and intervention, she and her mother expressed that the psychological stress caused by her unwanted biological puberty would have been overwhelming and likely would have resulted in further psychiatric decompensation.

SUBSET OF LATE-ADOLESCENT ONSET TRANSGENDER PATIENTS

Most adolescent patients who are seen in the GeMS clinic report histories of gender atypical behavior and severe gender dysphoria in childhood, and their parents recall this as well. These patients would likely have met the diagnostic criteria for gender identity disorder in childhood, had we evaluated them when younger. However, there is a subset of patients who have an atypical transgender identity development for one or more reasons.

Most of these late-adolescent onset transgender patients indicate that they always felt different or knew that something was not right, but were unable to identify it until puberty. Oftentimes these individuals report that they initially thought that their confusion was related to sexual orientation because they were unaware that transgenderism existed. Others report that they were aware of feeling like the other gender, but either thought that there was nothing that could be done about it so they tried to ignore the feelings, or they feared how others would react if they expressed their gender dysphoria. Some of these patients recall attempting to inform a parent of their cross-gender identity but feeling quickly dismissed or rejected, making it difficult to bring up again. We find it common among these patients to report little or no early body dissatisfaction as it relates to their male or female anatomy. Sometimes these patients report having been unaware of the anatomical differences between males and females when younger, thus being oblivious to what they were missing. The awareness of one's body not fitting with one's affirmed gender seems to occur at puberty for many of these patients.

Most parents of late-onset transgender patients are leery of their adolescent's newly affirmed gender identity, this is understandable given their child's lack of history supporting this. However, many of these adolescents report that their friends are not surprised by their declaration of their affirmed gender, often responding that they had suspected it for some time.

A more complicated subgroup among the late-adolescent onset patients fall within the autism spectrum, specifically with a question or previous diagnosis of Asperger's disorder. While we have also seen two younger patients with classic autism, Asperger's disorder has only been apparent in our adolescent patients, among whom we have not seen any classic autism cases. The GID-Asperger's and autism spectrum connection is perplexing and has begun to be studied. de Vries Noens, Cohen-Kettenis, van Berckelaer-Onnes, and Doreleijers (2010) found a 10 times greater incidence of autism spectrum disorders among children and adolescents referred to their gender clinic compared to the general population. However, this research examined primarily severe cases of autism, rather than milder versions, such as Asperger's disorder, which is more commonly seen in the GeMS clinic at Children's Hospital Boston. Although the question of whether gender dysphoria is simply a symptom of an autism spectrum disorder has been raised by mental health clinicians in the field, we feel it is equally worth questioning the validity of an autism diagnosis among transgender youth, particularly of those diagnosed with Asperger's disorder. Perhaps the social awkwardness and lack of peer relationships common among GID-Asperger's patients is a result of a lifetime of feeling isolated and rejected; and maybe the unusual behavior patterns are simply a coping method for dealing with the anxiety and depression created from living in an "alien body," as one patient described it. Continued research on the GID-Autism connection will help to further understand this link and assist in developing appropriate differential diagnostic and treatment guidelines. The GeMS clinic does not refuse medical treatment to autism-spectrum patients, but moves forward at a much slower and cautious pace, always working closely with the outside mental health provider in the assessment and treatment of these patients.

TREATMENT GOALS AND RATIONALE

Gender atypical behavior in childhood is not unusual. In most cases, the behavior and the accompanying moderate gender dysphoria can best be described as a disruptive phase (to the extent that it has an impact on one's daily functioning). However, we perceive those with severe gender dysphoria, cross-gender behavior, and strong identification with the other gender (usually accompanied by dissatisfaction with one's sexual anatomy, but not always), which either: a) began in childhood and persisted into adolescence with little or no wavering, or b) was recognized in adolescence with the onset of puberty and has persisted and intensified as puberty progressed (see earlier section on late-onset transgenderism) to be a primary physical rather than psychological condition. Our clinical experience has found that the psychological distress that exists for these patients is almost always due to: a) an extreme discomfort with one's body that is alleviated with medical intervention, and b) the social stigma that results from being different, specifically prior to transitioning. The patients we see who have been accepted by their friends, family, and school in their affirmed gender rarely exhibit psychological distress or inability to function in most areas of their life. The patients who have been both accepted by their networks of social support and are able to move forward with appropriate medical interventions are even less likely to exhibit psychological distress. Furthermore, of the 70 patients whom we have evaluated in our clinic and approved for cross-sex hormone treatment, none have changed their mind regarding their affirmed gender to date.

One early pubertal patient did change her mind after having puberty blocked for one year, ultimately identifying with the gender congruent with her biological sex. We certainly observe gender fluidity even in our clinic of severely gender dysphoric individuals in terms of the extent to which patients feel it necessary to alter their physical bodies in order to feel comfortable in their affirmed gender. For example, some individuals are only concerned about "passing" to the outside world (e.g., absence of large breasts in an affirmed male), while others care only about the body altering procedures that will provide them with the internal sense of being their affirmed gender (e.g., hormones used to eliminate spontaneous erections in an affirmed female). Moreover, for some individuals, possessing the correct body parts is essential for feeling completely feminine or masculine, while this is less important for others. This is not surprising when considering the variation in the non-gender identity disordered population (i.e., those who were fortunate enough to have their biological sex match their gender identity) regarding the degree to which one's secondary sex characteristics define his or her gender identity.

In the GeMS clinic, the primary individual treatment goal is assessing the patient to determine the severity of his or her gender dysphoria, and determining over time and with careful evaluation how to proceed with medical interventions that will result in the patient feeling comfortable in his or her body and capable of living as a psychological and physically healthy individual. The degree and type of medical intervention will vary based on all of the factors described above.

ADDRESSING SOCIETAL ISSUES

The treatment goals for individual patients may be considered straightforward when compared to the interventions necessary to address societal intolerance of transgender individuals. However, a societal shift must occur in order for these patients to truly be able to live without increased risk of psychological distress and potential physical harm by self or others caused by intolerance and discrimination. Like other medical and mental health providers addressing the psychological impact of other socially stigmatizing conditions (e.g., racial and ethnic differences, ageism, sexual orientation, sizeism), we wish to serve as advocates for the transgender population in the broader culture and community. This includes advocating for patients within school and legal systems, educating the public through organized discussions and appropriate media outlets, and of utmost need at the present time, training more mental health and medical providers to provide the care that these greatly underserved patients require.

CONCLUSIONS

We hope to learn from the progress made in the health care fields about providing services to gay, lesbian, and bisexual patients who initially could only find medical and psychological care from homosexual professionals or from clinics serving the gay and lesbian community. Perhaps someday we will have the long-term outcome data comparing transgender people treated too late with those who were fortunate enough to have been treated sufficiently early within an accepting society.

NOTES

1. The GeMS clinic provides a letter for each patient's outside mental health provider, which outlines the information we ask be included in their letter of support. This includes a description of the therapist's background and training in working with transgender youth; their assessment of the patient's gender dysphoria (severity, consistency, etc.); any psychiatric comorbidities that exist; and any other concerns they have about the patient moving forward with a medical treatment for their GID (e.g., difficult family situation; lack of gender identity history typical of transgender youth).

2. The largest lifetime expense for a male-to-female transperson in the USA is electrolysis.

REFERENCES

American Psychiatric Association. (2000). *Diagnostic and statistical manual of mental disorders* (4th ed., text rev.). Washington DC: Author.

Bradley, S. J., & Zucker, K. J. (1997). Gender identity disorder: A review of the past 10 years. *Journal of the American Academy of Child and Adolescent Psychiatry*, *35*, 872–880.

Cohen-Kettenis, P. T., Owen, A., Kaijser, V., Bradley, S. J., & Zucker, K. J. (2003). Demographic characteristics, social competence, and behavior problems in children with gender identity disorder: A cross-national, cross-clinic comparative analysis. *Journal of Abnormal Child Psychology*, *31*, 41–53.

de Vries, A. L. C., Cohen-Kettenis, P. T., Delemarre-Van de Wall, H., Holman, C. W., & Goldberg, J. (2008). Caring for transgender adolescents in BC: Suggested guidelines. 2006. Retrieved from http://www.vch.ca/transhealth

de Vries, A. L. C., Noens, I. L. J., Cohen-Kettenis, P. T., van Berckelaer-Onnes, I. A., & Doreleijers, T. A. (2010). Autism spectrum disorders in gender dysphoric children and adolescents. *Journal of Autism and Developmental Disorders*, *40*, 930–936.

Grossman, A. H., & D'Augelli, A. R. (2007). Transgender youth and life-threatening behaviors. *Suicide and Life-Threatening Behavio*r, *37*, 527–537.

Hembree, W. C., Cohen-Kettenis, P., Delemarre-van de Waal, H. A., Gooren, L. J., Meyer W. J., III, Spack, N. P., . . . Montori, V. M. (2009). Endocrine treatment of transsexual persons: An Endocrine Society clinical practice guideline. *Journal of Clinical Endocrinology and Metabolism*, *94*, 3132–3154.

Spack, N. P., Edwards-Leeper, L., Feldman, H. A., Leibowitz, S., Mandel, F., Diamond D. A., & Vance, S. R. (2012). Children and adolescents with gender identity disorder referred to a pediatric medical center. *Pediatrics*, *129*(3), 418–425.

Steemsa, T. D., Biemond, R., de Boer, F., & Cohen-Kettenis, P. T. (2011). Desisting and persisting gedner dysphoria after childhood: A qualitative follow-up study. *Clinical Child Psychology and Psychiatry*, *16*(4), 499–516.

Wallien, M. S. C., Swaab, H., & Cohen-Kettenis, P. T. (2007). Psychiatric comorbidity among children with gender identity disorder. *Journal of the American Academy of Child and Adolescent Psychiatry*, *46*, 1307–1314.

Wallien, M. S. C., & Cohen-Kettenis, P. T. (2008). Psychosexual outcome of gender-dysphoric children. *Journal of the American Academy of Child and Adolescent Psychiatry*, *47*, 1413–1423.

Zucker, K. J., & Bradley S. J. (1995). *Gender Identity disorder and psychosexual problems in children and adolescents*. New York, NY: Guilford Press.

From Gender Identity Disorder to Gender Identity Creativity: True Gender Self Child Therapy

DIANE EHRENSAFT, PhD
*Department of Pediatrics, University of California San Francisco,
San Francisco, California, USA*

True gender self child therapy is based on the premise of gender as a web that weaves together nature, nurture, and culture and allows for a myriad of healthy gender outcomes. This article presents concepts of true gender self, false gender self, and gender creativity as they operationalize in clinical work with children who need therapeutic supports to establish an authentic gender self while developing strategies for negotiating an environment resistant to that self. Categories of gender nonconforming children are outlined and excerpts of a treatment of a young transgender child are presented to illustrate true gender self child therapy.

My description amounts to a plea to every therapist to allow for the patient's capacity to play. . . . The patient's creativity can only be too easily stolen by a therapist who knows too much. (Winnicott, 1970, p. 57)

The form of therapy in which I engage with gender nonconforming and transgender children and youth is a treatment modality I have dubbed, *true gender self therapy* (TGST). As a child clinician deeply influenced by the work of D. W. Winnicott, I unexpectedly found myself turning to his concepts of the true self, false self, and individual creativity for the underlying principles of the form of therapy I engage in with any child who is sorting out gender issues. Winnicott's (1970) quote above reminded me that the therapist who knows too much about gender is typically the therapist who does not know enough, and that true knowing comes from listening to the patient.

In 2003, Cohen-Kettenis and Pflafflin (2003) wrote a comprehensive review of treatment options available at the time for transgender children and youth. They concluded: "Despite the many treatment approaches, controlled studies do not exist. It is therefore still unclear whether (an extreme) GID in childhood can truly be cured . . . .Nothing is known about the relative effectiveness of various treatment methods . . . . . .Pending controlled studies, psychotherapy directly aimed at curing GID has no place in the treatment arsenal" (p. 129). In 2012, as I write this piece, I regret to say that we have not traversed much further in executing such studies (Cf. Muller et al., 2009, for a review of studies to date). Yet, we now have research data indicating that gender nonconforming youth who receive support from their families for their sexual or gender identities show better mental health functioning than their peers who do not, as measured by direct assessment of the youth (Ryan, Huebner, Diaz, & Sanchez, 2009) or parent reports (Hill, Menvielle, Sica, & Johnson, 2010). In addition, listening to the patient has proved to be a vital source of information about the treatments we provide to transgender and other gender noconforming[1] youth as mental health professionals. Repeatedly, the children I work with tell me, in words and actions, that when allowed to express their gender as they feel it rather than as others dictate it, they become enlivened and engaged; when prohibited from that expression, they show symptoms of anxiety, stress, distress, anger, and depression.

With that said, it is my view, after reviewing the existing data, that significant harm is done to children when adults attempt to adjust the children's gender expressions and self-affirmed identities to match the gender listed on their birth certificates and from which the children show signs of transgression. Traditionally, mental health professionals have engaged in treatment approaches aimed at shaping a child to accept his or her assigned gender and adapt to the gender expressions "appropriate" to that assignation. True gender therapy is an alternative, or might I say opposing clinical model operating from the premise that gender is not a binary category, as our dominant cultural and theoretical canons assert, but is rather a complicated three-dimensional web. Each individual will spin his or her own unique gender web, from threads of nature, nurture, and culture. Like fingerprints, no two gender webs will be exactly alike.

In the majority of children, the gender assigned at birth will match the gender they feel themselves to be. A very small minority of children will experience a cacophony between their assigned and affirmed[2] gender, the latter defined as the gender that a child asserts him or herself to be. As with left-handed children, who are also a small minority of the population, I believe these children who experience this discord are not abnormal, they simply vary from the norm. Other children will accept the gender assigned to them at birth, but not the culturally defined expressions assigned to that gender. The true gender self model assumes that for all children, gender traditional and gender nonconforming alike, the primary locus of gender lies not between the legs but between the ears, or in Diamond's (2002) words, "It can be said that one is a sex and one does gender; that sex typically, but not always, represents what is between one's legs while gender represents what is between one's ears" (p. 323). In essence, the brain and mind work to establish an inner sense of self as male, female, or other, based on body, on thoughts and feelings, and absorption of messages from the external world, a sense of self that may or not match the sex that is found between one's legs. In this theory of gender development, individuals are the experts of their own gender identities and while gender expressions may vary over time, gender identity shows more temporal consistency. If we want to know how a child identifies, listen to the child, and if you pay close attention and provide a safe enough holding environment, over time he or she will tell you.

This model of gender development dispenses with the diagnosis of Gender Identity Disorder of Childhood (GIDC) of the *Diagnostic and Statistical Manual of Mental Disorders* (4th ed., text rev; *DSM-IV-TR*; American Psychiatric Association, 2000), a diagnosis and implied treatment that pathologize perfectly healthy children who are simply expressing their authentic gender identity. A boy who plays only with girls and with toys that have been culturally labeled as "girl toys" and dreams of being a girl when he grows up is not a child with a disorder, but rather a child who is creatively weaving his own gender web. The same applies to the girl who wants a boy's haircut, plays on the boys' soccer team, and blanches at the sight of a dress in her closet. The job of the clinician is not to ward off a transgender outcome, but to facilitate the child's authentic gender journey. This does not mean that gender can never be a symptom of some other underlying disorder rather than an expression of self. However, the most challenging task for the child clinician is to differentiate those symptomatic situations from the, albeit complicated but healthy, developmental journey of children who are reaching to establish their true gender identity and authentic gender expressions. If we are to place a gender diagnosis in any statistical manual of diagnoses, I would propose that the only diagnosis relevant and supportive of gender nonconforming and transgender children is *gender dysphoria*, a felt stress or distress about one's gender placement or identity. Therapeutic attention to relieve that stress involves sorting out internal conflicts about gender, working with parents to facilitate support for the child, or building a child's resilience to meet the unwelcome reception of a transphobic or genderist[3] milieu. The gender dysphoric stress or distress is not meant to be the parents' or social environment's angst, but solely the child's, defined not by others but by direct reports from or clinical observations of the child. TGST is also predicated on the observation that the vast majority of gender nonconforming and transgender children show up to their parents, rather than being shaped by them, suggesting an innate component to the gender nonconformity. The parents are responding to something exhibited by the child, rather than placing it there, and are often puzzled by the appearance of their child's gender nonconforming behaviors. In the words of one mother, "When he was two, he was always in my jewelry, my purses, always in the closet for my shoes, wanting to dress like me . . . I don't think anyone encouraged it'" (as reported in Green, 1987, p. 116).

From gender identity disorder to gender identity creativity, the rubric of the psychoanalytically informed treatment paradigm I would like to present, is a model that dispenses with the notion of binary gender categories, challenges assessments of perversion and inversion cast on gender transgressive people, and strives to help children discover their gender authenticity (Ehrensaft, 2011a, 2011b, 2011c). Central is the psychic importance of the true gender self, the potential dangers of the false gender self if left untreated, and the role of the child clinician in facilitating the child's gender creativity and authenticity. Although I focus on the development and treatment of children, I would like to emphasize that gender development is an unfolding life-long process and much of what I say applies to adults as well.

TRUE GENDER SELF, FALSE GENDER SELF, AND GENDER CREATIVITY

In Winnicott's (1960a, 1960b) concepts of human development, he identified the true self as the authentic core of one's personality, from which spontaneous action and a sense of realness come. He proposed that the original kernel of the true self is evident at birth. The potential for the true self to unfold is predicated on appropriate mirroring and emotional holding by the primary caretakers, in which the adults do not impose their own selves on the child's psyche but rather allow the child's authentic self to emerge. Winnicott defined false self as that part of the personality that accommodates to the demands of outer reality and functions to shield the true self from annihilation. According to Winnicott's theory, there are different points along a spectrum at which any one individual must call forth the false self to protect the true self's existence. One of those points is where the true self is acknowledged as a potential and allowed a secret life, while the false self holds forth to accommodate to the expectations and demands of the environment. The psychic intention at that point is the preservation of the individual in spite of abnormal environmental circumstances (Winnicott,

1960a). Individual creativity is the psychological function that launches the true self and allows it to stay afloat. It facilitates spontaneity, authenticity, and feeling real. In the beginning, individual creativity is reliant on a co-construction between the child and the people who comprise the holding environment, adults who in optimal circumstances will be responsive to the child's true self and able to follow the child's lead rather than imposing their own sensibilities about how that child should be. Individual creativity works to help an individual build a meaningful personal world for him or herself—a weaving together of internal desires with external realities to build one's subjectivity. When allowed to function unfettered, individual creativity leads to the discovery of one's quintessential self. Individual creativity is the opposite of compliance. In compliance one recognizes an external world into which one must fit. In creativity, an individual calls upon his or her own lens through which to view that external world while taking liberties to define the personal meaning of that vision. In existential terms, individuals will either find themselves living creatively and feel that life is worth living or end up finding no such creativity and doubting the value of living at all. Through creativity, the goal of life is to allow one's true self and individuality to blossom. Danger prevails when the false self takes over and suffocates the true self. In the most extreme case, an individual might want to stop living completely rather than let the false self continue to beat the true self into submission.

Although Winnicott (1960) never intended these concepts as defining features of gender, the three terms are remarkably adaptable to a nonbinary theory of gender development and treatment. This theory perceives gender as fluid rather than dichotomous, both within the individual and over a lifetime, and considers all human beings, not just the gender nonconforming child or adult, to carry within them the socially constructed attributes of both the feminine and the masculine along with characteristics that defy any such binary categorization (Corbett, 2009; Dimen, 1995, 2003, 2005; Goldner, 1991, 2003; Harris, 1991, 2000, 2005).

The true gender self begins as the kernel of gender identity that is there from birth, residing within us in a complex of chromosomes, gonads, hormones, hormone receptors, genitalia, but most importantly in our brain and mind. Once we are born, the true gender self is most definitely shaped and channeled through our experience with the external world, but its center always remains our own personal possession, driven from within rather than from without. Even in the face of imposed prescriptions, proscriptions, or repudiation, we strive to both establish and claim rights to our true gender self, which will include both our gender identity and our gender expressions, and which, although stable, may still shift over the course of our lives.

Gender expression is defined as those behaviors, actions, and choices we make to present ourselves as male, female, or some conglomeration or even negation of gender categories altogether (Brill & Pepper, 2008). The true gender self does not necessarily match one's gender expression. For example, a transgender woman reflects back on her high school experience: "I never dressed in women's clothes at school and usually I became alienated from my friends who did this. They caught a lot of heat. But I was different. For me, it wasn't the way I looked or dressed, it was the way I felt. It's who I was, it's how I identified at that particular time inside" (Glenn, 2009, p.109). Inner feelings, not outer accoutrements, are the cornerstone of the true gender self, which can be equated with the definition of *core gender identity* in traditional theories of gender development: "the sense of one's sex—of maleness in males and of femaleness in females, and in rare case of anatomic hermaphrodites, of being both, or even a vague sense of being a member of the opposite sex" (Stoller, 1985, p. 11). Remove the words "rare" and "vague" and replace hermaphrodite with "intersex" and "sex" with "gender" in Stoller's definition and what remains is a close approximation of the definition of the true gender self, absent the fluid variations and recognition of cultural specificity of the meanings of maleness and femaleness.

The false gender self is the face a child puts on for the world, based on the expectations of the external environment and the child's interpretations and internalizations of either appropriate or adaptive gender behaviors. Any child can and probably will develop a false gender self, running the gamut from the cisgender boy who puts on a macho mask to empower himself and please his Marine dad to the transgender child who hides dresses in the closet to avoid punishment from disapproving parents. Living an authentic gender life is a particular challenge for children who experience an extreme discrepancy between the gender assigned to them at birth and the gender they know themselves to be, particularly if that discrepancy is not welcomed by the world in which they live. The gender nonconforming and particularly the transgender child may need to wrap a blanket over the true gender self to ensure surviving in a world that might not be ready to embrace that child for who he or she is. That world qualifies as *abnormal environmental circumstances* in Winnicott's (1960) terminology and that blanket would be the false gender self. This process can occur either consciously or unconsciously. If such children are not given the opportunity for their true gender selves to emerge, they may find themselves at the most extreme end of the true self–false self spectrum, where intense efforts by the false gender self to shield the true gender self from annihilation, if failing, can result in the child's desire to die or be destroyed—from the despair of the true gender self never having a chance to emerge or the distress of being trapped in a life and/or body that feels too unreal. Studies document that incidences of suicide or suicide attempts are significantly higher in gender nonconforming youth than in the general population (Carver, Yunger, & Perry, 2003; D'Augelli, Grossman, & Starks, 2006; Morrow, 2004; Pilkington & D'Augelli, 1995; Yunger, Carner, & Perry, 2004), much of it attributed to the harassment and victimization from the external world but in so many cases, I believe, also a manifestation of the false gender self's strangulation of the true gender self's existence.

To guard against such morbid eventualities, gender creativity steps in, defined as each individual's unique crafting of a gender self that integrates body, brain, mind, and psyche, which, in turn, is influenced by socialization and culture, to establish his or her authentic gender identity and expressions. In the creative impulse of gender, a little child is drawn to make something of gender that is not based just on the inside (the child's body, the child's thoughts and feelings), nor just on the outside (the family, the culture's expectations), but a weaving together of the two, with the child in charge of the thread that spins the web. Every child's gender creativity will be unique. Every child will depend on a supportive environment to allow his or her gender creativity to unfold. Every child will suffer if an intrusive environment grabs the thread from the child and spins its own web around the child.

For gender nonconforming children, gender creativity works actively to circumvent the false gender self and privately keep the true gender self alive even in situations where it is not safe to let it come out. So, for example, Jeremy learns that he is not allowed to wear his favorite red velvet dress to school, only in the sanctity of his home. He does not like that, but he learns to accept it, as his parents have empathically explained to him that his school is not ready to accept a boy in dresses and the school still has more learning to do. He negotiates this conflict through reverie. Sitting at his desk at school, Jeremy imagines himself gliding through the classroom door in his beautiful dress. His hair is long and golden and all the girls gather around to admire him. But actually, it is not him. It is her—Genevieve, a perfect name for the girl he imagines himself to be. He has missed the math lesson, but in his musings he has let his gender creativity reign, asserting in fantasy the girl he knows himself to be but cannot yet express.

Therapeutically, it is important to differentiate gender creativity from gender creation. If a transgender child just shows up rather than being shaped by the parents, how is his or her core transgender self "creative" rather than "just is"? Would the concept of gender creativity erroneously suggest that a child made a decision to choose this identity, rather than coming into the world with it as the kernel of the true gender self? Like with any child, gender creativity is not the end product, that is, the gender identity and expressions, but rather the act of putting together the wardrobe of the affirmed true gender self, both literally and symbolically.

PRIMER OF TRUE GENDER SELF THERAPY

TGST has a simple goal: helping a child build gender resilience and explore his or her authentic gender identity while acknowledging social constraints that may work against its full expression. Whether working directly with a child, or indirectly through the parents, an objective is to facilitate acquisition of a psychological tool kit that will allow a child to internalize a positive self-identity while recognizing situations in which that identity may be in need of protection from an unwelcome or hostile environment. The specific tools for self-protection should be consciously constructed rather than unconsciously driven. In that regard, the therapist will need to differentiate the false gender self as a conscious artifice under the child's control from the false gender self as an embedded and constricting aspect of the child's personality, unavailable or resistant to conscious control. To minimize the need for either of those two self-constructions, it behooves the therapist to actively work not only with families but also with the community to facilitate transformations from an "abnormal environmental circumstance" (Winnicott, 1960b) to a supportive holding environment for the gender nonconforming or transgender child, so that Jeremy, for example, would be free to waltz into class in his red velvet dress.

Just as there is no infant without a mother (Winnicott, 1960b), there is no gender nonconforming child without an accompanying family or family substitute when it comes to treatment. Parents or caretakers bringing a gender nonconforming or transgender child to a therapist will come with two potentially opposing socialization tasks: allowing the child to unfold to be his or her healthiest and most authentic self; ensuring that the child is safe in the world. In TGST, there is no one formula for the appropriate balance between these two demands, except to say that the overriding principle is to foster the child's authentic gender. When parents deem it too dangerous to allow a child to fully express him or herself in certain settings or are themselves not psychologically ready to allow such expression, the function of the therapy is to ensure that a child externalizes rather than internalizes the potentially negative valence of those proscriptions. When parents find it necessary to ask a child to employ a false self presentation, when the family itself is not a safe environment for the child to fully express him or herself or when the child has actually been ejected from home because of a gender identity or presentation, ego-building will be a strong component of the therapeutic work. In these situations, the therapist can explore with the child the self-protective false gender self constructions that have evolved not because his or her inner self is bad or damaged, but because there is an external world that is not yet ready to receive it. This is a resiliency model facilitating the child's development of empowering responses to negative reactions from peers at school that are common and chronic occurrences in the lives of gender nonconforming children (Toomey, Ryan, Diaz, Card, & Russell, 2010).

This true gender self model does not give a free pass to a child's self-determined gender expressions and identities without assessment of the possibility of gender nonconforming presentations and ideations as a symptom of some other underlying psychological problem or a gender self that is not yet formed. To the contrary, every true gender self therapist will need to recognize that a child's gender is a developmentally unfolding process for which we must be able to suspend ourselves in a state of ambiguity and not knowing and understand that both the developmental unfolding and the therapeutic journey will be a process that takes time and careful and thorough explorations on the part of the therapist. Failure to accept this ambiguity would violate the very premise of the true gender self, for authenticity in these symptomatic cases may lie not in gender transformations but in sorting out other conflicts of self that express themselves through the portal of gender.

My own clinical experience is that in the vast majority of gender nonconforming children, there is no history of trauma or attachment disruptions. They come from stable families in which the most distinguishing features of their developmental histories are the parents' reports that their child just presented him or herself that way, typically in the second year of life, but even occasionally as early as nine months to one year of age (cf., Brill & Pepper, 2008; Ehrensaft, 2007, 2009). Yet, I have seen cases in which gender dysphoria was the manifestation of internal psychological disturbances rather than reactive behavioral distress in the face of societal stigma and prohibition or mismatch between assigned and affirmed gender. However, these are the exceptions rather than the rule. A key indicator of gender as a symptom of another underlying disorder or conflict, such as trauma, anxiety, social communication disorder, or psychosis, or a more global disorder of the self is when there is a more generalized disorganized, unintegrated sense of self, filled with anxiety and reflecting a lack of stable psychic structure. As described by Corbett (1996), the child's gender presentation is reflected in a nearly hysterical performance that is an overlay to chaotic states or regression or psychic pain. In other situations, rather than a consistent pattern over time, there is a sudden interest in gender bending or gender transformation, perhaps following a major psychological event in life and, perhaps, as a magical solution to life's challenges. The challenge for the therapist will be to differentiate the child who suddenly exhibits gender nonconformity with no preexisting history as an attempt to solve some other life or emotional problem from the child who has been suffering from what I would label a repressed true gender self that abruptly manifests itself with no forewarning. The latter is most often seen in children who are approaching puberty and are faced with a sudden trauma that forces to consciousness the horror that they are living in a body that is totally at odds with the gender they know themselves to be but which has been kept securely underground. Such youth are in gender crisis and need to be attended to immediately, with an evaluation for puberty blockers that will serve to temporarily stop the progression of the pubertal development with its unwanted secondary sexual characteristics and allow time to explore the true gender self in the light of day.

An example of gender as symptom of other problems is a young woman who implored her analyst to assign her a diagnosis of Gender

Identity Disorder and recommend top and bottom surgery for her. Her intent was to remove her breasts and sew up her vagina, to create a body that would repudiate any signs of sexuality altogether. She was not looking for a gender transformation, but rather a sex-neutered self-identity, driven by a frantic psychotic retreat from sex that had become equated with psychic and physical horror. An example of a gender response to a life event is the little boy who, after surviving a car crash in which his mother died, suddenly announced he was no longer a boy and would, henceforth, be living as a girl. This could be interpreted as a desperate attempt to retrieve his mother by embodying her. In this special case, this child's urgent wish to transition to a girl is a manifestation of traumatic attachment loss. A less dramatic example of a gendered response to a life event is Lucy. She returned from her first week at kindergarten suddenly announcing she would no longer wear girls' clothes, wanted a boy's haircut, and wanted a boy's name. Previously, she had been all about pink, frills, and Barbie dolls. The precipitating life event was the daily march to the principal's office because of disruptive behavior in class. She observed that some of the boys acted just as rowdy, but their behavior seemed more acceptable to the teacher. She concluded that boys had more leeway to act up in class, but girls got in trouble for the same behavior, ergo, she would switch to boy. She maintained a transgender façade for two years, at which point she announced, "I'm tired of pretending to be a boy." Lucy's transformation was not an expression of her authentic gender, but a magical solution to avoid school detentions. Other examples of magical gender solutions to psychological conflicts include the young man demanding cross-sex hormone treatment because of fears of his own repressed rages and desire to be a kinder and gentler human being; the molested girl who equates a change in gender with an escape from sexual predators; the teenage boy diagnosed with Asperger's Syndrome who demands transition because he has observed that girls are much better at making friends and being in relationships, believing that once he starts wearing dresses people will like him better and he will finally have friends.

There is often a simple ex post facto test that differentiates the child searching for his or her true gender self from the child who embraces gender nonconformity as a shibboleth to overcome psychic distress. The child who implores the world to listen to his or her pleas that the world has gotten it wrong and he or she is in the wrong gender or the child who is not allowed to express gender in the way that feels right to him or her often shows signs of stress, distress, or behavioral disruption. Once allowed to transition, these children typically relax and the signs of stress, distress, and disruption dissipate, if not disappear altogether (Interview with Dr. Norman P. Spack, as reported in Spiegel, 2008). In contrast, the child who has been mistakenly assessed as transgender will often get worse if precipitously allowed to transition to a pseudo true gender self and psychic distress escalates. Although not a universal phenomenon, one simple rule of thumb is that if the assessment is correct, the child shows signs of getting better; if the assessment was incorrect, the child gets worse, or at least no better.

CANDIDATES FOR TRUE GENDER SELF THERAPY

Not only is it difficult to separate gender as symptom from gender as journey toward an authentic self, we also have to differentiate the many different kinds of gender nonconforming children who are working toward a true gender self and who may benefit from therapeutic supports.

The rate of development moves much more swiftly in children than in adults and therefore children can go through many changes in a very short period of time. With that said, as in any situation of attempting to reliably predict adult outcomes from child experiences, we must be modest enough to say that we can never know with absolute certainty if a child who says she or he is transgender is expressing a stable, permanent lifelong identity or is just on a temporary stepping stone. Although not an exact science and certainly open to human error, better measures that are not binary biased are needed to decipher whether a child is truly gender nonconforming and may be suffering from gender dysphoria. Yet, until that time, I think the best means is simply listening to the child, attending not just to their words, but to their actions. Gender nonconforming children typically provide a consistent narrative over time in which they report that their real self is not determined by their assigned gender or the social expectations for that gender, but how they perceive themselves to be. A transgender child will most often declare, "I *am* a (child of the other sex than the one on the birth certificate)," whereas a gender nonconforming, but not transgender, child will more often make a statement, "I *wish* I were a_____" or "I *feel* like a _____." When allowed to match their gender expression with their inner gender identity, both transgender and gender nonconforming children relax and appear better regulated in most if not all aspects of life. If prohibited from matching their gender expression with their inner gender identity, the children become agitated, depressed, or even suicidal.

As a way to think about the myriad of children who may qualify for TGST, I have generated the following evolving categories for presentations of gender nonconforming children, with the caveat that these categories are somewhat reductionistic and potentially brittle if taken too literally or used inflexibly:

- *Transgender Children* affirm that the gender they are is opposite to the gender assigned at birth. They typically say they are a girl (boy), not that they want to be one. They represent a very small minority of gender nonconforming children.

- *Gender Fluid Children* do not abide by the binary norms of gender pre-scribed by the culture but instead flow along the spectrum from male to female, but not necessarily with a cross-gender identification or identity.
- *Gender Priuses* think of themselves as hybrids—half boy, half girl, or some combination thereof (e.g., "I'm 60% girl, 40% boy").
- *Gender Tauruses* are similar to Gender Priuses, except they assert they are one gender on top, another on the bottom—a creative solution to a mismatch between genitalia and the mind's messages to the child about his or her authentic gender.
- *Protogay Children* play at the margins of gender in the beginning stages of their gay development. They may remain gender fluid throughout their lives, or as they establish a gay identity may realize that earlier theories, like loving a boy means having to become a girl, are untrue and that boys can love boys and girls can love girls. In early childhood, they do not say that they are a boy (girl), but that they want to be a boy (girl).
- *Prototransgender Youth* first come out as gay or lesbian but then later discover that they are transgender. This is more common in female-to-male transgender than in male-to-female transgender youth and young adults.
- *Gender Queer Youth* defy all categories of culturally defined gender alto-gether and prefer to identify as gender-free, gender-neutral, or outside gender at all.
- *Gender Smoothies* Like gender fluid youth and gender queer youth, they metaphorically take everything about gender, throw it in the blender, and press the "on" button, creating a fusion of gender that is a mix of male, female, and other.
- *Gender Oreos* are layered in their gender, perhaps presenting as one gen-der on the outside, but feeling like another on the inside. These are the children who illustrate most poignantly the true gender self and false gender self in dialectical tension with each other.

This list is no doubt incomplete and will expand as my skills as a gender specialist grow.

WHO TO TREAT

Perrin, Tuerk, and Menvielle (2005) have provided a succinct summary of the reasons to treat a child who falls in any one of the categories above:

> Most [gender nonconforming] children will respond to parents' accep-tance and encouragement. Referral to a mental health specialist is appropriate if the child is anxious, depressed, or angry, exhibits self-destructive behavior, or experiences significant isolation—especially if

these problems do not improve with short-term counseling. Children who are victims of bullying can benefit from therapeutic approaches that teach skills to respond more effectively and provide strategies to reduce the impact. Children who are very shy or have difficulty making friends may benefit from training to improve social skills and reduce social anxiety. (p.3)

Even under the above circumstances, the bulk of the work in TGST may be not with the child, but with the parents in a parent consultation model. I would also include children in need of an evaluation for medical services, including consideration for hormone blockers or cross-sex hormones, children in need of a care letter to be placed in their permanent files and carried by parents, and children in need of assessment in legal disputes related to gender (typically custody battles) as candidates for services.

I start from the premise that a child whose main presenting problem (as reported by parents or others) is that he or she is gender nonconforming may be no more in need of treatment than the child whose main presenting problem is that he or she is gender normative. Yet, there are specific challenges to being a gender nonconforming child, and the challenges often fall most directly in the parents' laps. Work with parents gives them an opportunity to work out their own feelings, conflicts, and confusions about their gender nonconforming child, without depositing them into their child's psyche. The consultations also give parents time to adjust their parenting to the child they have, mourn the child they thought they had, and explore options for supporting the child they do have. While receiving their own emotional supports, the parents also become facilitators, taking ideas and emotional equanimity home to help their child, who may never know that a therapist exists and who can continue in the tasks of childhood without being put under the microscope of a "shrink," an experience that may lead the children to think that there is something wrong with them. The role of the therapist in the consultations is not to dictate what parents do, but to help them get their child in focus; deal with their own pain, suffering, and confusion, when evident; work through conflicts for parents who disagree about their child's gender presentation; and make a plan for their child that optimally will be gender enhancing rather than gender crushing. This necessitates starting where the parents are, not where the therapist hopes them to be; listening, but also knowing when to step in as the expert offering information about the developmental paths and risks for gender nonconforming children.

TGST work starts with parent consultations, with the exception of work with older adolescents, who may need to be seen alone first. Whether or not to see a child individually is decided collaboratively with parents. If a child asks to be seen, that should be reason enough. Other indications include signs of stress, distress, confusion, anxiety, depression, or social isolation that persist despite parent interventions and increased social supports both at home and at school; a nonsupportive environment that seems impervious to change or is characterized by warfare between disputing parents. Work with the child can last anywhere from a few sessions to years, weekly or intermittently, depending on the child's needs, and for some the psychotherapist can become the child's consultant over the course of development, not seen regularly, but only as issues arise.

Rather than trying to describe TGST, I will let the work speak for itself through excerpts from the case of Brady/Sophie. I have specifically chosen the case of a very young child evaluated as transgender since these children give most therapists the greatest pause in deciding between allowing a child so young to change gender versus waiting and exploring for an indefinite period of time.

Philip requested a parent consultation about his four-and-a-half-year-old child whom he suspected was transgender. He and his wife, Amy, provided the following history. Four months earlier, at Christmas, their child, Brady, announced that he wanted to be called Sophie all the time and that he felt like a girl on the inside and a boy on the outside (gender Oreo). Before that, Brady had given himself the nickname, Rainbow Love Heart. Philip had tried to talk more to Brady about his gender feelings, but Brady was resistant, saying only that he felt he was a girl, but could not be, because he had a boy's body. Soon after, Brady described himself as a girl with a penis and a boy's voice. Even before that Christmas, Brady had been longing for girls' clothes for some time. At age 3, Brady told his parents that he wanted to be a woman, not a man when he grew up and he asked if he cut off his penis, would it hurt. Amy and Philip were both concerned that Brady might actually try to cut off his penis to achieve his goal. During that same year, Brady saw a girls' shirt in a store and begged his mother to buy it for him, but Amy said no, that shirt was for girls and he was a boy. A year later, Amy had done reading on gender nonconforming children and felt more comfortable buying Brady the girls' clothes.

Amy and Philip came for several consultations; we decided together that Brady was showing enough signs of stress and discomfort to warrant individual sessions. He was presently attending a preschool where he only wanted to play with girls, but had few friends. He wished to let his hair grow long, but wear boy clothes and longed to be a princess. Most of the time Brady seemed steeped in his own internal world, and both parents described him as having a bit of an Asperger's quality. Brady strongly identified with an animated car in a Pixar film that he identified as Girly Girl, a car with boy paint but a girl engine. He had created a new category: Merman, a male mermaid. He was picking at his skin and generally seemed agitated. Amy and Philip saw Brady in turmoil about his gender identity. They wanted help from a professional to figure out what would be the right thing to do for Brady to ease his angst and give him a better go in life. They had a hunch that the answer was to allow him to express himself as a girl, but they did not want to do anything precipitous that might harm him.

Brady arrived at our first session in unisex clothes—a tie-dye tee shirt, shorts, and sandals. Almost the first thing Brady said to me when he met me was "I'm half and half. Half boy, half girl. A boy on the bottom (he points to his waist down), a girl on the top (he points to his waist up)" (gender Taurus). I asked, "What name should I use for you?" "Sophie. My nickname is Brady, but in kindergarten we'll sign me up as Sophie and I'll want everyone to call me 'she.'" Noteworthy, but not understood by me at the time in terms of Brady/Sophie's gender creativity, much of the play in that first session involved fierce aggression on the part of a giant sandworm who scares people and then eats them. After the first visit with me, Philip called to report that Brady declared, "I don't want to have to go to school if they have to call me Brady."

In a subsequent session, my patient arrived fully decked out as a girl, with a headband, girls' shirt, and multicolored sandals, and announced, "I'm all girl now—Sophie. It just happened real fast. I'm not half and half anymore." I asked Sophie where the boy half went. "Somewhere else." Throughout the session Sophie kept sucking in her tummy, in an attempt to make herself more girl on top. When asked, Sophie refused to do Draw-A-Person or a self-portrait, but she was eager to draw the car named Girly Girl. She assigned Girly Girl the number 53, which she explained is a girl's number. Her old number used to be 95, which is a boy's number: "8 is a boy's number, 76 is a girl's number, 6 is a boy's number, 70 is a girl's number." Later, I made a note that there is no gender fluidity for this little person—gender is as binary as a number system for her, just reversed.

In a later session, Sophie announced excitedly, "Did you hear? There's no more Brady. I threw Brady in the garbage, and Brady couldn't get out because the garbage can's too high, and then all the garbage got thrown on top of him. But Brady climbed to the top and still couldn't get out. Then Corky [their dog] came and ate him. Actually, Mom fed Brady to Corky. He tasted good, like a human. But a dead human, because Brady was already dead when Corky ate him." I simply listened and made a mental note about Sophie's creative, albeit gruesome, whimsical solution for consolidating a transgender identity. Sophie wanted to draw new portraits. A colorful mermaid replaced Girly Girl (mermaids appear as a common self-representation or identification figure for assigned male gender Tauruses and transgender little girls, which has an internal logic—a long-tail-y self on the bottom, a beatific, long and silky haired flow-y self on the top). In her play, not Brady but little mermaids were chased by a shark who tried to eat them, symbolizing the yet shaky consolidation or acceptance of her female self.

Sophie spent numerous sessions working through her feelings about her transition from Brady to Sophie. Sometimes I interpreted, but mostly I listened. In the last session, Sophie and I had the following conversation:

Sophie: You know what? Sophie is calm when she wakes up in the morning. But Brady, who got eaten, was wild.

D.E.: Does your mom know that?[4]

Sophie: I don't know.

D.E.: Should we ask her?

Sophie: No, I just want to tell Dr. Ehrensaft. But if you weren't Dr. Ehrensaft, I wouldn't tell you.

Later in that same hour, Sophie explained that Brady has never shown up again since Corky ate him. Throughout this session, Sophie clutched her penis over her shorts, having told me that when someone from preschool says she used to be a boy, so she can't be a girl, she just gets quiet and doesn't say anything. (Earlier, I had advised her parents to help her come up with language for responding to other children.) I reflected that she could be a teacher to others, because she knows more about this than they do. She asked how I knew that. I tell her because she was the expert of herself. She responded by expounding, "I have 8 baby dolls and 19 race cars." Through her play, I bore witness to her own unique gender web, which presently consisted of threads of nurturing baby doll play and violent racecar mayhem.

Over the course of these sessions, I met regularly with Amy and Philip, who reported Sophie's experiences both at home and at school. After a period of reflection, they had decided, with the school's acceptance, to allow their child to go to preschool as Sophie. The teachers reported that her behaviors now made more sense to them and that she was, for the first time, jumping right into the play, rather than anxiously clutching a baby doll carriage and literally freezing whenever a boy showed up in her vicinity. She now had her first real friend, a girl named Gina. One boy was giving her a hard time, telling her he was only going to call her Brady, and would not call her Sophie. Sophie's response: "Well, that's okay, but if you do, I'm not going to answer you."

During the initial transition period, Sophie's mother would set out three sets of clothes: girl clothes, tie-dye clothes, and boy clothes that Sophie had been wearing as Brady. Sophie consistently chose either the girl clothes or the tie-dye clothes. The first few days when she presented as a girl, her parents reported she was somewhat agitated, but then she seemed to settle down. Now that she was allowed to be Sophie all the time and wear girl clothes whenever she wanted, she reported, "I'm the happiest I've ever felt in my life."

As Brady transitioned to Sophie, she asked her parents if she would grow up to have "nomies" (breasts) like Mommy. Her parents wondered whether they should tell her about body change options—either surgical or hormonal. They had their doubts about whether this might be overwhelming or frightening information for a child as young as Sophie, and I confirmed those doubts when they brought them to me in our parent consultation. Together, we came up with a more age-appropriate response: "There are many ways to be a boy or a girl, and no, if you are born with a penis, you won't grow breasts on your own." They would then wait to see what Sophie, who is a very scientifically minded four year old, would do with that information.

The following summer, between preschool and kindergarten, I had completed sessions with Sophie but was available for parent consultations as needed. The parents reported that Sophie was adjusting to life as a girl and seemed to be enjoying herself, although she was showing some signs of stress, particularly fingernail biting. She worried that people would find out she used to be a boy or think she was a boy. She also feared that people who knew her before as a boy would not be accepting. On the other hand, she beamed with pleasure when she was acknowledged or recognized as a girl, as when a parent at the playground said to his own child, "Careful, there's a girl already on the slide," or when a young salesgirl commented, "I like your hair. It's cute."

As Sophie successfully settled into kindergarten with no apparent worries, my work with the family was finished for the time being, but was capped by the carry letter that I wrote for Sophie at the parents' request:

> To Whom It May Concern:
> I am writing this letter in regards to Sophie X, who has been in my care since xx. I am a clinical psychologist and gender specialist who is working with Sophie and her family, for the purpose of helping her clarify her gender identity. Sophie was assigned a male gender at birth but has shown signs of gender fluidity from early life. Under her care with me, Sophie (Ne. Brady X) has expressed both to me and to her parents that she is an affirmed female. With the support of her parents, Sophie is now living fully as a female and self-identifies as such. To promote her well-being and emotional health, it is imperative that Sophie be seen and treated as a female by her parents, her educational settings, and the community surrounding her. In school settings and the community, this would include such things as bathroom use, participation as a female in sports activities or any other programs that might be designated as "girl" activities, and so forth. Both of Sophie's parents have supported Sophie in her transition to an affirmed female gender identity and are in full agreement, as am I, that her well-being and mental health will be best served by recognizing and acknowledging her as a female.

Philip sent an E-mail thanking me for the carry letter, in which he shared that they had attended a picnic with other transgender children and their families. Some of the children were boys who had transitioned to girls. Others were girls who transitioned to boys. Afterward, Philip asked Sophie what she thought of the other children. Her reply: "They were okay, but I was the only girl."

CONCLUSION

There is now a little person named Sophie enrolled in kindergarten as a girl and by parent and teacher reports she is doing quite well. As Sophie grows older, she will have to decide, with the help of her parents, whether and to whom to disclose that she had once been Brady; whether to take hormone blockers; whether to take cross-sex hormones; whether to have surgery. In a fluid journey whose endpoint we can never fully predict, Brady may also make a reappearance, miraculously resurrected from the bowels of Corky. If that should occur, it will be imperative that Sophie feel free to express her desire to possibly switch back to male, rather than feel compelled to conform to the female gender that others have now supported and expect but who Sophie may no longer feel herself to be. If it should ever come to pass that Sophie would want to return to Brady, not making room for that transition back would simply be substituting one false gender self for another. To date, we have no research studies that indicate that a child who transitions gender and later transitions back in a gender fluid process rather than a frenzy of gender chaos or confusion suffers any damage to his or her psyche, and my own clinical observations are that such a process does indeed occur with no harm if the surrounding environment is accepting of the changes. Whatever course Sophie's life takes, it will continue to be the function of TGST to help Sophie and others like her tap into their gender creativity to establish, over time, the gender that will be true to them.

NOTES

1. Presently, many gender theorists and practitioners use the term *gender variant* to refer to children and youth who function outside binary gender norms. Others, including myself, have replaced gender variant with the term *gender nonconforming* for the reasons that *nonconforming* is a less pathologizing term and that *variant* has connotations of deviation rather than difference. Throughout this article, gender nonconforming will be used but is interchangeable with gender variant in its referents.

2. In the present terminology of the transgender community and some gender theorists and specialists, *affirmed gender* is used to denote the gender an individual asserts him or herself to be, perhaps more accurately to mean self-affirmed gender. Throughout this discussion I will be using the word *affirmed* to allude to an individual's assertion of his or her declared gender.

3. *Genderist* refers to a systematic belief system in the binary dichotomy of male/masculine, female/feminine as the only true, natural, or correct gender identities and expressions.

4. Amy was in the room with Sophie. Many parents of transgender or gender nonconforming children understandably are hesitant to leave their child alone with a therapist, either as a result of previous bad experiences with therapists who cast blame on them and tried to "repair" their child or in light of general mistrust of the mental health community's aspersion on children who do not fit their gender norms.

REFERENCES

American Psychiatric Association. (2000). *Diagnostic and statistical manual of mental disorders* (4th ed., text rev.). Washington, DC: Author.

Brill, S., & Pepper, R. (2008). *The transgender child*. San Francisco, CA: Cleis Press.

Carver, P. R., Yunger, J. L., & Perry, D. G. (2003). Gender identity and adjustment in middle childhood. *Sex Roles, 49*, 95–109.

Cohen-Kettenis, P. T., & Pfafflin, F. (2003). *Transgenderism and intersexualism in childhood and adolescence*. Thousand Oaks, CA: Sage.

Corbett, K. (1996). Homosexual boyhood: Notes on girlyboys. *Gender and Psychoanalysis, 1*, 426–461.

Corbett, K. (2009). *Boyhoods: Rethinking masculinities*. New Haven: Yale University Press.

D'Augelli, A. R., Grossman, A. H., & Starks, M. T. (2006). Childhood gender atypicality, victimization, and PTSD among lesbian, gay and bisexual youth. *Journal of Interpersonal Violence, 21*, 1462–1482.

Diamond, M. (2002). Sex and gender are different: Sexual identity and gender identity are different. *Clinical Psychology & Psychiatry, 7*, 320–334.

Dimen, M. (1995). Introduction to symposium on sexuality/sexualities. *Psychoanalytic Dialogues, 5*, 157–163.

Dimen, M. (2003). *Sexuality, intimacy, and power*. Hillsdale, NJ: The Analytic Press.

Dimen, M. (2005). Afterword. In E. Toronto, G. Ainslie, M. Donovan, M. Kelly, C. Kieffer, & N. McWilliams (Eds.), *Psychoanalytic reflections on a gender-free case* (pp. 298–305). New York, NY: Routledge.

Ehrensaft, D. (2007). Raising girlyboys: A parent's perspective. *Studies in Gender and Sexuality, 8*, 269–302.

Ehrensaft, D. (2009). One pill makes you boy, one pill makes you girl. *International Journal of Applied Psychoanalytic Studies, 6*, 12–24.

Ehrensaft, D. (2011a). Boys will be girls, girls will be boys: Children affect parents as parents affect children in gender nonconformity. *Psychoanalytic Psychology, 28*(4), 528–548.

Ehrensaft, D. (2011b). *Gender born, gender made: Raising healthy gender non-conforming children*. New York: The Experiment.

Ehrensaft, D. (2011c). "I'm a prius": a Child case of a gender/ethnic hybrid. *Journal of Gay & Lesbian Mental Health, 15*(1), 46–48.

Glenn, W. (2009). "For colored girls only": Reflection of an emerging male-to-female transgender and gender variant consciousness. In G. P. Mallon (Ed.), *Social work practice with transgender and gender variant youth* (pp.104–114). London, UK: Routledge.

Goldner, V. (1991). Toward a critical relational theory of gender. *Psychoanalytic Dialogues, 1*, 249–272.

Goldner, V. (2003). Ironic gender/authentic sex. *Studies in Gender and Sexuality, 4*, 113–139.

Green, R. (1987). *The "sissy boy syndrome" and the development of homosexuality*. New Haven, CT: Yale University Press.

Harris, A. (1991). Gender as contradiction. *Psychoanalytic Dialogues, 6*, 197–220.

Harris, A. (2000). Gender as a soft assembly: Tomboys' stories. *Studies in Gender and Sexuality*, *1*, 223–250.

Harris, A. (2005). *Gender as soft assembly*. Hillsdale, NJ: The Analytic Press.

Hill, D., Menvielle, E., Sica, K. M., & Johnson, A. (2010). An affirmative intervention for families with gender variant children: Parental ratings of child mental health and gender. *Journal of Sex & Marital Therapy*, *36*, 6–23.

Morrow, D. F. (2004). Social work practice with gay, lesbian, bisexual and transgender adolescents. *Families in Society*, *85*, 91–99.

Muller, B., Li, A., Schreier, H., & Romer, G. (2009). Gender identity disorder in children and adolescents. *Pediatric and Adolescent Health Care*, *39*(5), 113–143.

Perrin, E., Menvielle, E., & Tuerk, C. (2005). To the beat of a different drummer: The gender-variant child, *Contemporary Pediatrics*. Retrieved from http://www.hrc.org/files/assets/resources/transgender_to-the-beat-of-a-different-drummer-6-2007.pdf

Pilkington, N. W., & D'Augelli, A. R. (1995). Victimization of lesbian, gay, and bisexual youth in community settings. *Journal of Community Psychology*, *23*, 34–56.

Ryan, C., Huebner, D., Diaz, R. M., Sanchez, J. (2009). Family rejection as a predictor of negative health outcomes in white and Latino lesbian, gay, and bisexual young adults. *Pediatrics*, *123*, 346–352.

Spiegel, A. (2008, May 8). Parents consider treatment to delay son's puberty. *All things considered* [Radio broadcast transcript]. Retrieved from *www.NPR.org*

Stoller, R. (1985). *Presentations of gender*. New Haven, CT: Yale University Press.

Toomey, R. B., Ryan, C., Diaz, R. M., Card, N. A., & Russell, S. T. (2010). Gender-nonconforming lesbian, gay, bisexual, and transgender youth: School victimization and young adult psychosocial adjustment. *Developmental Psychology*, *46*(6), 1580–1589. doi:10.1037/a0020705

Winnicott, D. W. (1960a). Ego distortion in terms of true and false self. In D. W. Winnicott (Ed.), *Maturational processes and the facilitating environment* (pp. 140–152). Madison, CT: International Universities Press.

Winnicott, D. W. (1960b). The theory of the parent-infant relationship. In D. W. Winnicott (Ed.)., *Maturational processes and the facilitating environment* (pp. 37–55). Madison, CT: International Universities Press.

Winnicott, D. W. (1970), *Playing and reality*. London: Tavistock.

Yunger, J. L., Carver, P. R., & Perry, D. G. (2004). Does gender identity influence children's psychological well-being? *Developmental Psychology*, *40*, 572–582.

A Comprehensive Program for Children with Gender Variant Behaviors and Gender Identity Disorders

EDGARDO MENVIELLE, MD

Department of Psychiatry and Behavioral Sciences, Children's National Medical Center, Washington, DC, USA

This article describes a clinical program designed to address broadly defined mental health needs of children who experience stress related to not fitting into normative gender types and argues for the need for integrated services that address the spectrum of gender variance. An array of services useful to children and their families is proposed. The article describes the clinical population served, common clinical and social problems, and a rationale for the interventions provided.

Children with concerns about their gender may present to clinicians as young as age 3 years and all the way up through adolescence and the rate of clinical referrals appears to be increasing (Zucker, 2008). Presentations tend to cluster around two developmental events: The first is entering school and the second is entering adolescence. The main concerns that prompt consultation in the younger group include two broad areas: 1) etiologic, diagnostic, and prognostic questions that emanate from the parents' wish to understand the child's gender variance (i.e., "What is it?" "What causes it?" "Is this pathology?" "What lies ahead in the future?"); and 2) concerns about the social ramifications of gender nonconformity that may center on peers and school life or family life (i.e., "How do we deal with peer rejection and bullying?" How do we deal with negative attitudes toward gender variance among the parents, family members, and friends?").

While etiological questions may be very salient to some parents but of no consequence to others, questions related to social ramifications are nearly universal. Parents have presented to our clinic with a range of reactions to the gender variance in their children including the wish to do anything to change it, but increasingly we are seeing parents who deem gender variance to be a personality attribute that should not be interfered with. At the same time, all parents recognize that gender variance elicits hostile responses, at least among some, and puts the child at a social disadvantage.

THE CLINICAL PICTURE

Parent Views

Increasingly, consulting parents take for granted that gender identities and sexual orientations that vary from a heterosexual norm are not pathological and that not all people are meant to be heterosexual or to fit into a narrowly defined gender pattern (Ehrensaft, 2007; Richardson, 1999). Increasingly tolerant attitudes are expected as parallel changes in marriage and other laws, as well as public discourse and policies become more inclusive of gender and sexual diversity. Increasingly, visible messages from transgender and gay advocates as well as parents of transgender and gay persons, may also contribute to a greater awareness about gender and sexuality issues affecting children and families. Although diversity in class, education, ethnic-cultural background, immigrant status, political views, religious affiliation, and geographic location, may all contribute to the diverse reactions along the acceptance-rejection dimension, families that identify with traditional, socially conservative values regarding sexuality and gender seem to be increasingly represented among our patients and receivers of services. Forging supportive social enclaves for them within their families and communities is especially challenging. Such families may, therefore, receive greater benefit from group and community building interventions.

EMOTIONAL IMPACT

The emotional impact of gender variance in early childhood on the parents can be considerable, especially early on. Parents report a range of feelings at different stages, which may parallel the emotions experienced with losses, starting with distress and an urge to normalize, in the sense of shaping the child into a more conventional gender role, and then moving toward acceptance and affirmation. Overall, initial emotional responses are related to a perceived threat and may include fear, disgust, denial, sadness, and sorrow, while at later stages many parents experience positive reactions of pride, joy, and admiration. An important motive for parents to seek a clinical opinion may be to have the opportunity to express their emotions and to obtain validation of their emotional experience. Secondary emotional reactions about present or past responses and actions, such as guilt for having felt sadness or anger toward the child, or past efforts to normalize the child into gender-conventional behavior that are now deemed misguided, may be presented to the clinician. A nonjudgmental response that acknowledges the social imperatives that drive such feelings and actions reassures and soothes distressed parents. A frank discussion about the role of shame in keeping people within the confines of gender-appropriate behavior often offers relief regardless of whether shame has been brought up by parents.

Parents who express current discomfort with the child's gender variance benefit from a discussion about the possible sources of discomfort, which include internalized norms and expectations as well as from an acknowledgment of the stress that gender variance often brings to parents' social interactions. Negative or ambivalent parental feelings may linger in spite of the parents' wishes to become more embracing, but these do not necessarily preclude developing more positive attitudes of acceptance. As parents gain insight into the sources of their own discomfort and the discomfort of others, a more empathic understanding of the child's experience emerges. Parents may also develop a greater ability to observe interactions in which they participate from an outside perspective. Taking distance from their own circumstances and analyzing the situations in a more dispassionate way allows parents to better resist sanctioned discourses and social mechanisms that cast them as enforcers of gender difference. This shift in perspective can be liberating and transformative, and it probably is what is referred to when parents talk about "becoming a better person" through the experience of raising a child who resists gender molds (Hill & Menvielle, 2009).

Peer Relationships

The child's peer relationships are always a concern for parents. Fear that the young child will experience rejection often crystallizes at the time the child enters or is about to enter kindergarten. Parents who have accommodated to the child's gendered interests and behaviors within their home are faced with the prospect of a wider world that will not be so welcoming. The amount of rejection that children actually experience in the early school years varies significantly from severe to almost none. There is also great variation in children's social competence to secure a social position and to deal with rejection when it happens. Nevertheless, in the author's experience, as a group these children experience more social difficulties and social anxiety, perhaps related to the enforcement of gender rules in real time as well as the budding internalization of these rules by the child (Carver, Yunger, & Perry, 2003). Faced with a) pervasive girl–boy social segregation that develops in elementary school, b) the preference of many children to associate predominantly if not exclusively with same-sex peers, and c) children's enforcement of gender boundaries, often reinforced by adults, gender variant children may experience significant social isolation. Although in the preschool and early years of elementary school, children may integrate well with other-sex peers, over time opportunities for friendships across sex groups become fewer. This is particularly marked for feminine boys who tend to receive the brunt of mocking and ridicule for not living up to the normative masculine expectations by other boys, and who also may lose friendships as girls groups become more closed off.

Family Relationships

The impact of a child who does not conform to gender expectations on family relationships is variable; however, several themes are common. First, each parent's emotional and behavioral responses may differ from the others and this necessitates the therapist facilitating as much as possible a common ground of approaches. Divorced families and parents who, in general, have difficulty negotiating differences of opinion face the greatest challenges. Although the origins of personal world views are complex and ultimately untraceable, some of the differences among heterosexual couples may stem from the very difference in gender mandates that men and women embody: Deviations from conventional masculinity in men are met with stricter prohibitions than deviations from conventional femininity in women, making it generally harder for men to allow tolerance or to tolerate gender variance in themselves and in others, especially in other males. However, this by no means implies that mothers are always more flexible in accommodating to a gender variant child. Fear of homosexuality and transsexuality, distress stemming from being perceived as socially deviant or stigmatized, or from the fear that the child will not reproduce a heterosexual family in the future, and other factors alone or in combination may drive a person's inability to accept a child's gender variance. The stigma of gender nonconformity, the "spoiled identity," is, thus, borne not just by the child but also by all those associated with the child (Goffman, 1963/1986). The usual mechanism by which stigma by association is avoided, through the disavowing of the stigmatized person, is not possible here except in the extreme and rare cases of physical or psychological abandonment.

Second, the presence of a child with gender variant behaviors may complicate relationships with extended family and friends. Parents may be overtly or covertly criticized by relatives and friends for not enforcing limits on gender deviance. Parents may cope by distancing themselves from or confronting the critics. Feelings may be hurt and old interpersonal conflicts and grudges may be revived. The social circles that spring up around the child, parents of schoolmates, and neighborhood playmates can be tested along similar lines. As with any crisis, positive or negative change may result. A tested relationship may turn into a deeper and more meaningful relationship. Parents who display unwavering support of the child may find that other adults' respect for them increases as they witness parental support for their child. This flip side of the blame and criticism can occur when others are able to abandon the common notion that a child's gender variance is something that parents can contain or eradicate if they really wanted to, and respect and admiration may then ensue for the parent. However, relationships with other adults can also be strained and broken. Thus, raising a gender nonnormative child may be a catalyst for deeper relationships as well as for social losses. The threat of straining or losing important relationships is an important contributor to some parents' inability to suspend judgment about, let alone embrace, gender variance in their child. Families embedded in communities with commitments to certain religious or cultural traditions may experience a version of this, complicated by the threat of other losses of a symbolic nature (e.g., the threat of loosing full identification with the norms of their community and becoming cut off from a vital source of support and identity).

Children Actively Seeking to Present Socially as a Member of the Other Gender

A relatively small number of prepubertal patients overtly present socially as a member of the other gender. These are children who actively encourage peers to call them by a differently gendered name, or a gender neutral name, and who publicly assert membership in the other gender. These children can be characterized as asserting a transgender identity at an early age, since a) they experience a mismatch between their bodies and their identities; b) they are unable or unwilling to accommodate to the gender role and designation assigned to them; and c) they are capable of acknowledging their biological sex demonstrating that they are cognizant of their natal body. We have seen several children with this presentation, with parents who have in the end accommodated to the child's wish but who may have initially attempted for a period to persuade the child, to no avail, that their natal sex should determine their expression of gender.

The question of which individual children should be counted in this category presents one of the greatest clinical challenges. There are some children who are so assertive in this regard, that refusing to accommodate to their wish is at face value inappropriate. Their life in their assigned gender is very distressing and the relief they get from switching their gender presentation very palpable. On the other end of the spectrum, there are children who do not claim a cross-gender identity, whose longing to embody the other gender does not generalize to every social situation and whose wish to enact a cross-gender persona appears be more episodic and to stem from what they perceive to be the advantages of such embodiment free from judgment and restrictions (e.g., free to dress-up and fantasize the self as someone else as a source of creativity and enjoyment). The challenge lies in making a decision to move forward with a gender transition at this early stage for children who are in a category in between these two groups, when a child neither fits clearly into the group that insists on a cross-gender identity nor it seems to be a matter of pure cultural advantage, or for the child who sometimes expresses strong distress but also seems to waver between these two extremes. At this time, we lack the guidance of evidence regarding the potential long-term advantages and disadvantages of prepubertal gender-role transition (Dreger, 2009; Zucker & Cohen-Kettenis, 2008). Given that many, if not most, children who express childhood gender variance do not progress or persist into a transgender adult identity, a recommendation for social transition at this stage is given cautiously. In such cases, parents are advised to keep considering the possibility of a reversal at a later stage of development and to actively communicate to the child that the door is always open to reverse the gender role transition. We have observed two cases in which de-transition from an early childhood social transition (male to female) occurred. The potential long-term psychological effects of these actions remain to be studied.

Social Transition and Puberty Suppression

Studies show that fewer than 20% of children who meet diagnostic criteria for gender identity disorder of childhood (GIDC) before puberty will continue to experience gender dysphoria during and after puberty (see American Psychiatric Association, 2000). Those who do are called *persisters* and are the most likely candidates for puberty suppression and transgender hormones (Drummond, Bradley, Peterson-Badali, & Zucker, 2008). Some of these children may also seek cosmetic and surgical interventions when they are older. Because puberty suppression can have a long-term beneficial effect in this patient group, and since the timeframe for suppressing irreversible secondary sex characteristics is short, identifying children who will follow this path prior to the onset of puberty would permit beneficial interventions. At present, however, the only clinical predictor is intensity of gender dysphoria, with more intense dysphoria predicting a higher likelihood of persistence (Drummond, et al., 2008; Wallien & Cohen-Kettenis, 2008). Clinically, desisting children usually become more comfortable with their assigned gender role between the ages of 9 and 11, either coinciding with the early stages of puberty, or approaching the onset of puberty (Green, 1987).

Co-Occurring Conditions

The presence of psychopathology and comorbid disorders suggests that children need to be broadly assessed, a recommendation that is generally accepted (Zucker, 2008). Children who are in the autism spectrum are over-represented in gender clinics, suggesting the possibility that the cognitive characteristics of autism spectrum disorders (ASD) may somehow interact with feelings of gender or sexual difference. One hypothesis that needs to be tested is that children with social cognition problems may be more prone to be stressed by their own pubertal changes, making clinical distinctions between gender dysphoria and dysphoria due to body maturation challenging. Potential interactions between Autism Spectrum Disorders (ASD) and Gender Identity Disorder (GID) are complex and remain largely unexplored. Persons whose autism disorder causes problems in social functioning may be more challenged to manage or unable to manage gender transition.

CLINICAL PROGRAM

Our program bundles a set of diagnostic and treatment interventions aimed at helping parents affirm and support their children, while actively promoting their healthy adjustment. A premise of the program is that the development of children with gender behaviors, interests, and characteristics is not to be interfered with anymore than with children who are conventional in their gender. Resiliency in the child is best achieved through a supportive family environment that fosters the development of self esteem and social competences (Wyman, Sandler, & Nelson, 2000). Our assumption is that GID in children represents a normal developmental variation. Consistent with an affirmative goal, parents are encouraged to unconditionally value their child, acknowledge his or her difference, assist the child in navigating schools and society, and advocate for changes in the family and community to minimize social hazards (Lev, 2004). Nor does this imply that conflicts within the child, if present, are ignored.

The program encourages parents not to make rigid assumptions about long term outcomes, to accept and validate all possibilities (i.e., transsexuality, heterosexuality, homosexuality; gender ambiguity, noncommitment to a gender) and to privilege the child's lead to avoid imposing the parents' preferences. The program instills in parents the idea that, in time, the child will figure out who they are and in the meantime a supportive accompaniment by the parents is the child's best chance to lay a foundation of positive self-regard amidst the negativity of society toward difference (Hill & Menvielle, 2009; Hill, Menvielle, Sica, & Johnson, 2010).

Clinical Evaluation

Families are prepared for the visit with a set of instructions provided in writing. Due to the sensitive nature of the issue, and the fact that sometimes parents and young children have not had previous discussions of the parents' concerns, we recommend that the parents prepare the child for the appointment. We ask them to explain that the parent is looking for assistance from a specialized doctor to learn how to parent the child in the best possible way. We ask the parent to communicate to the child that they wish to learn how to help the child feel good about herself or himself and to get along and to be successful with peers.

Different explanations may be more appropriate depending on the child's age and circumstances. For example some children feel apprehensive about being asked potentially embarrassing questions. In such cases, it is important to reinforce that the appointment is more for the parent, and that the child can read a book or play with a toy while the parents see the doctor. The child would not have to answer any questions that make him or her feel uncomfortable. Other children may welcome the idea of talking with someone who can help them with their feelings. In that case, the child can be told that he or she will meet a doctor who understands and with whom they can talk privately about their feelings. We also ask the parents to bring medical and school records, drawings, writings, journals, and photos that would contribute to understanding the child. These messages may need to be repeated to the child in the session as well as a statement that we talk to "many boys who like girl things or that feel like girls inside" and the corresponding statement for natal girl patients. Sparing no effort to put the child at ease is critical to obtain the child's cooperation, particularly with children who already feel very self-conscious or ashamed of their difference. Some children with gender issues are exquisitely attentive to potential disapproval and are conditioned to expect it.

In our program, patients are initially evaluated by a team of professionals. An extended initial evaluation interview, supplemented by standard diagnostic instruments, allows for interviewing the child and the parents, separately and together, and to provide initial feedback and recommendations. Having the concurrent observation of more than one clinician increases the team's confidence in the recommendations, particularly regarding questions of later puberty suppression and gender transition.

Initial psychoeducational interventions may be provided to the parents and the child depending on the results of the clinical assessment. Some children present with gender variant behaviors and interests, but their expressed wishes to be the other gender or assertions about being a member of the other gender are not pervasive and do not suggest or represent deep and persistent convictions. Instead they may be expressions of a longing for the advantages a child perceives to accrue from being a member of the other gender. These children and their parents tend to benefit from a discussion about different ways of being a boy or a girl, some boys only like to play with certain toys, certain games (examples of male-typed toys and games) while other boys prefer female-typed toys and games, clothes, etc. The introduction of this language provides the parents and the child with the possibility of seeing themselves in a different light. It often has the effect of loosening up the ingrained associations of male-masculine and female–feminine by introducing the possibility that, for instance, there are boys whose main interests and identifications are conventionally feminine. The effect of this simple intervention may provide an alternative cognitive frame of reference that typically has not been considered and provides emotional validation. This intervention also has diagnostic value: for instance, if the natal male child does not respond positively, or reacts negatively to the suggestion that he is a different kind of boy, this is a suggestive clinical indicator that the child's cross-gender identity is stronger than previously suspected. A child who refuses this type of message may well be more likely to be transgender, although we currently lack empirical validation for this conjecture.

Children who are assessed to be more likely candidates for puberty suppression and cross-gender hormones may benefit from age-appropriate discussion about the various outcomes and intervention possibilities. This discussion should include the possibility of expressing one's gender regardless of body status, and the various choices people make: a) transitioning social gender with and without medical/surgical interventions; b) presenting oneself socially in the other gender full time or only in selected settings and circumstances; and c) adopting an in-between gender or completely embracing the other gender. The idea that is communicated is that all these are viable and valid options among which the patient can chose, and that the patient should make the best decision for themselves, free from external pressures to conform to gender ideals. The intention is trying to help patients and their parents to sort out internal motivation from societal normative expectations which may unduly influence a child and family's decision to, for example, pursue hormone treatment that the child would not have wanted if free from external pressures. This is to make sure, within what is possible, that choices are not made for the wrong reasons. When puberty suppression and hormone treatment are likely decisions down the road in a child who has not yet entered puberty, the child should be reevaluated on an ongoing or recurrent basis. In the absence of proven diagnostic tools to assist with this decision at present, the accumulation overtime of clinical evidence is our best hope for a correct decision.

Groups for Parent and Children

Our program provides an open-ended support and psychoeducational group intervention. Children assessed in our clinic can be referred to monthly simultaneous groups for children and for parents staffed by members of our assessment team and by additional staff members. The two simultaneous groups have a double purpose: to provide a supportive community for parents dealing with the challenges of raising children with gender variant behaviors and providing a socializing experience for the children.

The parent group allows us to provide ongoing education and problem solving in a medium in which parents are active participants and not merely passive recipients (Menvielle & Tuerk, 2002). The group experience is a powerful antidote to the common experience of families feeling like they are the only ones struggling with these issues. Through the group, we provide direct instruction about the benefits of a safe space at home where the child is free to explore his or her interests. Parents use the group process to work on their approach, including what limits to set and their own feelings, attitudes, and parenting approaches. The group experience is also a model for a safe space that transcends the boundaries of the home.

The child group is designed as a play and socialization group. A set of rules sets a tone of respect for the adults, each other and the environment, and an opportunity for play and artistic expression is provided. In addition to the child with gender variant behaviors, siblings are also encouraged to participate. This experience can be useful for siblings who may also struggle socially in relation to the child with gender variant behaviors. The group is generally very well received by the participating children although some children may be reluctant to attend before their first visit. The groups can also function as a springboard for friendships between parents or between children. In addition, the ongoing contact with the families through the group affords us the possibility of monitoring the child's development even for families who obtain psychotherapy by clinicians outside our institution. It is not uncommon that children who we assess are already receiving individual psychotherapy and that they wish to maintain this relationship after our consultation. Group participants also have the option to participate in our on-line community which includes families from across the country.

Online Community

The online community was developed as an extension of the parent support group and in response to requests from parents outside the DC metropolitan area looking for groups in their local community. This online community is part of a children's Web site (www.childrensnational.org/gendervariance). Parents of children with gender variant behaviors who have received a diagnostic evaluation are eligible to join and so are parents of children who have not come through our clinic. The latter are screened through telephone interview. Groups who share stigmatized traits can benefit from online communities (Camosy, 1996). Such communities offer alternative relationships in which parents feel included, valued, and respected (Dunham, Hurshman, & Litwin, 1998; Finn, 1996; McKenna & Bargh, 1998). Among the reasons that parents give for their continued involvement in the groups are that it is a place to be oneself, to find like-minded peers, and to help in coping with social exclusion (Major & Eccleston, 2005; Menvielle & Hill, 2011).

DISCUSSION

Our program is based on the notion that gender variance is not per se an indication of pathology (Bartlett, Vasey, & Bukowski, 2000), or at least that the problem is not located within the child, but that it is almost inevitably accompanied by stress and, in some cases, psychiatric disorders. Our clinical approach is one that centers on the family and strives to not interfere with the patient's development while trying to equip the patient and the parents with tools for better coping while also giving careful considerations to morbidities that may require concurrent interventions. We believe that the stress of social stigma can be buffered through participation in a supportive community and that such stress reduction facilitates the ongoing diagnostic questions as the child develops.

REFERENCES

American Psychiatric Association (2000). *Diagnostic and statistical manual of mental disorders* (4th ed., text rev.). Washington, DC: Author.

Bartlett, N.H., Vasey, P., & Bukowski, W.M. (2000). Is gender identity disorder in children a mental disorder? *Sex Roles, 43,* 753–785.

Camosy, P. (1996). Patient support networks: Something for everybody. *Journal of Family Practice, 42,* 278–286.

Carver, P. R., Yunger, J. L., & Perry, D. G. (2003). Gender identity and adjustment in middle childhood. *Sex Roles, 49,* 95–109.

Dreger, A. (2009). Gender identity disorder in childhood: Inconclusive advice to parents. *Hastings Center Report, 39,* 26–29.

Drummond, K. D., Bradley, S. J., Peterson-Badali, M., & Zucker, K. J. (2008). A follow-up study of girls with gender identity disorder. *Developmental Psychology, 44,* 34–45.

Dunham, P., Hurshman, A., & Litwin, E. (1998). Computer-mediate social support: Single young mothers as a model system. *American Journal of Community Psychology, 26,* 281–306.

Ehrensaft, D. (2007). Raising girlyboys: A parent's perspective. *Studies in Gender and Sexuality, 8,* 269–302.

Finn, J. (1996) Computer-based self-help groups: On-line recovery for addictions. *Computers in Human Services, 13,* 21–41.

Goffman, E. (1986). *Stigma: Notes on the management of a spoiled identity.* New York, NY: Simon and Schuster. (Original work published 1963)

Green R. (1987). *The "sissy boy syndrome" and the development of homosexuality.* New Haven, CT: Yale University Press.

Hill, D. B., & Menvielle, E. (2009). "You have to give them a place where they feel protected and safe and loved": The views of parents who have gender-variant children and adolescents. *Journal of LGBT Youth, 6,* 243–271.

Hill, D. B., Menvielle, E., Sica, K. M., & Johnson, A. (2010). An affirmative intervention for families with gender variant children: Parent ratings on child mental health and gender. *Journal of Sex & Marital Therapy, 36,* 6–23.

Lev, A. I. (2004). *Transgender emergence: Therapeutic guidelines for working with gender variant people and their families*. New York, NY: Haworth.

Major, B., & Eccleston, C. (2005). Stigma and social exclusion. In D. Abrams, M. A. Hogg, & J. M. Marques (Eds.), *The social psychology of inclusion and exclusion* (pp. 63–87). New York, NY: Psychology Press.

McKenna, K. & Bargh, J. (1998). Coming out in the age of the Internet: Identity "demarginalization" through virtual group participation. *Journal of Personality & Social Psychology, 75,* 681–694.

Menvielle, E., & Hill, D. B. (2011). Affirmative intervention for families with gender variant children: a process evaluation. *Journal of Gay & Lesbian Mental Health, 15,* 94–123.

Menvielle, E., & Tuerk, C. (2002). A support group for parents of gender non-conforming boys. *Journal of the American Academy of Child and Adolescent Psychiatry, 41*(8), 1010–1013.

Richardson, J. (1999). Response: Finding the disorder in gender identity disorder. *Harvard Review of Psychiatry, 7,* 43–50.

Wallien, M. S. C., & Cohen-Kettenis, P. T. (2008). Psychosexual outcome of gender-dysphoric children. *Journal of the American Academy of Child and Adolescent Psychiatry, 47,* 1413–1423.

Wyman, P. A., Sandler, I., Wolchik, S., & Nelson, K. (2000). Resilience as cumulative competence promotion and stress protection: Theory and intervention. In D. Cicchetti, J. Rappaport, I. Sandler, & R. P. Weissberg (Eds.). *The Promotion of Wellness in Children and Adolescents*. Washington, DC: Child Welfare league of America.

Zucker, K. J. (2008). Children with gender identity disorder: Is there a best practice? *Neuropsychiatrie de l'Enfance et de l'Adolescence,* 358–364.

Zucker, K. J., & Cohen-Kettenis, P. T. (2008). Gender identity disorders in children and adolescents. In D. L. Rowland & L. Incrocci (Eds.), *Handbook of sexual and gender identity disorders* (pp. 376–422). Hoboken, NJ: John Wiley & Sons.

A Developmental, Biopsychosocial Model for the Treatment of Children with Gender Identity Disorder

KENNETH J. ZUCKER, PhD, HAYLEY WOOD, PhD,
DEVITA SINGH, MA, and SUSAN J. BRADLEY, MD
Centre for Addiction and Mental Health, Toronto, Ontario, Canada

This article provides a summary of the therapeutic model and approach used in the Gender Identity Service at the Centre for Addiction and Mental Health in Toronto. The authors describe their assessment protocol, describe their current multifactorial case formulation model, including a strong emphasis on developmental factors, and provide clinical examples of how the model is used in the treatment.

In this article, we will outline the therapeutic approach for children that has evolved in the Gender Identity Service, Child, Youth, and Family Program at the Centre for Addiction and Mental Health in Toronto. Since our clinic was established in the mid-1970s, we have evaluated a total of 590 children (age range, 2–12 years) who were referred to our service. In organizing this article, we will attempt to address the majority of questions provided to the contributors by the guest editors.

WHAT CONSTITUTES AN ASSESSMENT?

Tables 1–2 show the assessment protocol that we currently use in our clinic. As is the case for most children referred for a psychiatric and psychologic

TABLE 1 Clinical assessment protocol

Interview schedule	Approximate duration
Telephone intake interview	.5–1.5 hours
Family interview	3 hours
Individual interviews with parents	2–5 hours/parent
Psychological testing of the child	4 hours
Individual interview with child	1 hour
Feedback session	1–2 hours

Note. In Canada, there is universal health care coverage. When a child is seen in a hospital setting, the Canadian health care plan covers the entire cost. A psychiatrist bills directly the health care system for all face-to-face contact. Psychologists who work in a hospital setting are paid an hourly rate, but do not bill the health care plan. For child psychiatrists in private practice, they also bill the health care plan for all face-to-face contact. Psychologists in private practice operate on a fee-for-service basis. Clients pay the psychologist directly. If they have private health insurance, at least some of the costs are covered by the individual health care plan.

TABLE 2 Psychological testing protocol and parent-completed questionnaires

Test/task/questionnaire	Comment/reference
Child measures	
IQ test	WPPSI-III or WISC-IV
Quality of attachment (mother-child observation)	Used with children 3–6 years of age. Cassidy and Marvin (1992)
Feelings, Attitudes, and Behaviors Scale for Children	Used with children 6–10 years of age. Beitchman (1996)
Youth Self-Report Form	Used with children 11–12 years of age. Achenbach and Edelbrock (1986a)
Rorschach	Zucker, Lozinski, Bradley, and Doering (1992)
Draw-a-Person test	Zucker, Finegan, Doering, and Bradley (1983)
Free play task	Zucker, Doering, Bradley, and Finegan (1982)
Playmate and Play Style Preferences Structured Interview	Fridell, Owen-Anderson, Johnson, Bradley, and Zucker (2006)
Color preference task	Chiu et al. (2006)
Gender Identity Interview for Children	Wallien et al. (2009) and Zucker et al. (1993)
Parent/teacher measures	
Separation Anxiety Interview schedule	Used for boys only. Zucker, Bradley, and Lowry Sullivan (1996)
Child Behavior Checklist	Achenbach and Edelbrock (1983)
Teacher's Report Form	Achenbach and Edelbrock (1986b)
Temperament questionnaire	Zucker and Bradley (1995)
Games Inventory	Bates and Bentler (1973)
Gender Identity Questionnaire for Children	Johnson et al. (2004)
Symptom Checklist-90	Derogatis (1983)
Dyadic Adjustment Scale	Spanier (1976)
Recalled Childhood Gender Identity/Gender Role Questionnaire	Zucker et al. (2006)

Note. We no longer use the two gender constancy assessment measures reported on by Zucker et al. (1999). The Children's Depression Inventory is used on an ad hoc basis.

assessment, a referral is invariably initiated on the part of parents or a health professional (e.g., the pediatrician, a family physician, a teacher or a mental health professional currently involved in the care of the child and the family). Upon receipt of the referral, the first phase in our assessment protocol is to conduct an intake telephone interview with a parent or another primary caregiver (e.g., a child protection worker). In this intake telephone interview, which varies between 30 and 90 minutes, parents provide information about why they have contacted us, their concerns, and their goals. We collect information about their child's gender development (asking questions about behaviors that correspond to the *Diagnostic and Statistical Manual of Mental Disorders* (DSM-IV-TR, American Psychiatric Association, 2000) diagnosis of Gender Identity Disorder), whether there are other concerns about the child's socioemotional development (including other *DSM* diagnoses), previous mental health contacts, the child's physical health, and whether or not there is a family history of psychologic problems/psychiatric disorders. If a child has had previous mental health contacts, this information is requested for review prior to our own assessment. An intake interview is as follows:[1]

An intake telephone interview was conducted with Zack's mother, lasting approximately 45 minutes. Ms. Aziz appeared to be quite distracted during the phone call, often excusing herself to attend to her children, who were heard screaming in the background. Zack, age 3, lives with his parents and 6-month-old sister. Both parents are employed full-time as managers of business firms.

Ms. Aziz explained why the referral to our clinic was initiated. She described Zack as exhibiting an array of behaviors that she believes to be female-typical. For example, he will color his fingernails to mimic nail polish, will wear her shoes, wrap a blanket around himself to make a skirt, and appears to be very fascinated by jewelry. She said that she first noticed these behaviors just over a year ago and that they have increased since then. Ms. Aziz said that she initiated contact with our clinic to learn how to deal with these behaviors.

Ms. Aziz stated that she believes that Zack knows that he is a boy and has a penis. She thinks that he notices the anatomical differences between himself and his sister. She said that she saw him "pushing his penis in" about 3 months ago. In terms of gender identity statements, Zack has said that he is a girl and that he wants to be a girl. Ms. Aziz said that she has responded to these statements by asking Zack, "Why?" Ms. Aziz explained that Zack is not able to express himself very well through speech, so has not been able to answer this question with clarity.

Ms. Aziz said that Zack displays a range of behaviors, acting in a gender-typical fashion at times. He enjoys playing with other children and has both male and female friends. It was reported that Zack's best friend is a boy and, together, they will play in a rough-and-tumble manner. However, Ms. Aziz believes that Zack likes being around same-aged girls more. With girls, Zack is said to be less active, sitting back and watching them with a look of fascination. He has made comments about liking the clothing of the girls in his class.

In terms of the feedback Zack has received regarding his cross-gender behaviors, Ms. Aziz said that she believes they have been inconsistent. Starting at the age of 1.5 years, Zack attended a daycare run by a woman, who Ms. Aziz thinks encouraged and taught some of his female-typical behavior because she found it "entertaining." For example, at this daycare, Zack was taught how to belly dance. Ms. Aziz sees the movements involved in belly dancing as being quite feminine and said that Zack enjoys showing them off. Zack's teachers have noticed some cross-gender behaviors but do not discourage them unless they are potentially harmful. For example, they will only intervene if they see him painting on his own skin.

Ms. Aziz said that her family identifies as Muslim. She explained that cross-gender behaviors are unacceptable in the Muslim faith, but said that their family is not very observant. Ms. Aziz has seen her husband get quite agitated by Zack's female-typical behavior and said that he "hates the idea" of Zack being girly. Mr. Aziz has made disapproving comments to Zack, like "you look silly" when he dresses up like a girl.

Ms. Aziz believes that she has contributed to Zack's gender confusion herself somewhat. Until recently, she has read him fairy tales like Cinderella, with female characters that Zack has seemed to really connect with. At first, she tried to ignore his cross-gender tendencies and not make any comments. However, she said that since reading online about Dr. Zucker's approach, she has tried to replace the feminine things that Zack is interested in with more masculine things. For example, she has taken away fairy tales and replaced them with stories about male characters, like Diego. Zack reportedly pays some attention to the newly introduced items, but appears to miss the female-typical things. Ms. Aziz said that he will throw a tantrum when something he likes is removed. For example, when his makeshift skirt was taken away, he cried and expressed that he wanted it back. She said that she still tries to remain neutral on the subject because she does not want to "cause harm," but has told him many times that he is a boy and has a penis.

Within the family, Zack is said to be closest with his mother, who has been his "primary caregiver." Ms. Aziz said that she has always been responsible for Zack's daily routine and she described Zack as being very attached to her. She has noticed separations from her, like when he goes to daycare, as being difficult for him. Zack is also said to be quite close with his grandmother, who is said to be very female typical. He often appears to be fascinated by her jewelry and makeup. She said that he just appears to like having someone around, even if he is playing by himself. He is also said to have a good relationship with his father. Together, they will read stories, build blocks, and ride bikes in the summer. Ms. Aziz said that Zack seemed to hate the idea of having a younger sister when she was pregnant. For example, he made a comment about sending the baby on a train to go to his aunt's house. Zack appears to have gotten used to the idea of having a younger sister. Ms. Aziz stated that Zack loves his sister and will sometimes appear to be frightened that something bad might happen to her.

Ms. Aziz said that her relationship with her husband has been contentious at times. When Zack was 1.5 years old, Ms. Aziz and her husband had their biggest fight. Ms. Aziz described this fight as "traumatic," as Zack witnessed his father hold a gun to his mother's chest. As a result, the police were involved. Ms. Aziz said that she is not sure if Zack remembers this incident because he has not said anything about it, but she believes it might have affected him. This fight was an isolated episode in terms of magnitude, but there have been other instances of argumentativeness. Zack is said to always take his mother's side in these arguments, asking his father why he is being "bad to mommy."

Ms. Aziz's pregnancy with Zack was the result of in vitro fertilization. He has been exposed to three languages all at once, so she believes that his speech has been slow to progress as a result. When asked why she thought Zack displayed these cross-gender behaviors, Ms. Aziz cited many environmental explanations. She said that she thinks it is likely related to his attachment to her. She noted that he sees her all the time and that she has always been the one to take care of his routine. She said that, although she does not see herself as being very "girly," she thinks that she has encouraged his identification with females by reading him fairy tales. Ms. Aziz also believes that his daycare provider is somewhat responsible for teaching and encouraging female-typical behaviors. Finally, she thinks that he is more likely to behave in this way if he is "lacking attention" or bored.

Prior to the assessment, parents are provided with information about the temporal course of the assessment (typically 3–4 visits) and what it will involve. Parents are asked what they will inform their child about the assessment, who they are going to see, and why they are coming to see us. In our experience, this is an important phase in the assessment process in terms of establishing appropriate assessment rapport, particularly with anxious parents. For the majority of parents, they do not have a particular difficulty or problem in explaining to their child that they are coming to see some "talking doctors who know a lot about families" (a script that we suggest). They are able to frankly discuss with their child that they are coming to see a talking doctor to understand better why their child wishes to be of the other gender. This is usually because the issue has been on the table within the family environment.

There are, however, a minority of parents who are very uncertain and torn about what to tell their child. A common comment is, "I don't know what to tell him. I don't want him to think that there is anything wrong with him." Our suggestion for these parents is to, first, state that the issue is not a matter of right or wrong. Rather, the issue is to understand better why their child feels the way that he or she does and the purpose of the assessment is to determine how to best help them and their child. For these parents, we have found this suggestion to usually be helpful and they might be able to say something like, "You know how you have been telling mommy that you want to be a girl, that you like 'girls' toys,' that you like to dress-up in mommy's clothes? Well, mom and dad want to understand better how you are feeling about yourself and we are going to go and see some talking doctors who know a lot about kids." In our experience, almost all reluctant parents who contact us are able to provide this information. However, for the very small minority who cannot provide this information due to severe anxiety or ambivalence, we will meet only with the parents. If after meeting us, they are comfortable bringing their child, the usual assessment protocol follows. If not, the assessment is conducted only with the parents. Since 1975, only five assessments were conducted only with parents.

The assessment protocol usually allows us to acquire enough information to decide whether or not the child meets the DSM criteria for Gender Identity Disorder (GID) and any other psychiatric disorder. Multiple sources of information are used, including the open-ended material gleaned from the clinical interviews, a review of the psychological testing of the child, and an examination of the relevant parent-report questionnaires. The assessment also attempts to understand the general functioning of the family matrix (e.g., the parent's relationship, parent-child relationships, sibling relationships, etc.) and how the child is functioning at school, in the peer group, etc. An effort is made to gain an understanding of how the parents have made sense of their child's gender development (e.g., its origins), how the parents have responded to their child's cross-gender behavior prior to the assessment, what goals the parents have with regard to their child's gender development, and so on.

ON WHAT BASIS IS IT DECIDED THAT TREATMENT IS INDICATED?

Prior to providing parents with feedback, we have a case formulation conference among the team members involved in the assessment. It is obvious that a case formulation requires some type of conceptual model to guide it. Accordingly, we will comment here on some of the parameters that underlie what we would like to characterize as a developmental, biopsychosocial model that we use in case formulations and in generating treatment decisions and recommendations. It is a model informed by a variety of theoretical and empirical advances that have emerged in the clinical and scientific literature over the past several decades.

1. Is gender identity fixed and unalterable in childhood? For the vast majority of children, it is probably safe to say that gender identity is a stable trait. A girl who "has" a female gender identity at age 3 is very much likely to have a female gender identity at age 13, at age 23, and so on

throughout the life course. In this sense, one might argue that the gender identity at age 3 was fixed and unalterable. But, for most children, no one tries to alter their gender identity after it is first expressed, for a host of psychological and social reasons. To formally answer the question of whether or not a young child's gender identity is fixed and unalterable, one would have to conduct a randomized psychosocial trial in which, for half the children, some type of intervention was attempted to alter the child's gender identity. It is unlikely that such an "experiment of nurture" would attract many volunteer parent participants.

For children who present clinically with the diagnosis of GID, long-term follow-up studies suggest that their gender identity is not necessarily fixed. The majority of children followed longitudinally appear to lose the diagnosis of GID when seen in late adolescence or young adulthood, and appear to have differentiated a gender identity that matches their natal sex (Drummond, Bradley, Badali-Peterson, & Zucker, 2008; Green, 1987; Singh, Bradley, & Zucker, 2010; Wallien & Cohen-Kettenis, 2008; Zucker, 2008a).[2] In this sense, one could argue that their childhood gender identity was alterable—that there was plasticity and malleability—although the mechanisms that underlie this change are far from fully understood. Thus, when we provide feedback to parents about their child's gender identity, we make use of the empirical information that is currently available about "natural history."

2. In our view, gender identity development can be best understood using a multifactorial model that takes into account biological factors, psychosocial factors, social cognition, associated psychopathology, and psychodynamic mechanisms. In the model, biological factors (e.g., possible genetic factors, prenatal sex hormones, temperament) are conceptualized as possible predisposing factors for the expression of a particular gender identity phenotype. They are not conceptualized as fixed factors leading to invariant gender identity differentiation across developmental time. The other parameters can be conceptualized as predisposing, precipitating or perpetuating factors.

Biological Factors

Let us use a dimension of temperament (activity level; AL) as an example of a possible predisposing biological factor. Activity level, the propensity for intense physical energy expenditure and the proclivity for rough-and-tumble play, is a sex-dimorphic trait, with likely genetic and prenatal hormonal influences (Campbell & Eaton, 1999; Eaton & Enns, 1986). Via a parent-report measure, we have shown that AL is inverted in children with GID: Boys with GID have a lower AL than control boys and girls with GID have a higher AL than control girls. Indeed, girls with GID have a significantly higher AL than boys with GID (Zucker & Bradley, 1995). If one construes

AL as a temperamental trait, one could conceptualize, for example, a boy with a low AL to find the behaviors of girls, on average, as more compatible with his own temperamental style than the behaviors of boys and could, conceivably, lead to a greater affiliation with girls regarding sex-of-playmate preference. In turn, this could lead to a greater interest in the toys and activities of girls which could, in theory, have a feedback effect on the child's gender identity, especially during early development when cognitive reasoning is fairly rigid and black and white.

> Frank was a 7-year-old boy who met the *DSM* criteria for GID. In contrast to his two brothers, Frank was described by his parents as more sensitive and emotional. He had a long history of an avoidance of rough-and-tumble play, complaining that other boys were both mean and aggressive. Indeed, one of his brothers, who had a history of severe disruptive behavior, had often been mean and aggressive towards him. The problematic relationship with his brother appeared to generalize to Frank's view of all boys, as he complained that all boys were mean. He affiliated primarily with girls and, with them, engaged in a variety of stereotypical feminine activities. By age 5, he began to voice the wish to be a girl, stating that if he were a girl, then all of his problems would be solved.
>
> If one conceptualized Frank's sensitive temperament as a predisposing, presumably biological factor, one could argue for an intervention that, in part, would focus on helping Frank recognize that there are a variety of ways to be a boy and that there are likely some boys in his social environment who are not pervasively mean or aggressive. Exposure of Frank to other boys whose temperament was more a match to his own could, in theory, help him to develop a more nuanced understanding of gender: that there are different ways to be a boy, that one does not have to be a girl as a fantasy solution to cope with his difficulties with his aggressive brother or the more boisterous boys in the school environment, and so on.

Psychosocial Factors

Psychosocial factors constitute a second parameter in case formulation. One example pertains to the parental response to cross-gender behavior as it emerges early in development. In our view, it is common for the initial parental response to cross-gender behavior to be either neutral or encouraging (reinforcement). Early cross-gender behavior is often viewed by parents as either cute or only a phase.[3] For some parents, they seek out a clinical assessment only after some kind of threshold is crossed, and they now no longer believe that the behavior is cute or only a phase (Zucker, 2000). The threshold might pertain to emergent social ostracism in the peer group, the child's intense verbalization that he or she either is or wants to be the other gender, or other factors. In our case formulation, parental neutrality or encouragement of cross-gender behavior is viewed as a perpetuating factor (in relatively rare cases, in which, e.g., the mother overtly cross-dresses her son, acting out her desire for a daughter, such behavior could be viewed as a precipitating factor).

> Roy was a 4.5-year-old boy with a two-year history of pervasive cross-gender behavior. At the time of assessment, Roy did not express the wish to be a girl; rather, he insisted that he was a girl. Since he first began to display signs of cross-gender behavior, the parental response was to "go with it." They bought him stereotypical girls' toys, allowed him to wear his mother's clothes on a daily basis, and would often videotape his activities when he dressed up as a girl. Apart from his gender identity development, the parents identified one other major concern about his socioemotional development, namely that he would have intense and extremely disorganized temper tantrums when frustrated. During these episodes, he was experienced as inconsolable. By history, the parents reported that they had never "challenged" Roy when he insisted that he "was" a girl. They came to the assessment wanting to know if this was "really who Roy was" and if they were doing the "right thing" by allowing Roy to consistently enact behaviors that allowed him to, in effect, see himself as a girl.

Social Cognition

In the literature on normative gender development, it has long been noted that young children do not have a full understanding of gender constancy. Gender constancy refers to a child's cognitive understanding that gender is an invariant part of the self. It has been argued that in the early stages of gender constancy (e.g., the capacity to self-label oneself as a boy or a girl or to understand the constancy of gender over time) that children do not fully understand its invariance. Until children develop the capacity for concrete operational thought, typically between the ages of 5 and 7 years, they often conflate gender identity with surface expressions of gender behaviors (Kohlberg, 1966; Ruble, Martin, & Berenbaum, 2006). Thus, it is not particularly unusual for a 4-year-old girl to express the belief that, if she wore boys' clothes and engaged in boys' activities, then this would mean that she was a boy. It has also been reported in the normative gender development literature that younger children tend to have more rigid beliefs than older children about what boys and girls can do or should do (Ruble et al., 2006). In our own research, we have reported that children with GID appear to have a developmental lag in gender constancy acquisition (Zucker et al., 1999). Although it is unclear if this developmental lag can be understood as a predisposing factor, it can certainly be understood as a perpetuating factor (e.g., pervasive enactments of surface cross-gender behaviors could contribute to the maintenance of cognitive gender confusion).

In some respects, gendered social cognition provides a window into how children with GID construct a subjective sense of self as a boy or as a girl. For example, when asked why he wanted to be a girl, one 7-year-old boy said that it was because he did not like to sweat and only boys sweat. He also commented that he wanted to be a girl because he liked to read and girls read better than boys. An 8-year-old boy commented that "girls are treated better than boys by their parents" and that "the teacher only yells at the boys." His view was that, if he was a girl, then his parents would be nicer to him and that he would get into less trouble at school. One 5-year-old boy talked about having a "girl's brain" because he only liked Barbie dolls. In this particular boy's treatment, he created drawings of his own brain, writing in examples of what made his brain more like a girl's brain and what made his brain more like a boy's brain (e.g., when he developed an interest in Lego). Over time, the drawings of the size of his girl's brain shrunk and the size of his boy's brain expanded.

It could, of course, be argued that gendered social cognition is merely an epiphenomenon of a more fundamental developmental process pertaining to gender identity, that is, it is simply a way that children attempt to explain to themselves their gender identity. On the other hand, it could be argued that young children's limited understanding of gendered social cognition calls for caution in assuming how fixed their gender identity is and that, with development, some children will develop a more flexible understanding that there are different ways one can be a boy or a girl.

Co-Occurring Psychopathology

When there is co-occurring psychopathology in children with GID, it can be understood in several ways: a) as a result of social ostracism; b) as related to generic family risk factors for psychopathology; and c) as a possible cause of the GID. Regarding this last possibility, Coates and Person (1985), for example, argued that severe separation anxiety preceded the expression of feminine behavior in GID boys, which emerged in order "to restore a fantasy tie to the physically or emotionally absent mother. In imitating 'Mommy' [the boy] confuse[s] 'being Mommy' with 'having Mommy.' [Cross-gender behavior] appears to allay, in part, the anxiety generated by the loss of the mother" (p. 708).

In recent years, various clinicians working with children with GID have noted that some of these youngsters also appear to show signs of autism spectrum disorder (ASD), particularly at the high-functioning end of the spectrum. This clinical observation, which is now supported by some systematic empirical data (de Vries, Noens, Cohen-Kettenis, van Berckelaer-Onnes, & Doreleijers, 2010), opens up another avenue regarding the role of associated psychopathology in children with GID. In our experience, children with GID generally show intense, if not obsessional, interests, in cross-gender activities. This propensity for intense interests may be magnified even further in those youngsters with a co-occurring ASD. Thus, a bridge between GID and ASD may be the predisposition for obsessional or focused interests and extreme rigidity in thinking. Moreover, any attempt to interfere with the obsessionality may evoke intense anxiety. It is common for parents of these youngsters to report a series of obsessions (e.g., with a particular color, with a particular book that must be read over and over in ritualistic fashion, with specific objects, such as washing machines, vacuum cleaners, etc.).

Gender can become a site for obsessionality, perhaps a magnification of intense interests in typically developing children (DeLoache, Simcock, & Macara, 2007). One 5-year-old boy with co-occurring GID and ASD had many obsessional interests that preceded his gender obsession. Unlike his earlier obsessions, which the parents tried to ignore, they were less certain if they should ignore his gendered obsessions and, thus, bought him an array of girls' toys and allowed him to wear his mother's clothes on a daily basis. At the time of assessment, this youngster had been insisting that he was a girl and, at school, where gendered line-ups were common, would join the girls in their line. In the course of the assessment, the mother reported that he was now developing a new obsession: "He now thinks that he is a computer." She thought that this was preferable to him believing that he was a girl. The child psychiatrist who has followed this youngster reported that, at age 12, the symptoms of GID had remitted. At age 12, this youngster had an "obsession" with male heavy metal rock stars (a particular musical genre) and wore his hair long to emulate them.

David was referred at the age of 5 by a child psychiatrist, following remarks to his parents that he wished to be a girl and to cut off his penis. Apart from a GID, David had a number of socioemotional difficulties, including persistent and pervasive struggles with self-regulation, behavioral rigidity, obsessive behaviors, anxiety, and poor social functioning. In our assessment, we concluded that he met criteria for Asperger's Disorder. Play therapy was initiated to help explore David's gender dysphoria. As appropriate, additional therapeutic strategies were drawn upon in order to support the development of self-regulation (e.g., with regard to sexualized behavior directed towards the therapist, temper tantrums), social skills, and the management of areas of obsessive focus. In the therapeutic context, struggles with the parent-child relationship, self-concept, peer relations, and anger and guilt were consistent themes.

Over the course of four years in therapy, David evidenced a strong tendency towards obsessions/restricted interests (e.g., trains, airports, certain television shows, and book series), with each lasting between 3 to 6 months in duration. The gender-related preoccupation stood out in terms of its relationship to identity. The gender dysphoria began to wane around age 7. At age 9 years, in the 112th therapy session, David initiated discussion about his history of obsessions/restricted interests. He requested that his therapist write out each of his areas of interest (in chronological order) and he proceeded to summarize the "rationale" behind each. Early in the list placed his preoccupation with cross-gender materials. David paused on this area and reflected it had carried special meaning for him. He went on to say that this may have been more than just an interest in this topic area, and that, in fact, he had wanted to *be* a girl. He reflected on the reinforcing aspects of many of the feminine interests and behaviors (e.g., the feeling of pretend long hair, how "beautiful" things looked, etc.), with a focus on the associated visual and tactile stimulation. When asked about his understanding of his involvement in therapy, starting at age 5 years, David reflected that his parents may have been concerned about his desire to be a girl, as they knew that he was "really a boy." He recalled his parents' efforts to curtail his cross-gender behaviors by limiting his time and access. He discussed his belief that this was not the right approach, and that they should have just allowed him to grow out of this interest, as he had all of the previous and subsequent ones.

In reflecting on his development of gender dysphoria, David discussed his experience of bullying from peers for his gender atypical areas of interest. He speculated that, in many ways, his desire to become a girl may have been an effort to avoid the bullying from peers. David again reiterated the very reinforcing aspects of many of his female-typical interests. Finally, he reflected on his negative feelings about himself and his behavior and we considered his gender dysphoria as an effort to cope with these feelings. David continues to demonstrate a tendency towards preoccupations but, at present, has no symptoms characteristic of GID. He continues to benefit from therapeutic support for self-regulation, social skills, and management of his restricted interests/preoccupations.

Psychodynamic Mechanisms

Psychodynamic mechanisms can be understood, in part, as a transfer of unresolved conflict and trauma-related experiences from parent to child. Sometimes these kinds of experiences are consciously recognized by parents (but, nonetheless, acted out), but certainly not always. Children, themselves, may vary in their understanding of what drives their behavior.

Tom was a 4-year-old boy with an approximate one-year history of pervasive cross-gender behavior, including the repeated wish to be a girl. Tom's mother was an intense, volatile, and extremely anxious woman, with strong narcissistic personality traits. She viewed Tom as a perfect child, until he began to express the desire to be a girl. She then experienced Tom as less than perfect, which, for her, was a severe narcissistic injury. Tom's father played little role in his day-to-day life, working 18-hour days, 7 days/week.

We understood Tom's GID to develop in the context of the birth of his younger sister when he was just shy of his third birthday. He felt abandoned by his mother, who seemed to transfer much of her psychologic investment to the sister. She adorned the baby sister in pink (in early therapy sessions with Tom, he only used the color pink in his numerous drawings). In part, we conceptualized Tom's GID as the result of feeling an intense psychologic abandonment by his mother and an intense jealous rage towards his sister ("If you could be a girl like Suzie, then mom would pay more attention to you"). In our view, one of the factors in helping Tom work through his gender identity conflict was to make him more conscious of his jealous feelings and how they organized his day-to-day life within the family matrix.

Rose was a 9-year-old girl with a long history of cross-gender behavior, including the strong desire to be a boy. Rose was raised by her biological mother. At the age of 4, Rose discovered her mother's body at the bottom of the staircase. She had been murdered by a boyfriend. For various reasons, there were no biological relatives to care for Rose and so she was adopted at the age of 6.

At the time of assessment, Rose looked like a boy, based on her hairstyle and clothing style. During the assessment, Rose commented that she wanted to be a boy because boys were stronger than girls. She told her adoptive mother that when they walked down the street together that her mother need not be afraid, because "I look like a boy and no one will hurt you." Rose acknowledged that she has had the recurring thought that, had she been a boy, then she would have been able to protect her mother from the boyfriend because "boys are stronger than girls."

We conceptualized Rose's desire to be a boy as an unusual symptom emanating from a Post-Traumatic Stress Disorder. Perhaps due to the rigid normative social cognitions about gender, Rose had constructed, for herself, an unusual fantasy solution: had she been a boy ("because" boys are stronger than girls), she could have saved her mother's life.

In the case of Roy described above, one issue that was discussed in the case formulation conference was why the parents had never attempted to tell Roy that he was, in fact, "a boy." We wondered about why the parents were so "paralyzed" in this regard. One element of the family history that seemed relevant was that his mother had been subject to a long history of psychological and physical abuse by her father. We wondered if any signs of more boy-typical behavior on Roy's part might be conflated with viewing him as an "abuser-in-the-making," like her own father. In addition, Roy's mother had been subject to very severe peer ostracism during her own childhood (e.g., being made fun of because she wore glasses, had dental problems, etc.). These experiences were extremely difficult for her and she cried profusely (30 years later) as she described them. She worried that, if she said anything to Roy about his insistence that he was a girl, he would experience this in the same traumatic way that she experienced the peer group teasing in her own childhood. Roy's father also had had a lot of difficult experiences in the peer group because of a speech impediment and he was also extremely worried that if he said anything to Roy about his girlish behaviors that Roy would experience this as representing a "defect," just like he experienced his speech problem as a defect.

Jim was the last of four boys born to a middle-class family. When seen at age 4, he had a strong desire to be a girl. Jim's mother acknowledged a very strong wish for a daughter, as she knew that this was her "last chance." Although rare, Jim's mother's reaction to giving birth to a fourth son was consistent with what we have characterized as pathological gender mourning (Zucker, Bradley, & Ipp, 1993). She became deeply depressed after his birth, wanting little to do with the baby for a couple of weeks. She had florid dreams about having given birth to a daughter. When Jim was a year old, her female friends bought her a life-sized female baby doll. As far as we could tell, Jim's mother had little insight into the significance of this gift. She asked plaintively, "Do you think it's because my desire for a daughter was so apparent to my friends?"

In the case formulation conference, we wondered whether or not it would be useful to organize treatment for the mother around helping her to understand the meaning of the wish for a daughter and what it represented for her and to help her mourn the loss of having given birth to a child of the non-preferred gender. We also wondered how the mother's disappointment/despondency might have been transmitted to Jim across his development.

WHEN TREATMENT IS INDICATED, WHAT ARE THE RATIONALES AND GOALS FOR TREATMENT AND, AS SPECIFICALLY AS POSSIBLE, HOW DOES TREATMENT PROCEED?

When treatment is recommended, it might include the following: a) weekly individual play psychotherapy for the child; b) weekly parent counseling or psychotherapy; c) parent-guided interventions in the naturalistic environment; and d) when required for other psychiatric problems in the child, psychotropic medication. The goals for treatment are formulated on a case-by-case basis. In some cases, the focus might be only on the child's GID, as the child shows little in the way of associated psychopathology and the parents are generally functioning well. In other cases, the focus of treatment is much broader: If the child has other significant socioemotional problems and if the parents have significant psychopathology or marital discord, then these issues also need to be addressed.

If the parents are clear in their desire to have their child feel more comfortable in their own skin, that is, they would like to reduce their child's desire to be of the other gender, the therapeutic approach is organized around this goal. Any co-occurring psychopathology is also treated and the approach depends heavily on the understanding of the sources of the associated psychopathology. If parents are uncertain about how best to address their child's GID, we offer to address this further in the course of therapeutic sessions and will suggest to the parents that we hold off on making any specific decisions about intervention options. Table 3 provides a summary of treatment recommendations and disposition for 26 children evaluated in 2008.

When we conduct open-ended play psychotherapy (or simply talk therapy) with children, like any psychotherapeutic intervention for any issue, therapy begins with educating the child about the reason that they are in therapy. This is tailored to the child's developmental level and cognitive sophistication. Some children are simply told that they are going to meet with an individual therapist to understand better their gender-related feelings and, during sessions, they are free to play with whatever they want (boys' toys, girls' toys, dress-up clothing, neutral and educational activities, etc.), to draw, to talk about day-to-day life, to report on their dreams, and so on. Principles of confidentiality are reviewed.

For other children, they have a very sophisticated understanding of why they are in treatment and the educative process is less formal. One 4-year-old girl, for example, had actually asked her parents to take her to see a therapist (she was very intelligent) because she was confused about why she wanted to be a boy. After the assessment, she seamlessly entered into a therapeutic process about her gender feelings. Other children are substantially more guarded and require a much longer period of time before they are comfortable discussing their feelings. One 3-year-old boy, for example, in the course of a two-year treatment, was never able to talk about his day-to-day life with his therapist: It was all enacted literally via play with repetitive family scenarios in which he labeled the characters as himself and his parents. In both of these cases, the GID remitted in full.

Individual open-ended psychotherapy enables many children with GID to discuss and to play out their gender identity issues, it affords them the opportunity to make sense of their internal representational world, and, in general, to master various developmental tasks with which they may be struggling. There is a reasonably large psychoanalytic case report literature on GID, for which the interested reader can glean some good examples of the process of open-ended psychotherapy (see Zucker, 2006a, 2008b; Zucker & Bradley, 1995).

TABLE 3 Treatment recommendations for cases evaluated in 2008 ($N = 26$)

ID	Sex	Age	Individual Therapy	Parent Therapy	Medication	Other	Comment
1	F	10	No	Yes	On Concerta for ADHD prior to assessment	Support provided to child by school psychologist	Diagnosed with ODD and ADHD Outpatient services difficult to access in community
2	F	7	Yes	Yes	Consult recommended for ADHD	Feedback provided to school psychologist	Dropped out of treatment; mother sought advice from a nurse practitioner who specialized in naturopathy; significant discord between parents, who were separated; diagnosed with ODD and ADHD
3	F	5	Yes	Yes	No		Mourning the sudden death of father was one focus of treatment
4	M	6	Yes	Yes	Consult recommended for ADHD	In day treatment for behavioral problems (diagnosed with ODD and ADHD)	Father seen in counseling; mother refused treatment (has bipolar disorder and on long-term disability); parents separated; father has custody
5	M	9	No	No	No		Sibling of ID 2; subthreshold for GID; feminine behaviors of no concern to mother; father "denies" observing any feminine behaviors
6	M	5	No	Yes	No	Feedback provided to school psychologist and to child protection agency	Subthreshold for GID; behavioral problems at school; in foster care

7	M	3	No	No	No	Recommendations to parents for interventions in naturalistic environment	Family lives in a small town, with no mental health resources available
8	M	7	No	No	No	Recommendations to parents for interventions in naturalistic environment	Parents wanted to try interventions on their own prior to considering formal therapy
9	M	6	Yes	Yes	No	Recommendations to parents for interventions in naturalistic environment	When informed that the "odds" of persistent gender dysphoria were quite low for the patient, the mother "sobbed" with relief. She did not feel that formal therapy was, therefore, required, that she could "handle the rest" on her own.
10	M	8	Yes	Yes	No		Referred for immediate surgery for undescended testicles
11	F	12	Yes	Yes	On Celexa, Strattera, and Serequel prior to assessment		Patient had transitioned to living as a boy prior to assessment; diagnosed with PDD-NOS
12	M	8	Yes	Yes	No		Raised by maternal grandmother; both biological parents were drug addicts; father diagnosed with Schizophrenia

(*Continued*)

TABLE 3 (Continued)

ID	Sex	Age	Individual Therapy	Parent Therapy	Medication	Other	Comment
13	M	7	Yes	Yes	No	Consult recommended for pharmacologic treatment for anxiety	Diagnosed with ASD prior to our assessment; referred to a child psychiatrist in private practice
14	M	6	No	No	No	Recommendations to parents for interventions in naturalistic environment	Parents wanted to try interventions on their own prior to considering formal therapy
15	M	7	Yes	Yes	No		Parents, who were separated, refused treatment; parent-initiated a social gender change in child after assessment; diagnosed with Separation Anxiety Disorder query ODD
16	M	6	Yes	Yes	No		
17	M	4	Yes	Yes	No		
18	F	10	Yes	Yes	No		adopted
19	M	6	Yes	Yes	No	Recommendations to parents for interventions in naturalistic environment	Parents wanted to try interventions on their own; query ASD; r/o chronic motor tic disorder; local mental health resources not available

20	M	3	Yes	Yes	No		Co-occurring disorder of sex development (46,XX ova-testicular DSD); male gender assignment shortly after birth; speech and language delay; significant behavior problems
21	F	10	Yes	Yes	Yes	On Concerta prior to assessment; Risperdal recommended	adopted at 20 months from Russia; language delay; Reactive Attachment Disorder (in remission); query PDD-NOS; significant behavior problems (one brief in-patient hospitalization)
22	M	6	Yes	Yes	No		Marfan syndrome; significant obsessional behavior; query Separation Anxiety Disorder; significant family stress, including OCD in older sister; discontinued treatment because of distance and family stress; referred to local resources for continued therapeutic support
23	M	4	Yes	Yes	No		Parents agreed to therapy, but then did not follow up
24	F	5	Yes	Yes	No		Referred mother for local mental health support
25	M	4	Yes	Yes	No		
26	F	5	No	Yes	No		

Note. F = natal female; M = natal male; ADHD = attention-deficit/hyperactivity disorder; ASD = autism spectrum disorder; ODD = oppositional defiant disorder; OCD = obsessive-compulsive disorder; PDD-NOS = pervasive developmental disorder not otherwise specified.

With parents, the focus of treatment that is specific to GID considers two issues: a) the potential role of parental factors in the genesis and maintenance of the GID, and b) naturalistic interventions. For parents for whom there may be significant psychodynamic and interpersonal factors in the genesis/maintenance of GID, we attempt to work on these issues. For example, we have posited that "identification with the aggressor" may be one factor involved in GID in girls (Zucker & Bradley, 1995). One 7-year-old girl, for example, had a long-standing conflicted relationship with her father. Her father was extremely critical, abrasive, and mean to this her. She had numerous socioemotional problems: extreme oppositional behavior with the parents, intense jealousy directed toward a younger sister, many sensory sensitivities that resulted in ritualistic behaviors, and was, in general, a very challenging child to parent. A large part of the treatment with the father focused on discussing how his rage toward his child was not helpful and likely made matters worse.

When parental psychopathology revolves around a gender-related axis, effort is made to explore the impact of this on their feelings toward the child. One mother of an 8-year-old boy wanted little to do with him. She was extremely depressed and withdrawn from her parenting role. She had been date raped as an adolescent and recalled that she dealt with this by becoming promiscuous ("Better to fuck them than to get fucked"). She acknowledged that she hated men. The only maneuver this boy could use to be close to his mother was to comb her hair (she was a hairdresser). In our view, these kinds of pathological processes require a long time to work on in psychotherapy with parents and are not particularly amenable to brief interventions.

When parents have significant reservations about setting limits on their child's cross-gender behaviors and to provide alternative activities, this requires considerable discussion. In our work, we emphasize that authoritarian limit setting is not the goal (limit setting per se is not the goal of treatment, but part of a series of interventions); rather, the goal is to help the child feel more comfortable in his or her own skin. Limit setting is discussed in context of the overall case formulation. If, for example, a young boy is driven by the desire to cross-dress, we explore with parents their understanding of what might underlie it.

For example, one 8-year-old boy was cared for by his mother (the father had died in a car accident) who worked two jobs. He was often left in the care of a neighbor while his mother worked the swing shift. In this context, he began to cross-dress and created a transitional mother object that he slept with. Helping the mother understand the possible link between his separation anxiety and his gender identity issues motivated her to spend more time discussing with him why she needed to work long hours, provided him with pictures of her to sleep with while she worked, called him a couple of times prior to his bedtime, and made more of an effort to be with him on her days off. This resulted in a significant reduction in both the separation anxiety and his desire to be a girl. In general, our approach with parents is to make the point that the surface behaviors of GID are, in effect, "symptoms" and that symptoms can best be helped if the underlying mechanisms are better understood. As an example, we might explain to parents of girls that forcing them to wear dresses or other feminine clothing (which creates severe anxiety in many girls with GID) should not be the focus of treatment and that it would likely be unhelpful. Instead, it would be more helpful to focus on the underlying gender dysphoria.

In the naturalistic environment, we typically target the improvement of same-sex peer relations, since peer relationships are often the site of gender identity consolidation (Maccoby, 1998; Meyer-Bahlburg, 2002). For young children, this can be implemented via parent-arranged play dates with temperamentally compatible same-sex peers; with older children, this can be implemented via enrollment in community activities, such as gymnastics, drama clubs, and team sports. The goal here is to see if children with GID are able to develop a broader range of friendships that include same-sex peers. For parents who are free of major life stressors or significant psychopathology that interferes with their parenting role, this task can be implemented fairly easily; however, when parents are overwhelmed with their own difficulties, they often feel depleted and unable to work on these kinds of interventions.

WHAT IS THE DISPOSITION OF REFERRED CASES FOR WHICH NO CLINICALLY SIGNIFICANT GENDER-VARIANT BEHAVIOR IS OBSERVED?

In our clinic, we almost never receive a referral in which we conclude from the intake interview that the case is a false positive. About 70% of the children we evaluate meet the complete *DSM* criteria for GID; the remainder of referrals are subthreshold (gender variant), some of whom had met the full criteria when younger. Of the 26 cases evaluated in 2008 (Table 3), only one youngster (ID 6) showed no signs of GID although he had voiced to the referring child psychiatrist a strong wish to be a girl. Psychological testing confirmed the absence of clinically significant gender identity issues. In this case, this youngster was dealing with the stressor of having been placed in foster care because of maternal neglect and had significant behavior problems at school and at home. Another youngster (ID 5) was the sibling of ID 2 and was subthreshold for GID. As noted in Table 3, the mother did not have any concerns about his feminine behavior and the father denied observing any. Because his sister had a severe GID, oppositional behavior, and ADHD, and because the parents had significant relational discord (they were separated), the focus of the recommendations were directed elsewhere.

The question posed by the guest editors of this special issue of the *Journal of Homosexuality* is relevant especially for children who are subthreshold for GID. Do these youngsters still have clinically significant gender identity issues that need to be monitored or even treated? In our view, the answer is sometimes yes and sometimes no. Some children may be subthreshold for GID, yet, the clinical impression is that these children may well be struggling with their gender identity and, for these children, a trial of therapy can certainly be beneficial to explore the issue further. If they have substantial other psychologic or psychiatric issues, these can also be a focus of treatment. One could argue that some children who are subthreshold for GID may be at risk for the later development of a full-blown GID (e.g., see Zucker, 2004, 2006b).

HOW ARE THE RELATIVE RISKS AND BENEFITS OF TREATMENT AS WELL AS THE IMPACT OF TREATMENT ON OUTCOME EXPLAINED TO CAREGIVERS?

In providing feedback to parents, we attempt to articulate our case formulation in a manner that is understandable. We identify the factors that we have found useful in understanding the child and the family. Parents vary in their psychologic sophistication and capacity for reflective functioning, so feedback is done in a way that is client centered. We provide a rationale for our treatment recommendations.

In the era of the Internet, some parents are quite familiar with the controversies about treatment of children with GID; others are not. For parents who are interested in discussing the philosophical differences among care providers, we discuss the varying perspectives. Benefits of treatment that we argue in favor of include the reduction in gender dysphoria, the attendant social ostracism that can ensue from GID persistence, the complexities of sex-reassignment surgery and its biomedical treatment, and the importance of reducing family psychopathology and stress, when it is present. The risks of treatment are discussed: Perhaps the child will not respond to the treatment; perhaps the parents will find it too stressful to attempt naturalistic interventions. As noted earlier, we explain that the goal of treatment is not to prevent the child from developing a future homosexual sexual orientation. For some parents, this is a non-issue; for other parents, it remains their goal. One concern parents have is that their child may go underground with his or her gender dysphoric feelings. We are mindful of this concern (the development of a false self in the Winnicottian sense) and emphasize that this is not a good outcome–the goal is to help the child work through their gender dysphoric feelings.

IS PREVENTION OF ADULT TRANSSEXUALISM
A REASONABLE TREATMENT GOAL, AND GIVEN THE LOW FREQUENCY WITH WHICH GID PERSISTS INTO ADULTHOOD, HOW IS IT POSSIBLE TO DETERMINE THE EFFICACY OF TREATMENT IN ATTAINING THAT GOAL?

... we cannot rule out the possibility that early successful treatment of childhood GID will diminish the role of a continuation of GID into adulthood. If so, successful treatment would also reduce the need for the long and difficult process of sex reassignment which includes hormonal and surgical procedures with substantial medical risks and complications. (Meyer-Bahlburg, 2002, p. 362)

Relatively little dispute exists regarding the prevention of transsexualism, though evidence about the effectiveness of treatment in preventing adult transsexualism is also virtually nonexistent. (Cohen-Kettenis & Pfäfflin, 2003, p. 120)

The guest editors of this special issue have posed a provocative question about the prevention of transsexualism (GID) in adulthood. Here, we can pose an ancillary question to illustrate, in part, the centrality of social values: Is prevention of homosexuality a reasonable treatment goal? On this point, most secular clinicians would answer "no." In our own clinic, we have never advocated for the prevention of homosexuality as a treatment goal for GID in children. At the same time, we are sensitive to the fact that some parents bring their child to the clinic, in part, because they are worried that their child will grow up to be gay or lesbian (for all the reasons one might imagine—parental homophobia, worries about social ostracism, worries about HIV/AIDS, worries that this will result in a more difficult life, cultural factors, religious factors, etc.).

Over the years, our approach has been a psychoeducational one and also a pragmatic one: a) we explain to parents that there are no empirical studies that suggest that alteration of a child's gender identity will also alter their eventual sexual orientation; b) that homosexuality per se is not considered a mental disorder; c) that gay men and lesbians can lead productive and satisfying lives (as banal as this sounds) and that, over time, if their child develops a homoerotic sexual orientation, then it will be their job (and ours) to support their child in adapting to whatever stressors may be associated with their sexual identity. In our experience, the majority of parents are satisfied with this psychoeducational approach and, for some, it involves mourning the loss of the expected heterosexual child and whatever fantasies and aspirations are associated with this. Many of the parents that we work with do not have a particular problem if their child were to grow up gay or lesbian. Many of these parents do, however, hold the aspiration that they would like their child to be comfortable in his or her skin. In other words, they can see that growing up transsexual or transgender may augur a more complicated life.

Although we do not have a particular quarrel with the prevention of transsexualism as a treatment goal for children with GID, we believe that this should be contextualized. If, for example, children with GID who persist in their desire to be of the other gender showed a better psychosocial adjustment and adaptation than children with GID who desist (e.g., become gay or lesbian or heterosexual without gender dysphoria), then one could, quite reasonably, question the prevention of transsexualism as a legitimate treatment goal. If a child grew up comfortable in their own skin, but was generally miserable otherwise, one could hardly argue with unabashed enthusiasm for the prevention of transsexualism.

From a developmental perspective, we take a very different approach when we work with adolescents with GID than when we work with children with GID. This is because we believe that there is much less evidence that GID can remit in adolescents than in children. Whether this is due to different populations of clients seen in adolescence versus childhood or whether this is due to a narrowing of plasticity and malleability in gender identity differentiation by the time of adolescence is open to debate. But, if the clinical consensus is that a particular adolescent is very much likely to persist down a pathway toward hormonal and sex-reassignment surgery, then our therapeutic approach is one that supports this pathway on the grounds that it will lead to a better psychosocial adaptation and quality of life (Zucker, Bradley, Owen-Anderson, et al., 2011).

Because the treatment literature is lacking in terms of rigorous comparative evaluations (e.g., Treatment X vs. Treatment Y or Treatment X vs. no treatment, etc.), one has to rely on a patchwork of empirical evidence about natural history. Thus, for example, natural history data suggest, to date, a much higher rate of desistance of GID in child samples than in adolescent or adult samples (Zucker et al., 2011).

The guest editors have made reference to the low frequency with which GID persists into adulthood and the implications of this fact in the evaluation of treatment efficacy. Persistence rates have varied fairly substantially in long-term follow-up studies. For example, Green (1987) reported that only 1 of 44 previously feminine boys appeared to be gender dysphoric at the time of follow-up. In contrast, Wallien and Cohen-Kettenis (2008) reported that 50% of 18 GID girls were persisters at follow up. In our own follow-up studies, we have found a persistence rate of 12% for GID girls ($n = 25$; Drummond et al., 2008) and a persistence rate of 13.3% for GID boys ($n = 135$; Singh et al., 2010). Thus, there is a fair bit of variation in persistence rates.

How can this variation be understood? One possibility is sampling differences. Another possibility pertains to the degree of GID in childhood.

Both Wallien and Cohen-Kettenis (2008) and Singh et al. (2010) showed that several metrics of GID severity in childhood predicted persistence at follow-up. Another possibility is to contextualize the natural history data.

Is there really such a thing as natural history for GID or does its developmental course vary as a function of contextual factors? If, as in our clinic, treatment is recommended to reduce the likelihood of GID persistence, perhaps the data can only be interpreted in that context. In any event, we require more comparative data to draw conclusions about the natural history of GID in children and its relation to contextual factors.

WHAT CONSTITUTES A SUCCESSFUL OUTCOME? WHAT CONSTITUTES A TREATMENT FAILURE?

If one goal of treatment is to reduce the gender dysphoria, then, by definition, a successful outcome would be its remission and a failure would be its persistence. If, however, a successful outcome also takes into account a child's more general well-being and adaptation to various developmental tasks, then the definitions of success and failure must be broader. Consider, for example, the vignette described earlier of the 7-year-old girl who had an extremely strained relationship with her father. Six years after therapy commenced (and still continues), the GID has fully remitted and there has been a lessening of the sensory sensitivities and rituals. Although this now young adolescent girl functions reasonably well at school and has friends, parent-child relations remain severely strained and there continues to be substantial parental psychopathology (in each parent and in their marriage). Success? Failure? In between?

For Tom, the 4-year-old boy who experienced his younger sister's birth as an extreme threat to his relationship with his mother, at the age of 13 his GID has remitted fully. In the course of many years of therapy, he has intermittently struggled with various issues (episodic encopresis, peer conflicts, behavioral compliance with parental expectations), but he functions extremely well at school and has many close friends. Although his development has been marked with various stressors and challenges, we would gauge his current outcome as pretty successful.

For children whose gender dysphoria persisted into adolescence or adulthood, some are functioning quite well; others are not. One natal male, originally seen at age 5, was seen for follow up at age 35. At follow up, she was living as a woman, but had elected to neither take exogenous female hormones or to have genital reassignment surgery ("A woman does not need a vagina to be a woman"). Because this individual was quite overweight, idiopathic gynecomastia was sufficient for the appearance of female breasts. She had a boyfriend who was sexually attracted to "she-males." She engaged in sex work, also attracting men interested in she-males. She used, on a daily basis, oxycontin and heroin. She was on long-term psychiatric disability, with various diagnoses: ADHD, bipolar disorder, and adult baby syndrome (she and her boyfriend planned on getting an apartment and creating a baby's room for her). Apart from the ADHD, the patient had no complaints about her life. Success? Failure?

Another natal female was originally seen for assessment at the age of 12 years and followed up at the age of 26. He had transitioned to the male gender in adolescence, but had not sought out either hormonal suppression or cross-sex hormonal therapy. He was very content living as a man. Ben worked full time, owned his own house, and had had long-term relationships with women. However, he struggled with severe alcohol abuse, abused recreational drugs, had been frequently arrested for getting into fights while intoxicated, and was occasionally suicidal. Success? Failure? In between?

Our long-term follow-up studies of both girls and boys with GID suggest that many of these youngsters, regardless of their later gender identity and sexual orientation, are a psychiatrically vulnerable group (Drummond, 2006; Drummond et al., 2008; Singh et al., 2010). Although some of this vulnerability might be understood in relation to the stressors associated with an atypical gender identity and/or sexual orientation, it is our belief that it is also related to other risk factors, including biological and psychosocial parameters within their families.

NOTES

1. We have used Clifft's (1986) guidelines for confidentiality in reporting clinical material.

2. These children are sometimes referred to as *desisters*, while those who do not "lose" the diagnosis are referred to as *persisters*.

3. There are more parents nowadays who interpret the cross-gender identification as a marker of the child's "essential" gender identity (Brill & Pepper, 2008; Dreger, 2009; Kilodavis, 2009).

REFERENCES

Achenbach, T. M., & Edelbrock, C. (1983). *Manual for the Child Behavior Checklist and Revised Child Behavior Profile*. Burlington, VT: University of Vermont: Department of Psychiatry.

Achenbach, T. M., & Edelbrock, C. (1986a). *Manual for the Youth Self-Report and Profile*. Burlington, VT: University of Vermont Department of Psychiatry.

Achenbach, T. M., & Edelbrock, C. (1986b). *Manual for the Teacher's Report Form and Teacher Version of the Child Behavior Profile*. Burlington, VT: University of Vermont Department of Psychiatry.

American Psychiatric Association. (2000). *Diagnostic and statistical manual of mental disorders* (4th ed., text rev.). Washington, DC: Author.

Bates, J. E., & Bentler, P. M. (1973). Play activities of normal and effeminate boys. *Developmental Psychology, 9,* 20–27.

Beitchman, J. H. (1996). *FAB-C^{TM}: Feelings, Attitudes, and Behaviors Scale for Children*. Toronto, ON, Canada: Multi-Health Systems.

Brill, S., & Pepper, R. (2008). *The transgender child: A handbook for families and professionals*. San Francisco, CA: Cleis Press.

Campbell, D. W., & Eaton, W. O. (1999). Sex differences in the activity level of infants. *Infant and Child Development*, *8*, 1–17.

Cassidy, J., & Marvin, R. S., with the Attachment Working Group of the MacArthur Network on the Transition from Infancy to Early Childhood. (1992). *Attachment organization in three- and four-year-olds*. Unpublished manual, University of Virginia at Charlottesville.

Chiu, S. W., Gervan, S., Fairbrother, C., Johnson, L. L., Owen-Anderson, A. F. H., Bradley, S. J., & Zucker, K. J. (2006). Sex-dimorphic color preference in children with gender identity disorder: A comparison to clinical and community controls. *Sex Roles*, *55*, 385–395.

Clifft, M. A. (1986). Writing about psychiatric patients: Guidelines for disguising case material. *Bulletin of the Menninger Clinic*, *50*, 511–524.

Coates, S., & Person, E. S. (1985). Extreme boyhood femininity: Isolated behavior or pervasive disorder? *Journal of the American Academy of Child Psychiatry*, *24*, 702–709.

Cohen-Kettenis, P. T., & Pfäfflin, F. (2003). *Transgenderism and intersexuality in childhood and adolescence: Making choices*. Thousand Oaks, CA: Sage.

de Vries, A. L. C., Noens, I. L., Cohen-Kettenis, P. T., van Berckelaer-Onnes, I. A., & Doreleijers, T. A. H. (2010). Autism spectrum disorders in gender dysphoric children and adolescents. *Journal of Autism and Developmental Disorders*, *40*, 930–936.

DeLoache, J. S., Simcock, G., & Macari, S. (2007). Planes, trains, automobiles–and tea sets: Extremely intense interests in very young children. *Developmental Psychology*, *43*, 1579–1586.

Derogatis, L. (1983). *SCL-90: Administration, scoring and procedures manual for the revised version*. Baltimore, MD: Clinical Psychometric Research.

Dreger, A. (2009). Gender identity disorder in childhood: Inconclusive advice to parents. *Hastings Center Report*, *39*, 26–29.

Drummond, K. D. (2006). *A follow-up study of girls with gender identity disorder*. Unpublished master's thesis, Ontario Institute for Studies in Education of the University of Toronto.

Drummond, K. D., Bradley, S. J., Badali-Peterson, M., & Zucker, K. J. (2008). A follow-up study of girls with gender identity disorder. *Developmental Psychology*, *44*, 34–45.

Eaton, W. O., & Enns, L. R (1986). Sex differences in human motor activity level. *Psychological Bulletin*, *100*, 19–28.

Fridell, S. R., Owen-Anderson, A., Johnson, L. L., Bradley, S. J., & Zucker, K. J. (2006). The Playmate And Play Style Preferences Structured Interview: A comparison of children with gender identity disorder and controls. *Archives of Sexual Behavior*, *35*, 729–737.

Green, R. (1987). *The "sissy boy syndrome" and the development of homosexuality*. New Haven, CT: Yale University Press.

Johnson, L. L., Bradley, S. J., Birkenfeld-Adams, A. S., Kuksis, M. A. R., Maing, D. M., Mitchell, J. N., & Zucker, K. J. (2004). A parent-report Gender Identity Questionnaire for Children. *Archives of Sexual Behavior*, *33*, 105–116.

Kilodavis, C. (2009). *My princess boy: A mom's story about a young boy who loves to dress up*. Seattle, WA: K D Talent LLC.

Kohlberg, L. (1966). A cognitive-developmental analysis of children's sex-role concepts and attitudes. In E. E. Maccoby (Ed.), *The development of sex differences* (pp. 82–173). Stanford, CA: Stanford University Press.

Maccoby, E. E. (1998). *The two sexes: Growing up apart, coming together*. Cambridge, MA: Harvard University Press.

Meyer-Bahlburg, H. F. L. (2002). Gender identity disorder in young boys: A parent- and peer-based treatment protocol. *Clinical Child Psychology and Psychiatry*, 7, 360–377.

Ruble, D. N., Martin, C. L., & Berenbaum, S. A. (2006). Gender development. In W. Damon & R. M. Lerner (Series eds.) and N. Eisenberg (Vol. ed.), *Handbook of child psychology (6th ed.). Vol. 3: Social, emotional, and personality development* (pp. 858–932). New York, NY: Wiley.

Singh, D., Bradley, S. J., & Zucker, K. J. (2010, June). *A follow-up study of boys with gender identity disorder*. Poster presented at the University of Lethbridge Workshop, The Puzzle of Sexual Orientation: What Is It and How Does It Work?, Lethbridge, AB, Canada.

Spanier, G. B. (1976). Measuring dyadic adjustment: New scales for assessing the quality of marriage and similar dyads. *Journal of Marriage and the Family*, 38, 15–28.

Wallien, M. S. C., & Cohen-Kettenis, P. T. (2008). Psychosexual outcome of gender dysphoric children. *Journal of the American Academy of Child and Adolescent Psychiatry*, 47, 1413–1423.

Wallien, M. S. C., Quilty, L. C., Steensma, T. D., Singh, D., Lambert, S. L., Leroux, A., . . . Zucker, K. J. (2009). Cross-national replication of the Gender Identity Interview for Children. *Journal of Personality Assessment*, 91, 545–552.

Zucker, K. J. (2000). Gender identity disorder. In A. J. Sameroff, M. Lewis, & S. M. Miller (Eds.), *Handbook of developmental psychopathology* (2nd ed.; pp. 671–686). New York, NY: Kluwer Academic/Plenum.

Zucker, K. J. (2004). Gender identity disorder. In I. B. Weiner (Ed.), *Adult psychopathology case studies* (pp. 207–228). New York, NY: Wiley.

Zucker, K. J. (2006a). I'm half-boy, half-girl": Play psychotherapy and parent counseling for gender identity disorder. In R. L. Spitzer, M. B. First, J. B. W. Williams, & M. Gibbons (Eds.), *DSM-IV-TR casebook, volume 2. Experts tell how they treated their own patients* (pp. 321–334). Washington, DC: American Psychiatric Publishing.

Zucker, K. J. (2006b). Gender identity disorder. In D. A. Wolfe & E. J. Mash (Eds.), *Behavioral and emotional disorders in adolescents: Nature, assessment, and treatment* (pp. 535–562). New York, NY: Guilford Press.

Zucker, K. J. (2008a). On the "natural history" of gender identity disorder in children [Editorial]. *Journal of the American Academy of Child and Adolescent Psychiatry*, 47, 1361–1363.

Zucker, K. J. (2008b). Enfants avec troubles de l'identité sexuée: y-a-t-il une pratique la meilleure? [Children with gender identity disorder: Is there a best practice?]. *Neuropsychiatrie de l'Enfance et de l'Adolescence*, 56, 358–364.

Zucker, K. J., & Bradley, S. J. (1995). *Gender identity disorder and psychosexual problems in children and adolescents*. New York, NY: Guilford Press.

Zucker, K. J., Bradley, S. J., & Ipp, M. (1993). Delayed naming of a newborn boy: Relationship to the mother's wish for a girl and subsequent cross-gender identity in the child by the age of two. *Journal of Psychology and Human Sexuality*, *6*, 57–68.

Zucker, K. J., Bradley, S. J., Kuksis, M., Pecore, K., Birkenfeld-Adams, A., Doering, R. W., et al. (1999). Gender constancy judgments in children with gender identity disorder: Evidence for a developmental lag. *Archives of Sexual Behavior*, *28*, 475–502.

Zucker, K. J., Bradley, S. J., & Lowry Sullivan, C. B. (1996). Traits of separation anxiety in boys with gender identity disorder. *Journal of the American Academy of Child and Adolescent Psychiatry*, *35*, 791–798.

Zucker, K. J., Bradley, S. J., Lowry Sullivan, C. B., Kuksis, M., Birkenfeld-Adams, A., & Mitchell, J. N. (1993). A gender identity interview for children. *Journal of Personality Assessment*, *61*, 443–456.

Zucker, K. J., Bradley, S. J., Owen-Anderson, A., Singh, D., Blanchard, R., & Bain, J. (2011). Puberty-blocking hormonal therapy for adolescents with gender identity disorder: A descriptive clinical study. *Journal of Gay & Lesbian Mental Health*, *15*, 58–82.

Zucker, K. J., Doering, R. W., Bradley, S. J., & Finegan, J. K. (1982). Sex-typed play in gender-disturbed children: A comparison to sibling and psychiatric controls. *Archives of Sexual Behavior*, *11*, 309–321.

Zucker, K. J., Finegan, J. K., Doering, R. W., & Bradley, S. J. (1983). Human figure drawings of gender-problem children: A comparison to sibling, psychiatric, and normal controls. *Journal of Abnormal Child Psychology*, *11*, 287–298.

Zucker, K. J., Lozinski, J. A., Bradley, S. J., & Doering, R. W. (1992). Sex-typed responses in the Rorschach protocols of children with gender identity disorder. *Journal of Personality Assessment*, *58*, 295–310.

Zucker, K. J., Mitchell, J. N., Bradley, S. J., Tkachuk, J., Cantor, J. M., & Allin, S. M. (2006). The Recalled Childhood Gender Identity/Gender Role Questionnaire: Psychometric properties. *Sex Roles*, *54*, 469–483.

The Dynamic Development of Gender Variability

ANNE FAUSTO-STERLING, PhD

Department of Molecular Biology, Cell Biology and Biochemistry, Brown University, Providence, Rhode Island, USA

We diagram and discuss theories of gender identity development espoused by the clinical groups represented in this special issue. We contend that theories of origin relate importantly to clinical practice, and argue that the existing clinical theories are under-developed. Therefore, we develop a dynamic systems framework for gender identity development. Specifically, we suggest that critical aspects of presymbolic gender embodiment occur during infancy as part of the synchronous interplay of caregiver-infant dyads. By 18 months, a transition to symbolic representation and the beginning of an internalization of a sense of gender can be detected and consolidation is quite evident by 3 years of age. We conclude by suggesting empirical studies that could expand and test this framework. With the belief that better, more explicit developmental theory can improve clinical practice, we urge that clinicians take a dynamic developmental view of gender identity formation into account.

Parents of gender variant children face a multitude of questions and dilemmas. Should they discourage the gender variance? Should they "go with the flow"? How can they protect their children from harm—both physical and mental? How can they deal with their own feelings about their gender variant child? Is the gender variance treatable? Is it their fault? What will become of their child as he or she grows to adulthood? The clinicians invited to address these and other questions for this special issue of the *Journal of Homosexuality* bring decades of boots on the ground clinical experience to the discussion. Indeed, we have come a long way both in terms of knowledge and of attitudes since the 1960s when Robert Stoller first analyzed children struggling with gender identity issues (Green, 2010; Kessler & McKenna, 1978; Stoller, 1968).

We congratulate the clinicians writing for this issue for their persistent, thoughtful, and pioneering work. Since I am a biologist and gender theorist, not a clinician, I do not intend in this commentary to reach conclusions about clinical practice. Rather, I have used several of the texts as a jumping off point to examine what we might and might not know about the origins of gender variance, and further, to offer some thoughts on how we might frame or model gender development in childhood.

Two housekeeping points: First, I am restricting my discussion to early presenting (within the first five years of life) gender identity issues. I do so because my own theoretical inclination is to think developmentally about the first emergence of difference and because children are the explicit topic of the focus articles. Second, because language choice betokens a theory of origin, people dispute the very language used to describe these children. The terms *gender identity disorder, gender dysphoria, gender variant children and gender nonconforming* each suggest different behaviors that may or may not warrant clinical treatment. Indeed, if one views these terms as representing conditions along a continuous spectrum of gender identity and expression, then the question becomes: is there a normative line along this spectrum and where should it be drawn? The word "gender" in the context of this article, is the culturally local behavioral expressions of an internalized individual identity that includes understandings of masculine and feminine. In this sense, gender is not universal, but is tailored to the specific culture in which a child develops.

EXTRACTING THEORIES OF DEVELOPMENT

The clinicians represented in this issue operate from different theoretical and practical points of view. To simplify the discussion I have assigned them to one of two kinship groups. The first joins Zucker, Wood, Singh, and Bradley (this issue) and de Vries and Cohen-Kettenis (this issue) as theoretical "kissing cousins"; the second links Ehrensaft (this issue) and Menvielle (this issue) between whom—in my opinion—run common theoretical threads. Finally, I found it difficult to extract any theory from Edwards-Leeper and Spack (this issue), although their point of view may be made clear elsewhere. The Zucker et al. kin group uses multipronged analyses, accepts pathology as part of the mix, and has published extensive numerical and qualitative details of the children visiting their clinics, including prospective follow-up studies. At the same time that they consider the possibility of multiple factors contributing to childhood gender identity variance, they seem unwilling and—due to what they view as a lack of data—unable to draw causal conclusions. Therefore, I call this kin group the "agnostics." They assume a practical, one case at a time approach to treatment.

I call the group represented by Menvielle and Ehrensaft "naturalists." Ehrensaft's (this issue) notion of a true gender self that shows up to the parents "rather than being shaped by them, suggesting an innate component to gender nonconformity" (p. 340) is softened by the idea that subsequent to showing up, the true self gets woven into a nonbinary gender web. The naturalists believe that most gender nonconformist children are mentally healthy and come from healthy families; they argue that the stress and anxiety felt by gender variant kids results from external pressures, sometimes including the inability of parents to cope with these curious children who have shown up on their doorsteps. For the naturalists, therapeutic goals include helping children to accept their true selves as they learn how to negotiate gender in a complicated and often hostile world (Ehrensaft, 2011). In addition to individual psychotherapy, an important innovation has been the development of social networks for gender variant families, providing a safe social space with others of like mind and constitution (E. Menvielle & Tuerk, 2002; E. J. Menvielle, Tuerk, & Perrin, 2005).

Finally, the agnostics and the naturalists agree on certain things. They both see biology as a scaffolding on which the psyche is built. They both agree that there are probably several kinds of gender variance. And they concur that at least on occasion, psychopathology and gender variance coexist, possibly reinforcing one another.

The Agnostics

Figure 1 stylizes the apparent elements of the agnostics' model. They propose that predisposing biological factors (e.g. genes, hormones, temperament, brain structure) provide a structural scaffolding that may precipitate other events or perpetuate other responses. In Figure 1, predisposing biology appears as a background, but no arrows link biology to the other factors; nor do the other theoretical elements feed back to biology. This essential point is missed by both Zucker et al. (this issue) and de Vries and Cohen-Kettenis (this issue). Brain development itself, especially in children, is to a large extent directed by social and sensory experiences; so too is hormone biology and physiological regulation (Field, Diego, & Hernandez-Reif, 2006; Petanjek, Judaš, Kostović, & Uylings, 2008; Schore, 2005). A well-developed theory of gender identity needs to place this dynamic at its center.

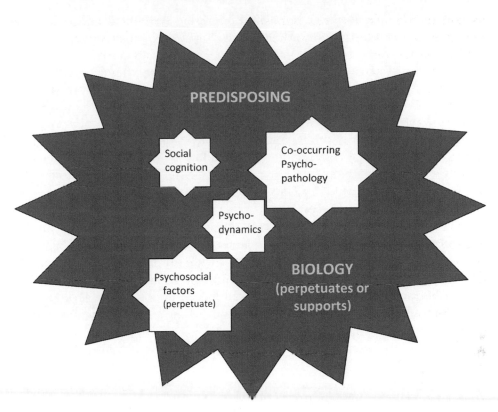

FIGURE 1 The agnostic's model of gender identity formation (based on Zucker, Wood, Singh, & Bradley, this issue) (color figure available online).

The biopsychosocial model conceptualizes psychosocial factors as conscious parental responses to their child's cross-gender interests. Zucker et al. (this issue) view parental neutrality or encouragement of cross-gender behavior "as a perpetuating factor" (p. 377). As used by the agnostic group, social cognition seems to involve how a child applies his or her own reading of gender in his or her social world to his or her sense of self. The agnostics provide strong evidence of co-occurring psychopathology for many, but not all of the gender variant kids they see in their practice. For example, S. Coates (1992; Coates & Wolfe, 1995) has focused over the years on severe separation anxiety as a precursor to GID in some boys; more recently, the Dutch group has proposed an elevated co-occurrence of autistic-like rigidity and obsessiveness in gender dysphoric kids (de Vries, Noens, Cohen-Kettenis, van Berckelaer-Onnes, & Doreleijers, 2010). The naturalists, it should be pointed out, also report such co-occurrences, but consider them to be rare and unrelated to mainstream (if I may call it that) gender variance. Some clinicians treat the anxiety or obsessiveness and find that the cross-gender obsessions abate. It seems likely that the succession of childhood obsessions is one of the underlying systems to be explored as we try to understand gender identity development (DeLoache, Simcock, & Macari, 2007).

Last, the biopsychosocial model proposes psychodynamic mechanisms. These mechanisms may involve the child's assumption of unresolved family conflict and traumas. In family systems lingo, the child manifests the symptoms of a distressed family system; cross-gender interests are the symptoms of a poorly functioning family, and treatment needs must be a family affair. Importantly, different children may have different response thresholds for similar traumatic incidents, possibly explaining why what appears to be similar family stresses could, in one case, result in a gender-focused coping response but not in another.

The biopsychosocial model contains important elements for understanding gender development. The agnostics supply evidence from case studies to support their contention that each of these systems has the potential to play a role in the development of cross-gender identities and behaviors. Yet, they are curiously unlinked and static. It would seem the same elements ought to be a component of gender development in all kids.

The Naturalists

In truth, the naturalists don't offer a theory of gender identity origins. Instead, they posit a preformed, but unexplained true gender self and focus on how the true self develops and takes individual shape within a particular nexus of culture, nature and nurture. None of these latter terms are precisely defined, but the naturalists develop an important point: gender identity is not binary. They conceptualize it as a three dimensional web, although neglecting that important fourth or developmental dimension. The strength in this approach is the emphasis on individual difference. The weakness is the loss of insight into how previous form shapes subsequent structure (Thelen, 2000).

Using the following passage from Ehrensaft (this issue) I have created an image of the naturalist's theory of gender identity (Figure 2A).

> The true gender self begins as the kernel of gender identity that is there from birth, residing within us in a complex of chromosomes, gonads, hormones, hormone receptors, genitalia, secondary sex characteristics, but most importantly in our brain and mind. (p. 341)

After birth, each true gender self is "channeled through (individual) experience with the external world . . . but its center always remains . . . driven from within . . ." (p. 341). This postnatal shaping is depicted in Figure 2B.

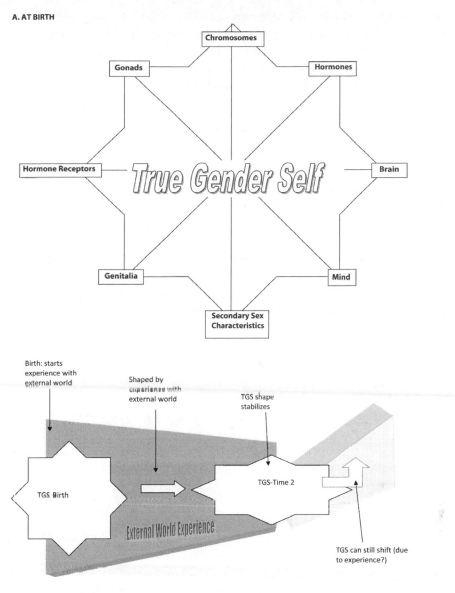

FIGURE 2 The naturalist's model of gender identity formation (Based on Ehrensaft, this issue) (color figure available online).

Two noteworthy characteristics emerge from both the agnostics' and the naturalists' theories. First, the working parts seem peculiarly unconnected. Second, gender identity is strangely disembodied and outside of the world. How do the precursors of gender identity manifest themselves through the body—a pleasure in the soft or the pink, an aversion to rough play, for example? I argue that such signs of gender are in the body, yet, these clinical theories seem to work only from the mind. Following the extraordinary lead provided by Thelen and colleagues (2000), and by psychoanalysts such as Harris (2005) and Corbett (2009), I argue that gender development be placed in a dynamic embodied systems framework. First, I provide some general principles, then, I explore the presymbolic origins and early symbolic manifestations of gender identity. (Presymbolic representations are prelinguistic, physiologically embodied memories.) I end by suggesting that the transition from presymbolic to internalized symbolic representations of gender lies at the heart of the matter.

A DYNAMIC SYSTEMS FRAMEWORK FOR GENDER IDENTITY DEVELOPMENT

General Considerations

Thelen (2000), and biologists such as Chiel and Beer (1997), insist that behaviors and cognition arise from the coupling of several contributing systems. Cognition, for example, depends on particular kinds of experiences had by particular bodies with particular perceptual and motor abilities. These sensory and motor capacities link to form a matrix within which reason, emotion, memory, language, and more reside. The developmental issue is to understand the timing, strength, and history of the coupling between these critical systems.

The world is the matrix in which all elements embed. This contrasts with predisposing factors that provide the underlying matrix (Figure 1). By "the world," I intend all the experiences encountered by a child from before birth and throughout life. Postnatally, these include caregiving, touching, dressing, feeding—that is, all of the emotional and physical interactions a newborn and developing infant encounters in his or her immediate world (see, e.g., Fausto-Sterling, 2010a, 2010b, 2011). The world has other people in it and the infant cannot develop without them. But also, the infant's behaviors influence and shape how others respond. At birth an infant's behaviors relate importantly to the state of development of his or her nervous and digestive systems and physiological capacities to self-regulate. Beyond, but also reaching into the nursery, the world brings specific gender attachments—flowery wallpaper, toy trucks, pink onesies, gendered parental assumptions and expectations, and more (J. F. Feldman, Brody, & Miller, 1980; Rheingold & Cook, 1975; Shakin, Shakin, & Sternglanz, 1985). At birth the world subsumes what Zucker et al. (this issue) call psychodynamics; in late infancy, toddlerhood and childhood it also includes social cognition.

The body is the next largest collection of systems found within the world. It is not the foundation of all things, but rather is in the middle—sustained within the world, responding to it, but also reshaping it. Obviously, as I have displaced the idea of predisposing biology (Figure 1), I have also rendered it an untenable concept. To understand this, consider the work of biologist David Crews. A long and productive career analyzing the role of genes and environment in sex determination has led Crews to espouse a systems view of gonad formation and the regulation of sociosexual behavior. He understands that both complex behaviors and their genetic underpinnings (a.k.a., predisposing biology) are cumulative processes both resulting from past events and setting the stage for responses to future experience (Crews, Lou, Fleming, & Ogawa, 2006; Putz & Crews, 2006). Such a general framework is the appropriate starting point for thinking through the development of human gender variability.

At heart, Ehrensaft's (this issue) true gender self is a biological concept, similar in many ways to the idea that one is born gay. The true gender concept is a homunculus that grows within the world and, in so growing, is shaped by it, much as, I imagine, a plant grown without enough light becomes etiolated and spindly while one raised with good light becomes bushy, green, and strong. But we gain little sense of the systems out of which the true gender self emerges, no sense of the multiple feedback systems which sustain or shape it.

Finally the brain/mind is integrated into the body. Through its sensory and motor abilities the exterior layers of the body bring the world into the central nervous system. Neural plasticity lies at the heart of the matter. A toddler's mind emerges from experience in a particular body and particular world. The brain's very synapses form, take shape, die back, or reconnect in response to the world and body that envelops it. The same is true of the forming neuromuscular connections—links from the central nervous system to the muscles that control motor ability and visceral responses (Thelen, 1994, 1995a, 1995b, 2001).

Chiel and Beer (2007) suggest the following metaphor. Traditionally, behaviorists think of the nervous system as the body's conductor—choosing the program for the players and influencing how they play. But consider instead that the nervous system is only one player in a jazz improv group. The music results from a continued give and take between the player, a continuous interaction between the nervous system, the rest of the body and the environment. If gender identity were the performance piece it would succeed or fail based on the contributions of all the instruments in the band, how they integrate into a coherent system and how the couplings ebb and flow during the time course of the performance.

Gender identity is located in all three interacting networks, a product of the coupling of critical systems—including those postulated by Zucker and colleagues (this issue). I have already suggested that gender-related behaviors and identity formation emerge as a pattern of several cooperating parts; since we need each part to sustain the whole, one is not more fundamental than another. Not a thing, gender identity is a pattern in time. In any one individual, it is shaped by the preceding dynamics and becomes the basis of future identity transformations.

As a set of systems moving through time, gender identity varies in its relative stability. When the components (see following sections) cohere tightly, gender identity is stable. When the elements cohere poorly, the system becomes chaotic; more loosely bound elements are better able to make new connections out of which more stable patterns can possibly emerge. Thelen (2000) phrases it this way: "the components of the system are coupled in a particular way . . . development consists of the progressive ability to modulate the coupling so as to meet different and changing situations . . . There is no point in time when these dynamic processes stop and something else takes over" (p. 8). My working premise is that enormous individual variation exists within the general processes outlined above. By individual I mean both the infant as he or she develops in utero and first appears outside of the womb and the adult-infant dyads, which become the units of self-regulation, mutual regulation and learning through which infants gain an understanding of the world and of self.

I agree with Meyer-Bahlburg (2010) when he laments the lack of a general theory of gender identity development. Corbett (1996, 2009) reminds us that there can be no measurable norm without variance around it. Whether or not some variants—either in the child or in the family unit might get labeled as productive of psychopathology is a different debate. Instead, in this article, I want to refocus discussion on what amounts to the prior question: How does any type of gender identity develop? Even here we confront a prior question: What is gender identity? How, clinically and experimentally, do we make it operational?

IN THE CLINIC

Clinical definitions and the criteria from the *Diagnostic and Statistical Manual of Mental Disorders* (4th ed., text rev; *DSM-IV-TR*; American Psychiatric Association, 2000) for childhood Gender Identity Disorder create, in essence, a negative film of gender identity. The supposed disorder is said to consist of some combination of: a child's insistence that he/she is the other sex, preference for cross-dressing, persistent, or strong preferences for cross-sex roles in make believe or play, strong desire to participate in the stereotypical games and pastimes of the other sex, and strong wish for playmates of the other sex. The positive print of this image, then, is that gender identity in general must consist of several rather different but interwoven features. The acquisition of a gender identity usually involves the ability to self-identify as male or female, development of feelings about one's genitalia, and a set of pleasures and repulsions that concern styles of dress and play. Thus, gender identity is not a thing, but a name given to a weaving together into a subjective self of aspects of the masculine and the feminine.

Corbett's (1996, 2009) work on boyhood femininity is helpful. First, he rejects a world of binary rules. He sees gender as a dynamic of "gendered codes, behaviors, and traits circulate and transform . . . within modern families" (2009, p. 103) which reside in a larger, social field of relatives, schools, television, social workers, and more. The family, in this view, is the locale of concrescence for the gender rules and representations encountered in the outside world. "The 'outside' society is indelibly 'inside' the family" (p. 103). Such a notion of the outside has not seriously penetrated the skin of attachment or social learning theory.

DEVELOPMENTAL TIMING

Operationally, gender identity lies partly inside the body—in the shape of sensitivities, desires, preferences, and interests; but it is partly outside the body in that it is always an oppositional concept. Corbett (2009), for example, quotes Robert Stoller that "The first order of business in being a man is don't be a woman" (p. 91). A version of that web we call gender identity is first visible in early toddlerhood and transforms over a period of years. That which we call gender identity in a 3 year old differs in important ways from that which we call gender identity in a 7 year old. As Harris (2005) has so aptly put it, gender is a softly assembled system. In the first five or so years of life, the system itself develops fairly rapidly; thereafter, it usually stabilizes even as it transforms more modestly. Occasionally, the systems that stabilize gender identity fall into chaos and reorganize on a substantially new plain (Martin, as cited in Meyer-Bahlburg, 2010).

Soft assembly contrasts with Zucker and colleagues (this issue) "developmental, biopsychosocial model" which asserts that in the majority gender identity is a "fixed and unalterable" (p. 375) trait. Zucker et al. contrast this fixity with a lack of stability in gender variant kids. Agnostics seem to set up a binary division between majority development, and that which must be explained, that is, deviation from the majority. In contrast, by understanding the acquisition of gender identity and gender expression as a process common to all people, we can weave elements of the agnostics' model into an account in which the processes for both gender variant and gender congruent kids are similar in kind, but differ in timing and or execution. In a process model, gender identity may be stable, but it is never fixed.

THE PRESYMBOLIC PHASE OF GENDER
IDENTITY FORMATION

A better understanding of the many and complex pathways that lead to human variation can produce a greater tolerance for variability in children and adults alike. Offering families a deeper conceptualization of the dynamics of gender identity formation in childhood may well be the best therapy of all. The framework developed in the following pages sets us on the path toward that end.

The newborn infant does not have a self-concept as either male or female. Indeed, on the surface of things, the foremost agenda item for an infant is to attract the adult attention needed for survival. In the first several months all children have a set of tasks, the successful accomplishment of which provides a sound physiological and emotional basis for the emergence of individual gender identity. We postulate that the building blocks that enable gender identity differentiation, including a developing awareness of symbolic and culturally specific gender knowledge, takes shape during the first year of life, while gender identity itself becomes increasingly evident to adult observers during the second.

The achievement of universal developmental tasks (e.g., dyad competence and physiological regulation) provides the skills needed to internalize and symbolize gender; these universal tasks, however, are always individually and culturally specific. The developmental state of the newborn, the emotional and skill states of the parents, their financial resources, the cultural accoutrements of parenthood structured by social gender norms all matter (Fausto-Sterling, García Coll, & Lamarre, in press).

In the beginning there is touch. Through skin-to-skin contact the infant gains hold of temperature regulation. Through touch, the infant develops control of crying and sleeping (de Weerth, Zijl, & Buitelaar, 2003; Korner & Thoman, 1970; Sadeh, Dark, & Vohr, 1996; Weller & Bell, 1965). Early affectional touch improves the quality of reciprocal communication in the adult-infant dyad. Infants who are held and touched have lower circulating stress hormones and careful massage of preterm infants decreases metabolic rate, improves sleep, decreases stress behaviors, and improves immune function. Proper touch is essential to the embodiment of emotions and the development of self (Ferber, Feldman, & Makhoul, 2008; Field, 2010; Field, Diego, et al., 2006; Field, Hernandez-Reif, & Diego, 2006).

Touch co-occurs with vocalizations, facial expressions, body tone, and movement. All these come from the caring adult—usually called the mother, but the importance of other adult-infant contact requires a great deal more study (Lamb, 1977); these behaviors are a response to infant demands but also meet infant needs and enable infant development. The dyadic exchanges affect and attune autonomic, neurological, and hormonal systems of each partner in the dyad (Schore, 1994). By two to three months, parent-infant interactions have a clear structure and timing; Observers note cycles of behavior that include looking, touching and affective expression. At four months, the direct social gaze becomes all important. Periods of synchronous gazing, are often integrated with affectionate touch and vocalization. Importantly, this pattern is culturally specific, more typical of North America and Western Europe. Parents from other parts of the world offer more bodily contact but less gaze, voice, and object use. As development passes the half year mark, objects become the center of adult-child play; with this transition gaze synchrony lessens and shared attention turns toward an object (R. Feldman, 2007a, 2007b).

In this pas-de-deux, sex and gender matter. From birth to 6 months most studies focus on behaviors related to the function of the mother-infant dyad. In addition to differences in weight, brain size, and motor and sensory development (Fausto-Sterling et al., 2011a), neonatal starting points may include greater average brain cortical maturity in girls (Thordstein, Lofgren, Flisberg, Lindecrantz, & Kjellmer, 2006) and average differences in crying and fussing at birth, 3–6 months (Moss, 1967; Phillips, King, & DuBois, 1978; Sadeh et al., 1996).

A study of the mother infant dyad from birth to 3 months reveals sex-related variability in dyadic communication (Lavelli & Fogel, 2002). If, for example, the critical factors that shape early dyadic communication include levels of neural development, sleep and fuss patterns and physical size, these variables might correlate with the development of dyadic communication patterns. If these variables, in turn, correlated with the sex of the infant as suggested by the findings of Weinberg, Tronick, Cohn, and Olson (1999), then a process by which the development of early sex differences is initiated might be identified. Studies of the gender dynamics of adult-infant dyad formation and coordination suggest that at 3–9 months a mutually engaged state has stabilized in mother-daughter dyads but is more likely to still be unilateral in mother-son dyads. (Hsu & Fogel, 2003; Malatesta, Culver, Tesman, & Shepard, 1989; Tronick & Cohn, 1989; Weinberg et al., 1999).

Parents also bring sex and gender to the nursery. R. Feldman (2007b) found that first time mothers and their 5-month-old infants cycled between low and medium peaks of arousal, with the occasional peak of high positive emotion. The father-infant dyad involved greater emotional and physical arousal. Peaks of laughter and exuberance became more frequent as play progressed. Although, father and infant achieved the same degree of synchrony as did mother and child, when dyads were gender matched (father-son or mother-daughter) synchrony was at its highest. Such differing dyad interactions provide infants with the opportunity to form presymbolic representations, or models, for masculine and feminine styles of activity and emotional output.

To sum up our argument to this point: a) from the beginning (possibly even before birth) the dyadic interaction shapes individual nervous systems in such a way that groups with overlapping but statistically differentiable behaviors start to emerge; b) at birth great individual variability in developmental parameters exists; some of which rises to the level of average group differences between male and female infants; c) from birth on, average sex-related differences in (parent-infant) communication take shape, developing into varied patterns of vocal, physical, and emotional interactions. Between

3 and 6 months other dyadic patterns emerge, some of which appear to be sex-differentiated.

PRESYMBOLIC REPRESENTATIONS OF DIFFERENCE

Piaget defined the presymbolic stage as lasting roughly from birth to 18 months (Piaget & Inhelder, 1972). Relying primarily on sensorimotor representations, the infant in this period interacts with the world through actions such as crying and regulated gestures. Infants enter the world with surprisingly advanced capabilities. Using auditory, visual, motor, touch, and circadian insights infants take the measure of their surroundings even in utero. As they measure, they also learn to manipulate the adults whose care they need, and begin the life-long process of honing a capacity for self-regulation (Beebe, Lachmann, & Jaffe, 1997). The environmental trappings of gender, from the voices, faces, modes of holding and touching, dress, hair, and grooming, to the colors in the room, the toys offered and the baby clothing used, are ever present. From birth or before an infant absorbs them, commits them to memory, develops expectations about them, and receives bodily messages about their own sex and gender.

Beebe and Lachmann (1994) articulate three working hypotheses about how presymbolic representations of social relatedness form in infancy. First, ongoing regulations in adult-infant interactions create regularities that organize an infant's experience. Second, infants further learn to regulate their environment through a process of disruption and repair. An expectancy (e.g. feeding at a certain hour) may be disrupted, the infant expresses distress, adults repair the disruption by (belatedly) feeding or otherwise attempting to comfort the infant. Finally, during heightened affective moments infants respond to heightened adult emotion evident in facial or vocal expression with an arousal pattern measured physiologically as changes in brain waves, heart rates and/or respiration. The high moments of excitement in father-infant dyad play is one example. The differential between maternal and paternal interactive styles could be one of the early inputs that shapes presymbolic representations of gender and links them to emotional development.

Beebe and Lachmann (1994) believe that both self-representation (obviously relevant to the emergence of a sense of oneself as male or female) and object representations (with regard to gender, an understanding of familial and cultural gender categories), result from "the expected moment to moment interplay of the two partners (p. 131). Representations are "persistent, organized classifications of information about an expected interactive sequence" (p. 131). Infants and children base representations on past interactions, but continuously modify and restructure them as the environment—including the human interactions within it—transforms.

How might the idea that infancy involves a continuous organizing process based on developing expectancies, their disruption and their repair, apply to gender development? The experiences that organize gender might include, first, the daily physicalities of care. How do parents carry, touch, sooth, and play with their children and how do specific infant nervous systems experience the resulting physical sensations? What pleasurable or discomforting expectations develop from sensory input including emotive faces, voice timbre and expression, touching while playing, bathing (including genital touch) and feeding? Are these linked in ways that differentiate gender? At a more removed level, male and female adults in the infant environment shape infant expectations. From the start, toys are available in different types and quantities, the colors and tactile features of clothing and stuffed animals also shape infant expectations and are highly differentiated even for neonates (Rheingold & Cook, 1975; Shakin et al., 1985). Thus, taking seriously Beebe and Lachmann's (1994) framework for the infant phase of representing and individualizing opens a little-explored field of study for those interested in the emergence of gender identity in toddlers and beyond.

As infants perceive regularities in their experience they begin to form categories. In the case of gender, both visual and auditory categories can be noted by 6–9 months (faces and voices) and by 12 months cross-modal abilities emerge including an association of male and female voices with gender related objects (Fausto-Sterling, García Coll, & Lamarre, in press). By the time an infant has become a toddler, gender knowledge has progressed from presymbolic representations such as recognition and association of voice pitch and faces to a far more sophisticated, increasingly symbolic representation of gender in self and others. It seems likely that this transition from presymbolic to symbolic and to increasingly internalized representations of gender, which must start in the vicinity of one year of age and carry on for several years, is an especially important period for understanding the developmental dynamics of gender identity.

FROM PRESYMBOLIC TO SYMBOLIC REPRESENTATIONS OF GENDER

R. Feldman (2007a) and others (see, e.g., (Beebe & Lachmann, 1994) argue that symbolic representations emerge toward the end of year one as specific infant responses to the training afforded by perceptual, affective and motor experiences organize into coherent structures Early synchrony between parent and child correlates positively with more complex symbolic play at age 3. At 3 and 9 months it correlates with how well a child can use words to refer to mental states such as thoughts or feelings attributed to self or others, while parent-infant synchrony at three months predicts how well a five year old can perceive that his or her own emotions might differ from those of others.

Gender differentiation becomes most evident as children develop symbolic representations. Gender specific toy preference, for example, begins to emerge at about one year of age (Jadva, Hines, & Golombok, 2010). At 18 months, children are startled at culturally gender inappropriate images (e.g., a man putting on makeup) and have also developed a system of gender-related metaphors (Poulin-Dubois, Serbin, Eichstedt, Sen, & Beissel, 2002). Gender identity itself—which lies at the heart of the discussion—comes on line gradually. Before 2 years of age, children learn to label others as boy or girl—using external (symbolic?) features such as hair length or dress. They next develop the ability to self-label and can exhibit a nonverbal gender identity. However, the notion that gender itself is stable and sex constant as children grow to adulthood does not usually take root until a child is 5 or 6 years old (Fagot, 1995; Fagot & Leinbach, 1989, 1993; Fagot, Leinbach, & Hagan, 1986; Fagot, Leinbach, & O'Boyle, 1992).

GENDER METAPHORS AND WORDS

Zosuls et al. (2009) studied the development in toddlers of the ability to utter basic gender labels (girl, boy, man, lady). At 17 months, about a quarter of the kids they studied had used at least one verbal label, and by 21 months this number had increased to 68%. However, boys developed this ability more slowly. In this same time period, children accurately associate gendered objects such as a fire hat or a tiara with male or female faces and they have acquired a view about what links, symbolically to one or the other sex (Eichstedt, Serbin, Poulin-Dubois, & Sen, 2002). Such symbolic knowledge seems to affect children's' belief systems about which sex should play with which toys. Eichstedt et al. (2002) suggest that symbolic gender knowledge in the pre-two year old set can drive or enhance the acquisition of a variety of gender stereotypes.

OPPOSITIONAL KNOWLEDGE

In this same time period, we first detect a surprisingly sophisticated understanding of gender roles. When asked to choose either male or female dolls to act out activities deemed by adults to be masculine stereotyped, feminine stereotyped or, or gender neutral, 2-year-old girls used the male dolls to play act masculine activities 70% of the time. For neutral activities, they used the male doll 30% of the time and for feminine-stereotyped activities they used the male dolls 48% of the time. Despite a range of variability from 23 to 95%, these 2-year-old girls clearly had some knowledge about gender stereotyped behavior. The same cannot be said for the boys, who used male and female dolls pretty much equally regardless of the task's stereotypy

(Poulin-Dubois & Forbes, 2002). In studies using a looking rather than a playing method, however, both male and female 2-year-olds looked longer at photos of women behaving in gender-inappropriate ways, such as hammering a nail, fixing a toy, or taking out the garbage, but seemed unimpressed by photos of a man putting on lipstick, feeding a baby, or ironing (Serbin, Poulin Dubois, & Eichstedt, 2002). These studies suggest that even 2 year olds know some pretty complicated things about gender roles. As they also develop the capacity to label themselves according to gender, they may put this knowledge to use in building their own identities.

SELF-LABELING

Zosuls et al. (2009) found a significant relationship in months 17–21 between the ability of kids to label themselves as a boy or a girl and increased levels of gender-typed play. Thus, the application of some knowledge of gender in the world to a sense of self happens between the second and third year of life and provides self-feedback on behavioral preferences. Some argue that this is the moment in which a child acquires a gender identity. For Ehrensaft (this issue), this might be the point in time in which a child presents his or her parents with a true gender self. But clearly, this version of gender identity, gradually acquired as knowledge about experienced gender roles, forms a dynamic network which gradually ensnares the child.

INTERNALIZING A GENDER SELF

Harris (2005) states it beautifully:

> Brought into an intense, embodied responsiveness and contact with the material world, caught up in the conscious and unconscious reverie of parents, prenatally already an object of intense fantasy, a child finds the experience of self within a relationship in which he or she is already seen ... The internalization ... of the gender/body mirror becomes a part of the child's procedural knowing, available for many complex remappings and reassemblies in the course of development. (p. 181)

Children with individualized nervous systems, genes, hormone levels, and physiologies are born into a gender differentiated world. Even during the last weeks of uterine life, fetuses can perceive gender outside the womb. These differences take shape or disappear at first through the dyadic formations of early infancy and with time, through increasingly independent knowledge acquisition and behavioral patterns. Gender is never absent. There is never a point at which it begins. Still, the $64,000 question remains: How do increasing levels of gendered embodiment, knowledge about gender in the world, the growing abilities to self-label and modulate behaviors to correlate with labels, become part of an internal sense of self?

In Figure 3, we recap the elements contributing to presymbolic gender embodiment and representation, indicating a period of transition—critically

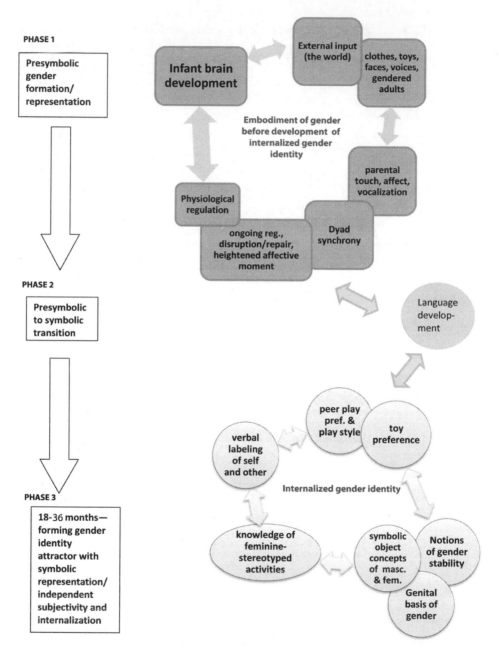

FIGURE 3 Three phases of gender representation and identity internalization (color figure available online).

mediated by language development—to symbolic gender knowledge. Such knowledge builds on previous embodiment and enmeshes in a web of behavior, self-labeling and preferences that are the subsystems of that dynamic web we call *internalized gender identity*. In each developmental phase, there are dynamically interacting subsystems; but the developmental time line is unidirectional.

Psychoanalyst Susan Coates distilled several important characteristics from a study of over 130 young boys (2–4 years of age) brought to therapeutic attention because of their cross-gendered behaviors, interests or identities. First, the boys' cross-gendered behaviors emerged during a critical period of development (2–4 years). Second, GIDC often appeared and consolidated quite suddenly, and, for the boys who came to Coates' practice, frequently (but not always) in the context of some kind of psychic trauma. Coates associated several biopsychological markers with these boys including a sense of physical fragility, the avoidance of highly physical play, anxiety in new situations, high sensitivity to others' emotional states, high vulnerability to separation or loss, an unusually acute ability to imitate others, and extraordinary sensory sensitivity to sound, color, texture, smell and pain (S. Coates, 1992; S. W. Coates & Wolfe, 1995).

Analyst Ken Corbett (1996) argues that boyhood gender nonconformity does not represent a continuum of femininity. Instead, he suggests these boys fall on "a continuum of ego integration and psychic structure" in which GID and gender-nonconforming boys may be equally feminine, but in the latter group "the femininity is contained within a more stable psychic structure" (p. 438). Corbett insists that the very category of Gender Identity Disorder demands that we develop theoretical approaches that explain how the psyche, the soma and the social build one another.

As should be clear, I agree with Harris and Corbett (and thank Coates for her expanded framing, which initially broadened my own perspective on early gender identity development) that to understand the emergence of gendered behaviors and their attachment (or not) to natal sex we need first to become more knowledgeable about the presymbolic, dyadic processes through which gender becomes embodied in infancy. Such embodiment forms the basis for the transition to symbolic understandings of gender as a relational and oppositional concept coincident with the internalization and dynamic stabilization of gender as a component of the self.

WHAT NEXT?

A lot of work remains to fully develop and shape these ideas. Beebe and colleagues (Beebe, Jaffe, et al., 2010; Beebe & Lachmann, 1994; Beebe, Lachmann, et al., 1997) have published a series of studies of dyad formation and interactions. What still must be done here is to incorporate sex of infant as a variable into such studies. Some such work exists, but more is needed (Fogel, Dickson, et al., 1997; Fogel, Garvey, et al., 2006; Fogel & Thelen, 1987). To understand the dynamics of gendered embodiment investigations of presymbolic gender formations must be longitudinal.

Dyad formation and input from the physical environment likely affect brain development, but neither has been studied in relationship to neural growth and development. While the measurement of functional brain activity in infants is still fairly crude, the development of noninvasive scanning methods seems to be coming into its own (Bell & Fox, 1992; Dawson et al., 1999; Kuhl, 2010). It should be possible to link the development of dyad synchrony to brain development both generally and with regard to gender. Similarly, studies testing the importance of exposure to a skewed physical environment (e.g., many toy cars, few dolls) to brain activity and development during the first year of life should illuminate gendered developmental systems.

More detailed knowledge of gender formations and embodiment during infancy should enrich our thinking about the transition from presymbolic to symbolic gender representation and the concomitant internalization of identity. Writ large this is a question about how sense memories and bodily knowledge transform into psychic knowledge. In terms of gender, for the time being, it makes sense to operationalize identity via the study of gendered behaviors and self-assessments. If the transformation really is a dynamic system, then we might expect this period to be chaotic and unstable relative to the stability of well-formed dyadic synchrony that precedes, and the relative rigidity of gender identity evidenced by, children by the time they are 4–5 years of age (Hollenstein, 2007).

As the developmental details and dynamic interactions of phase 1, the transition and phase 2 come into clearer focus, a supportable theory of gender identity development will emerge, allowing us to get a handle on individual variations in identity formation and expression. Given the number of subsystems contributing to the outcome as seen by age 5 or so, it seems likely that several roads can lead to similar-appearing variations in gender identity. Furthermore, no single item—be it parental behavior or infant genes—can be held responsible for the outcome. Improved understandings of the many and complex pathways that underlie human variation can lead to a greater tolerance for variability in children and adults alike. Offering families a more profound knowledge of the dynamics of gender identity formation in childhood may well be the best therapy of all.

REFERENCES

ABC, N. (2011). J. Crew Ad with boy's pink toenails creates stir.

American Psychiatric Association. (2000). *Diagnostic and statistical manual of mental disorders* (4th ed., text rev).Washington, DC: Author.

Beebe, B., Jaffe, J., Markese, S., Buck, K., Chen, H., Cohen, P., . . . Felstein, S. (2010). The origins of 12-month attachment: a microanalysis of 4-month mother-infant interaction. *Attachment & Human Development, 12,* 3–141.

Beebe, B., & Lachmann, F. M. (1994). Representation and internalization in infancy: Three principles of salience. *Psychoanalytic Psychology, 11,* 127–165.

Beebe, B., Lachmann, F. M., & Jaffe, J. (1997). Mother-infant interaction structures and presymbolic self-and object representations. *Psychoanalytic Dialogues, 7,* 133–182.

Bell, M. A., & Fox, N. A. (1992). The relations between frontal brain electrical activity and cognitive development during infancy. *Child Development, 63,* 1142–1163.

Chiel, H. J., & Beer, R. D. (1997). The brain has a body: Adaptive behavior emerges from interactions of nervous system, body and environment. *Trends in Neuroscience, 20,* 553–557.

Coates, S. (1992). The etiology of boyhood gender identity disorder: An integrative model. In J. W. Barron, M. N. Eagle, & D. L. Wolitzky (Eds.), *The Interface of psychoanalysis and psychology* (pp. 245–265). Washington, D.C.: American Psychological Association.

Coates, S. W., & Wolfe, S. M. (1995). Gender identity disorder in boys: The interface of constitution and early experience. *Psychoanalytic Inquiry, 15,* 6–38.

Corbett, K. (1996). Homosexual boyhood: Notes on girlyboys. *Gender and Psychoanalysis, 1,* 429–461.

Corbett, K. (2009). *Boyhoods: Rethinking masculinities.* New Haven, CT: Yale University Press.

Crews, D., Lou, W., Fleming, A., & Ogawa, S. (2006). From gene networks underlying sex determination and gonadal differentiation to the development of neural networks regulating sociosexual behavior. *Brain Research, 1126,* 109–121.

Dawson, G., Frey, K., Panagiotides, H., Yamada, E., Hessl, D., & Osterling, J. (1999). Infants of depressed mothers exhibit atypical frontal electrical brain activity during interactions with mother and with a familiar, nondepressed adult. *Child Development, 70,* 1058–1066.

de Vries, A. L. C., & Cohen-Kettenis, P. T. (this issue). Clinical management of gender dysphoria in children and adolescents: The Dutch approach. *Journal of Homosexuality, 59,* 301–320.

de Vries, A. L., Noens, I. L., Cohen-Kettenis, P. T., van Berckelaer-Onnes, I. A., & Doreleijers, T. A. (2010). Autism spectrum disorders in gender dysphoric children and adolescents. *Journal of Autism and Developmental Disorders, 40,* 930–936.

de Weerth, C., Zijl, R. H., & Buitelaar, J. K. (2003). Development of cortisol circadian rhythm in infancy. *Early Human Development, 73,* 39–52.

DeLoache, J. S., Simcock, G., & Macari, S. (2007). Planes, trains, automobiles— and tea sets: Extremely intense interests in very young children. *Developmental Psychology, 43,* 1579–1586.

Edwards-Leeper, L., & Spack, N. (this issue). Psychological evaluation and medical treatment of transgender youth in an interdisciplinary "gender management service" (GeMS) in a major pediatric center. *Journal of Homosexuality, 59,* 321–336.

Ehrensaft, D. (2011). "I'm a prius": A child case of a gender/ethnic hybrid. *Journal of Gay and Lesbian Mental Health, 15,* 46–57.

Ehrensaft, D. (this issue). From gender identity disorder to gender identity creativity: True gender self child therapy. *Journal of Homosexuality*, *59*, 337–356.

Eichstedt, J. A., Serbin, L. A., Poulin-Dubois, D., & Sen, M. G. (2002). Of bears and men: Infants' knowledge of conventional and metaphorical gender stereotypes. *Infant Behavior and Development*, *25*, 296–310.

Fagot, B. I. (1995). Psychosocial and cognitive determinants of early gender-role development. *Annual Review of Sex Research*, *6*, 1–31.

Fagot, B. I., & Leinbach, M. D. (1989). The young child's gender schema: environmental input, internal organization. *Child Development*, *60*, 663–672.

Fagot, B. I., & Leinbach, M. D. (1993). Gender-role development in young children: From discrimination to labeling. *Developmental Review*, *13*, 205–224.

Fagot, B. I., Leinbach, M. D., & Hagan, R. (1986). Gender labeling and the adoption of sex-typed behaviors. *Developmental Psychology*, *22*, 440–443.

Fagot, B. I., Leinbach, M. D., & O'Boyle, C. (1992). Gender labeling, gender stereotyping, and parenting behaviors. *Developmental Psychology*, *28*, 225–230.

Fausto-Sterling, A. (2010a). Nature versus nurture (part 1): It's time to withdraw from this war! Sexing the body: The dynamic development of gender and sexuality. *Psychology today*. Retrieved February 15, 2012 from http://www.psychologytoday.com/blog/sexing-the-body/201007/nature-versus-nurture-part-1-it-s-time-withdraw-war

Fausto-Sterling, A. (2010b). Nature versus nurture (part 2): Building brains. Sexing the body: The dynamic development of gender and sexuality. *Psychology today*. Retrieved February 15, 2012 from http://www.psychologytoday.com/blog/sexing-the-body/201008/nature-versus-nurture-part-2-building-brains

Fausto-Sterling, A. (2011). Nature versus nurture (part 3): QUACK? Sexing the body: The dynamic development of gender and sexuality. *Psychology today*. Retrieved February 15, 2012 from http://www.psychologytoday.com/blog/sexing-the-body/201103/nature-versus-nurture-part-3-quack

Fausto-Sterling, A., García Coll, C., & Lamarre, M. (in press). Sexing the baby: Part 1—What do we really know about sex differentiation in the first year of life? *Social Science and Medicine*.

Fausto-Sterling, A., García Coll, C., & Lamarre, M. (in press). Sexing the baby: Part 2 Applying dynamic systems theory to the emergences of sex-related differences in infants and toddlers. *Social Science and Medicine*.

Feldman, J. F., Brody, N., & Miller, S. A. (1980). Sex differences in non-elicited neonatal behaviors. *Merrill Palmer Quarterly*, *26*, 63–73.

Feldman, R. (2007a). On the origins of background emotions: from affect synchrony to symbolic expression. *Emotion*, *7*, 601–611.

Feldman, R. (2007b). Parent-infant synchrony and the construction of shared timing; physiological precursors, developmental outcomes, and risk conditions. *Journal of Child Psychology and Psychiatry and Allied Disciplines*, *48*, 329–354.

Ferber, S. G., Feldman, R., & Makhoul, I. R. (2008). The development of maternal touch across the first year of life. *Early Human Development*, *84*, 363–370.

Field, T. (2010). Touch for socioemotional and physical well-being: A review. *Developmental Review*, *30*, 367–383.

Field, T., Diego, M., & Hernandez-Reif, M. (2006). Prenatal depression effects on the fetus and newborn: a review. *Infant Behavior and Development*, *29*, 445–455.

Field, T., Hernandez-Reif, M., & Diego, M. (2006). Newborns of depressed mothers who received moderate versus light pressure massage during pregnancy. *Infant Behavior and Development, 29*, 54–58.

Fogel, A., Dickson, L., Hsu, H.-c., Messinger, D., Nelson-Goens, G. C., & Nwokah, E. (1997). Communication of smiling and laughter in mother-infant play: research on emotion from a dynamic systems perspective. *New Directions in Child Development, 77*, 5–24.

Fogel, A., Garvey, A., Hsu, H.-C., & West-Stroming, D. (2006). *Change processes in relationships: A relational-historical research approach.* Cambridge, UK: Cambridge University Press.

Fogel, A., & Thelen, E. (1987). Development of early expressive and communicative action: reinterpreting the evidence from a dynamic systems perspective. *Developmental Psychology, 23*, 747–761.

Green, R. (2010). Robert Stoller's sex and gender: 40 years on. *Archives of Sexual Behavior, 39*, 1457–1465.

Harris, A. (2005). *Gender as soft assembly.* Hillsdale, NJ: The Analytic Press.

Hollenstein, T. (2007). State Space Grids: Analyzing dynamics across development. *International Journal of Behavioral Development, 31*, 384–396.

Hsu, H.-C., & Fogel, A. (2003). Stability and transitions in mother-infant face-to-face communication during the first 6 months: a microhistorical approach. *Developmental Psychology, 39*, 1061–1082.

Jadva, V., Hines, M., & Golombok, S. (2010). Infants' preferences for toys, colors, and shapes: Sex differences and similarities. *Archives of Sexual Behavior, 39*, 1261–1273.

Kessler, S. J., & McKenna, W. (1978). *Gender: An ethnomethodological approach.* New York, NY: Wiley.

Korner, A. F., & Thoman, E. B. (1970). Visual alertness in neonates as evoked by maternal care. *Journal of Experimental Child Psychology, 10*, 67–78.

Kuhl, P. K. (2010). Brain mechanisms in early language acquisition. *Neuron, 67*, 713–727.

Lamb, M. E. (1977). Father-infant and mother-infant interaction in the first year of life. *Child Development, 48*, 167–181.

Lavelli, M., & Fogel, A. (2002). Developmental changes in mother-infant face-to-face communication: birth to 3 months. *Developmental Psychology, 38*, 288–305.

Malatesta, C. Z., Culver, C., Tesman, J. R., & Shepard, B. (1989). The development of emotion expression during the first two years of life. *Monographs of the Society for Research in Child Development, 54*, 1–104.

Menvielle, E. (this issue). A comprehensive program for children with gender variant behaviors and gender identity disorders. *Journal of Homosexuality, 59*, 357–368.

Menvielle, E., & Tuerk, C. (2002). A support group for parents of gender-nonconforming boys. *Journal of the American Academy of Child and Adolescent Psychiatry, 41*, 1010–1013.

Menvielle, E. J., Tuerk, C., & Perrin, E. C. (2005). To the beat of a different drummer: The gender variant child. *Contemporary Pediatrics, 22*, 38–39.

Meyer-Bahlburg, H. F. (2010). From mental disorder to iatrogenic hypogonadism: dilemmas in conceptualizing gender identity variants as psychiatric conditions. *Archives of Sexual Behavior, 39*, 461–476.

Moss, H. A. (1967). Sex, age, and state as determinants of mother-infant interaction. *Merrill Palmer Quarterly*, *13*, 119–135.

Petanjek, Z., Judaš, M., Kostovic, I., & Uylings, H. B. (2008). Lifespan alterations of basal dendritic trees of pyramidal neurons in the human prefrontal cortex: A layer-specific pattern. *Cereb Cortex*, *18*(4), 915–929

Phillips, S., King, S., & DuBois, L. (1978). Spontaneous activities of female versus male newborns. *Child Development*, *49*, 590–597.

Piaget, J. & Inhelder, B. (1972). *The Psychology of the Child*. New York, NY: Basic Books.

Poulin-Dubois, D., & Forbes, J. N. (2002). Toddlers' attention to intentions-in-action in learning novel action words. *Developmental Psychology*, *38*, 104–114.

Poulin-Dubois, D., Serbin, L. A., Eichstedt, J. A., Sen, M. G., & Beissel, C. F. (2002). Men don't put on make-up: Toddlers' knowledge of the gender stereotyping of household activities. *Social Development*, *11*, 166–181.

Putz, O., & Crews, D. (2006). Embryonic origin of mate choice in a lizard with temperature-dependent sex determination. *Developmental Psychobiology*, *48*, 29–38.

Rheingold, H. L., & Cook, K. V. (1975). The contents of boys' and girls' rooms as an index of parents' behavior. *Child Development*, *46*, 459–463.

Sadeh, A., Dark, I., & Vohr, B. R. (1996). Newborns' sleep-wake patterns: the role of maternal, delivery and infant factors. *Early Human Development*, *44*, 113–126.

Schore, A. N. (1994). *Affect regulation and the origin of the self : The neurobiology of emotional development*. Hillsdale, NJ: L. Erlbaum.

Schore, A. N. (2005). Back to basics: Attachment, affect regulation, and the developing right brain: Linking developmental neuroscience to pediatrics. *Pediatric Review*, *26*, 204–217.

Serbin, L. A., Poulin Dubois, D., & Eichstedt, J. A. (2002). Infants' response to gender-inconsistent events. *Infancy*, *3*, 531–542.

Shakin, M., Shakin, D., & Sternglanz, S. H. (1985). Infant clothing: Sex labeling for strangers. *Sex Roles*, *12*, 955–964.

Stoller, R. (1968). *Sex and gender: On the development of masculinity and femininity*. New York, NY:Science House.

Thelen, E. (1994). Three-month-old infants can learn task-specific patterns of interlimb coordination. *Psychological Bulletin*, *5*(5), 280–285.

Thelen, E. (1995a Motor development: A new synthesis. *American Psychologist*, *50*(2), 79–95.

Thelen, E. (1995b). Origins of motor control. *Behavioral and Brain Sciences*, *18*, 780–783.

Thelen, E. (2000). Grounded in the world: Developmental origins of the embodied mind. *Infancy*, *1*, 3–28.

Thelen, E. (2001). Dynamic mechanisms of change in early perceptual-motor development. In J. L. McClelland & R. S. Siegler (Eds.), *Mechanisms of cognitive development: Behavioral and neural perspectives* (pp. 161–184). Mahwah, NJ: Erlbaum.

Thordstein, M., Lofgren, N., Flisberg, A., Lindecrantz, K., & Kjellmer, I. (2006). Sex differences in electrocortical activity in human neonates. *Neuroreport*, *17*, 1165–1168.

Tronick, E. Z., & Cohn, J. F. (1989). Infant-mother face-to-face interaction: age and gender differences in coordination and the occurrence of miscoordination. *Child Development*, *60*, 85–92.

Weinberg, M. K., Tronick, E. Z., Cohn, J. F., & Olson, K. L. (1999). Gender differences in emotional expressivity and self-regulation during early infancy. *Developmental Psychology*, *35*, 175–188.

Weller, G. M., & Bell, R. Q. (1965). Basal skin conductance and neonatal state. *Child Development*, *36*, 647–657.

Zosuls, K. M., Ruble, D. N., Tamis-Lemonda, C. S., Shrout, P. E., Bornstein, M. H., & Greulich, F. K. (2009). The acquisition of gender labels in infancy: Implications for gender-typed play. *Developmental Psychology*, *45*, 688–701.

Zucker, K. J., Wood, H., Singh, D., & Bradley, S. J. (this issue). A developmental, biopsychosocial model for the treatment of children with gender identity disorder. *Journal of Homosexuality*, *59*, 369–397.

Supporting Transgender Children: New Legal, Social, and Medical Approaches

SHANNON PRICE MINTER, JD

Transgender Law and Policy Institute, Washington, DC, USA

The author, a lawyer who advocates for transgender children and youth, explores how clinical approaches to transgender children and youth are keeping pace with social and legal changes affecting these young people and with recent evidence suggesting that children are harmed by family and societal rejection as well as by attempts to change their gender identity or gender expression. The author urges providers and legal advocates to work with policymakers and the families of transgender children and youth to create a future in which these young people can reach their full potential and be embraced as fully equal, respected, and participating members of society.

As a lawyer who advocates for transgender children and youth, I appreciate the opportunity to comment on the important articles submitted by some of the leading clinicians and mental health professionals who work with this unique population. Although we approach these young people from the perspective of different disciplines, we share a deep commitment to their best interests and long-term health and wellbeing. In this article, I explore how clinical approaches to transgender children and youth are keeping pace with social and legal changes affecting these young people and with recent evidence suggesting that children are harmed by family and societal rejection and by attempts to change their gender identity or gender expression. I end by urging providers and legal advocates to work with policymakers and the families of transgender children and youth to create a future in which these young people can reach their full potential and be embraced as fully equal, respected, and participating members of society.

During the past 15 years, public awareness and acceptance of transgender children and youth in the United States have increased at breathtaking speed. In 1997, the Belgian film *Ma Vie En Rose* [*My Life in Pink*] portrayed a family's journey from rejection to acceptance of a transgender child who was born male but identifies as a girl. Despite receiving an R rating solely because it dealt with transgender issues, the film played to popular audiences in the United States and received a Golden Globe award for best foreign film. Two years later, Hilary Swank won an Oscar for her portrayal of the murdered transgender youth Brandon Teena in *Boys Don't Cry,* a major Hollywood film that portrayed Brandon with compassion and humanity.

In 2002, Gwen Araujo, a transgender teenager, was murdered by four young men in Newark, California. Gwen's death attracted national attention and shined a spotlight on the terrible vulnerability of many transgender youth. The subsequent trial was one of the first in which prosecutors brought hate crimes charges in a case involving a transgender victim. Gwen's mother, Sylvia Guerrero, expressed wholehearted acceptance of her deceased daughter and became one of the first public role models for other parents of transgender youth.

In the wake of this growing public awareness, more parents have begun to recognize that their gender variant children may be transgender and to seek out information and support. Informal networks for families of transgender children have begun to proliferate. In 2002, the influential national group Parents, Family, and Friends of Lesbians and Gays (PFLAG) launched a special affiliate, called the Transgender Network (TNET), for parents of transgender children and youth. Around the same time, nonprofit organizations dedicated to supporting parents and advocating for transgender children, such as Gender Spectrum and TransYouth Family Allies also emerged. In 2008, Stephanie Brill and Rachel Pepper published the first mainstream book for parents of transgender children: *The Transgender Child: A Handbook for Families and Professionals.*

In 2007, the popular television show *20/20* aired an hour-long special on families raising young transgender children, and cited research on family rejection from Ryan, Huebner, Diaz, and Sanchez's (2009) study of lesbian, gay, bisexual, and transgender (LGBT) young people and their families. Hosted by Barbara Walters, the show provided the mainstream public with its first intimate glimpse into the lives and psyches of these children and the challenges faced by their parents, portraying both with great insight and nuance. A year later, National Public Radio taped interviews with a number of parents and children attending an annual conference for families of transgender children. The segment focused on the benefits to children of being permitted to express their gender identities and of having parental support ("The Conversation," 2007; "All Things Considered," 2008).

Also during the past decade, states and localities began to enact legal protections for transgender children and youth in schools. California was the first to do so in 1999, followed by New Jersey (2002), Washington and the District of Columbia (2006), Iowa and Vermont (2007), Oregon (2008), Colorado, North Carolina, and Hawaii (2009), New Hampshire and Illinois (2010), and Arkansas, Connecticut, and New York (2011). These laws generally protect transgender children and youth against discrimination and bullying in schools. In addition, some school districts have adopted detailed policies requiring that schools use appropriate names and pronouns for transgender students, permit them to dress according to their gender identity, and provide them with access to restrooms and locker rooms based on their gender identity (see, e.g., L.A. Unified School District, 2011; San Francisco Unified School District, 2004).

In 2000, a state court in Massachusetts became the first to hold that a public high school had to accommodate a male-to-female transgender teenager by permitting her to wear female clothing to school and, generally, to be treated like any other girl. The court based its decision in part on testimony from the girl's therapist, finding that "plaintiff's ability to express herself and her gender identity through dress is important to her health and well-being, as attested to by her treating therapist. Therefore, plaintiff's expression is not merely a personal preference but a necessary symbol of her very identity" (Doe ex rel. Doe v. Yunits, 2000). The court held that "Defendants are essentially prohibiting the plaintiff from expressing her gender identity, and thus her quintessence, at school" and concluded that it could not "allow the stifling of plaintiff's selfhood merely because it causes some members of the community discomfort" (Doe ex rel. Doe v. Yunits, 2000).

In 2008, the Washington Association of High Schools adopted the nation's first policy for high school transgender athletes. The policy requires that schools accommodate transgender students and permit them to play on the teams that correspond to the student's gender identity regardless of the student's biological gender or the sex designated on the student's official identity documents or records. In 2009, the National Center for Lesbian Rights and the Women's Sports Foundation, with participation from the National Collegiate Athletic Association (NCAA), hosted a think tank on transgender athletes in high school and intercollegiate sports. The think tank—which included high school and college administrators and coaches, athletes, and medical and legal experts—resulted in the publication of the first recommended national guidelines for the inclusion of transgender athletes on high school and college teams ("On the Team," 2000). In 2011, the NCAA adopted an official policy based on those guidelines ("NCAA Adopts New Policy," 2011). The Transgender Law & Policy Institute (2009) has issued similar national recommendations for the inclusion of younger transgender children in recreational sports.

In 2010, Kye Allums, a basketball player for the George Washington University Colonials, became the first openly transgender student to play on an NCAA team. He was strongly supported by his teammates and coaches, and his story received national attention (Orton, 2010). In 2011, the students at Mona Shores High School in Muskagon, Michigan, elected a transgender boy, Oak Marshall, to be their prom king (see Melloy, 2010). Since 2010, the popular television series *Degrassi* has featured a recurring transgender character, Adam, played by young actress Jordon Todosey (see, e.g., Jancelewicz, 2011).

As social and legal support for transgender children and youth have grown, youth are disclosing their identities at younger ages, and the demand for information and supportive care from physicians and mental health providers is increasing dramatically. In response, a number of children's hospitals have created or expanded programs for transgender children and youth, including facilities in Boston, Denver, Los Angeles, Minneapolis, Oakland, Seattle, and Washington, DC. Not coincidentally, most of the articles in this special issue are authored by clinicians affiliated with one of these programs, which have played a leading role in developing contemporary approaches and protocols for treating transgender children and adolescents. In addition, private practitioners who work outside these hospital clinics are also treating growing numbers of transgender children and youth, as evidenced in this issue by the valuable contribution of psychologist Diane Ehrensaft (2011), whose recent publication of *Gender Born, Gender Made: Raising Health Gender Non-Conforming Children* marks the first book length study of this topic by a clinical psychologist. Generally, the number of scholarly and professional articles on how to recognize and provide appropriate care to transgender children and youth is burgeoning.

The new scholarship being generated by clinicians who work with these young people and their families is remarkably consistent and points to a strong emerging consensus about the best ways to work with this population. In their article in this issue, Edwards-Leeper and Spack (this issue) aptly note that "[w]e are in a transitional period regarding the treatment of transgender youth," citing in particular a marked decrease in the age at which gender variant children disclose their identities and the corresponding need for practitioners to "reexamine the framework from which we understand Gender Identity Disorder (GID)" to protect these young people from the harmful consequences of "delaying proper diagnosis" (pp. 321–322). As more youth seek treatment and more practitioners gain experience working with these young people and their families, the benefits of a supportive, nonpathologizing approach are becoming increasingly clear—as are the dangers of pathologizing these identities. Many mainstream practitioners have shifted from a pathologizing model that locates the problem within an individual child whose gender variance must be altered to avoid external social disapproval, to a supportive model that seeks to help the child self-actualize. This is a major shift from early clinical responses to transgender and gender variant children and youth.

As the contributions to this special issue reflect, many of the leading practitioners working in this field agree on a number of key points—first, and perhaps most important, that transgender children exist. As fundamental as this premise may seem, it marks an important milestone. As recently as the 1960s and 1970s and even early 1980s, many mental health professionals would have considered a child who insisted that he or she was "really" the other gender to be psychotic or, at the least, deeply disturbed. The treatments meted out to those children were often damaging and cruel, albeit motivated by a sincere belief that the child's gender variance could be eliminated and that doing so would benefit the child.

When I first began to advocate for transgender people in the early 1990s, I was shaken by meeting older transgender people who shared painful stories of being confined in psychiatric hospitals, subjected to electro-shock, and given debilitating drugs—not only as adults, but as teenagers and in some cases even children. One woman described being taken to a psychiatric facility by her parents when she was five years old. After a few initial visits, she never saw her parents again. Over the years, she was repeatedly sexually abused by other patients and staff and endured multiple exposures to electro-shock therapy and a variety of psychotropic drugs (including Thorazine, which left her with tardive dyskinesia). She remained institutionalized until her early 20s, when she walked in paper slippers through the woods adjacent to the hospital until she came to a road and hitchhiked to freedom. She soon made her way to San Francisco, where she worked in drag shows and eventually had sex-reassignment surgery in the basement of a house on Van Ness Street, because at that time, in the 1980s, no hospitals in San Francisco would permit sex-reassignment surgeries to be performed. As an adult, she is a fierce advocate for transgender children, and surprisingly forgiving of her own family. She tells me that she often dreams of her father, and believes that her parents loved her and simply did not have the information to understand her identity.

Today, the dominant clinical response to cross-gender identified children has changed dramatically. In this era, few if any children are likely to be subjected to such extreme efforts to change their identity by reputable therapists, although some parents continue to punish gender nonconformity in their children severely, and there still are religion-based programs that encourage this punitive approach. Increasingly, clinicians recognize that transgender children exist and that, at least for some children, "GID in children represents a normal developmental variation" (Menvielle, this issue, p. 363). Accordingly, they recognize that while a child's cross-gender identification may be symptomatic of other issues, it may also represent a child's authentic core identity.

Once clinicians accept that transgender children and youth are part of the normative spectrum of gender expression and presentation, the goals of therapy change. In the past, therapeutic interventions with these children were focused on trying to prevent the child from growing up to be gay or transgender. With near unanimity, however, the clinicians contributing to this issue recognize that efforts to change or suppress a child's gender identity or gender expression to alter the child's adult identity are ineffective and damaging. Rather than attempting to eliminate or reduce a child's cross-gender behavior or identity, the goal of therapy, in Ehrensaft's (this issue) phrase, is "to facilitate the child's authentic gender journey" (p. 339). Menvielle similarly notes that "[a] premise of the program [at the Children's National Medical Center in Washington, DC] is that the development of children with cross-gender behaviors, interests, and characteristics is not to be interfered with, anymore than with children who are conventional in their gender" (p. 363).

This does not mean that every child who exhibits cross-gender behaviors or identity is presumed to be transgender. One of the most striking features of recent scholarship, including the articles submitted for this issue, is the growing sensitivity of practitioners to the differences between children who are simply tomboys or gender nonconforming boys, children for whom gender variance is limited to a particular developmental stage (de Vries & Cohen-Kettenis, this issue), children for whom gender variance or a stated wish to be the other gender is a transient symptom of their struggle with other issues (such as dealing with a traumatic death or separation),[1] and children who are developing a genuine aspect of their identity. As Menvielle (this issue) notes, "[s]ome children present with gender variant behaviors and interests, but their expressed wishes to be the other gender or assertions about being a member of the other gender are not pervasive and do not suggest or represent deep and persistent convictions" (p. 364). Ehrensaft (this issue) similarly explains that adopting a nonpathologizing view of transgender children "does not mean that gender can never be a symptom of some other underlying disorder rather than an expression of self." Rather, she explains, "the most challenging task for the child clinician is to differentiate those symptomatic situations from the albeit complicated but healthy developmental journey of children who are reaching to establish their true gender identity and authentic gender expressions" (p. 339).

Even when a child's developing identity appears to be clear, practitioners emphasize the need to avoid prematurely labeling the child or assuming the inevitability of any particular outcome. For example, Edwards-Leeper and Spack (this issue) "support the use of early individual and family therapy that encourages acceptance of the child's budding gender development while simultaneously emphasizing the importance of remaining open to the fluidity of his or her gender identity and sexual orientation" (p. 330). Even when social transition is the right step for a particular child, they stress the need to emphasize to parents "the importance of remaining open to the possibility of the child's gender shifting back at some point" (p. 331). Ehrensaft (this issue) similarly stresses that "we must be modest enough to say that we can never know with absolute certainty if a child who says s/he is transgender is expressing a stable, permanent lifelong identity or just on a temporary stepping stone" (p. 347).

At the same time, contemporary practitioners increasingly acknowledge that prepubertal gender transition is appropriate for children who cannot live in their assigned gender without intense suffering and for whom social transition offers clear relief. As Menvielle (this issue) explains, "[t]here are some children who are so assertive in this regard, that refusing to accommodate to their wish is at face value inappropriate. Their life in their assigned gender is very distressing and the relief they get from switching their gender presentation very palpable" (p. 361). Edwards-Leeper and Spack (this issue) present a particularly thoughtful discussion of the factors that clinicians should consider when dealing with younger children who express a desire to socially transition, including the child's wishes and desires, how the social transition will affect the child's siblings, and the safety of the child and the child's family in light of the surrounding community.

In addition to this growing consensus (particularly among U.S.-based practitioners) that social transition is appropriate for some younger children who are not approaching puberty,[2] there is an even stronger consensus that as youth enter the first stages of puberty, the best practice for dealing with significantly gender dysphoric adolescents is to prescribe hormone blockers that suppress puberty.[3] This treatment usually coincides with the youth living in (or continuing) to live in the social role of his or her desired gender. Suppressing puberty provides these youth with an opportunity to explore their identities without the distress of developing the permanent, unwanted physical characteristics of their biological sex. For example, hormone blockers prevent a female-to-male transgender youth from the trauma of growing breasts, starting to menstruate, and developing typically female patterns of fat distribution around hips and thighs. They prevent a male-to-female transgender youth from developing unwanted facial and body hair, roughening of skin texture, muscle mass, a deep voice, a masculine facial structure, and other unwanted secondary sex characteristics. The relief provided by this intervention can be enormous and gives a transgender youth the opportunity to develop a strong, positive sense of self.

Credit for breaking new ground on this issue must go to Cohen-Kettenis and her colleagues at the Amsterdam Clinic, who have treated over 100 adolescent patients with puberty blocking medication and carefully tracked their outcomes. The article, contributed by deVries and Cohen-Kettenis to this issue, provides the first comprehensive description of what has come to be known as the "Dutch protocol" for treating gender dysphoria in adolescents, which two studies have now shown to produce extremely positive results for the young people who have received this treatment. As they note, while "[m]any studies in gender dysphoric adults have demonstrated that gender reassignment treatment is effective," their "initial results demonstrate that this is also the case in young people who have received [hormone blockers] to suppress puberty at an early age, followed by the actual gender reassignment" (p. 315).

Edwards-Leeper and Spack (this issue) helpfully identify four psychological benefits of suppressing puberty for transgender adolescents. First, it "can prevent needless emotional and psychological suffering, which can be severe for some adolescents" (p. 329). As Edwards-Leeper and Spack elsewhere note, the psychological problems and symptoms that many transgender youth experience— often as a result of social isolation and rejection, in addition to gender dysphoria—frequently "decrease and even disappear once the adolescent begins a social and/or physical transition" (p. 327). Second, it buys time for the youth to continue exploring his or her identity and to make a more informed and less pressured decision about whether to pursue a full physical transition. Third, it provides an opportunity to see whether suppressing the unwanted secondary sex characteristics has a positive impact on how the youth functions, thereby confirming or disconfirming that the youth's distress was likely caused by gender dysphoria. Finally, for youth who go on to physically transition, it "allows for a much easier full transition to the other gender at a later time because the individual's body remains in a neutral, early pubertal state" (p. 329).

Contemporary experts also recognize, however, that there are a wide range of transgender identities, and medical interventions such as hormone blockers may not be appropriate for all transgender-identified youth.[4] For example, some children and youth may strongly identify as the other gender, but may be comfortable with their bodies. Others may identify as neither a boy nor a girl, or may identify as some combination of the two—and may or may not experience distress about their bodies. In every case, it is important to give children and young people the space to discover and determine who they are and to respect their emerging identities.

The contributors to this special issue and other practitioners also stress the therapeutic importance of providing transgender youth and their parents with tools to navigate societal discrimination and hostility. Here again, there is a marked break with past approaches, which often sought to justify efforts to prevent children from being transgender as a means of protecting them from social rejection and mistreatment as well as the potential need for medical transition with its limitations and risks. Zucker, Wood, Singh, and Bradley (this issue) continue to defend this approach[5]; however, many contemporary experts believe that seeking to alter a child's identity in order to avoid social discrimination is neither effective nor appropriate, and that "the problem is not located within the child" (Menvielle, this issue, p. 367). Instead, they seek to provide these young people and their families with support, resources, and strategies for dealing with external discrimination and stigma. These include participation in support groups with other parents and youth, "helping a child build 'gender resilience' and explore his or her authentic gender identity while acknowledging social constraints that may work against its full expression," (Ehrensaft, this issue, p. 343) and practical advice for addressing "homophobia and transphobia among family members, schools, and the broader communities (neighbors, religious affiliations)" (Edwards-Leeper & Spack, this issue, p. 330). The goal, as Ehrensaft (this issue) notes, is to provide "a psychological tool kit that will allow a child to internalize a positive self-identity while recognizing situations in which that identity may be in need of protection from an unwelcome or hostile environment" (p. 344).

Research by Ryan and colleagues (Ryan, Huebner et al., 2009; Ryan, Russell, Huebner, Diaz, & Sanchez, 2010) at the Family Acceptance Project at San Francisco State's Marian Wright Edelman Institute for the Study of Children, Youth, and Families lends support to this approach by showing the compelling relationship between family acceptance and rejection of transgender and gay children and their health and wellbeing as young adults. This work provides an empirical framework for helping families support their children's gender identity. For example, Ryan et al.'s research shows that transgender and gay young people who are supported by their families have significantly higher levels of self-esteem, social support and general health in adulthood, compared to peers with low levels of family acceptance. In particular, this research has found that specific parental and caregiver behaviors—such as advocating for their children when they are mistreated because of their LGBT identity or supporting their gender expression—protect against depression, substance abuse, suicidal thoughts and suicide attempts in early adulthood. Moreover, supporting a child's gender expression is among the most important protective factors for supporting a gay or transgender child's long-term health and wellbeing. Conversely, this research has found that parental or caregiver behaviors such as making a child keep his or her identity secret from other family members, pressuring a child to be more or less masculine or feminine, or telling a child that how he or she acts or looks will shame or embarrass the family dramatically increases the child's risk for depression, substance abuse, unprotected sex, and suicidality in adulthood (Ryan, 2009).[6] Other researchers (Crocket, Brown, Russell, & Shen, 2007) are finding similar results.

In light of this suggestive research, as well as the growing body of data being generated by therapists and doctors working with transgender and gender nonconforming youth, legislators, policymakers, and courts are becoming more aware of the need for laws and policies that protect these youth.

Similarly, medical practitioners are increasingly united in the view that one of their most important roles is "serv[ing] as advocates for the transgender population in the broader culture and community," recognizing that "a societal shift must occur in order for these patients to truly be able to live without increased risk of psychological distress and potential physical harm by self or others caused by intolerance and discrimination" (Edwards-Leeper & Spack, this issue, p. 334–335). Historically, medical practitioners such as Harry Benjamin and many others have shown tremendous foresight and courage in advocating for increased social and legal acceptance of transgender people. In the courts, individual therapists have supplied critical expert testimony on behalf of transgender youth and adults that has helped courts understand the reality of transgender identity and the need to treat transgender individuals with dignity and respect. In many important legal cases, the World Professional Association for Transgender Health (WPATH) has filed friend-of-the-court briefs on behalf of transgender plaintiffs, explaining why legal recognition and protection is essential to the health and wellbeing of transgender people. This legacy of collaboration between providers and legal advocates bodes well for the future and lays a strong foundation for clinicians, lawyers, policymakers, and families to work together to create a better future for transgender children and youth.

NOTES

1. Zucker et al. (this issue) describe various scenarios in which gender variance appears to be symptomatic rather than indicative of a child's authentic identity; Ehrensaft (this issue) describes scenarios in which children manifest gender variance "in an attempt to solve some other life or emotional problem" (p. 345).

2. In contrast to the U.S.-based clinicians represented in this volume, the Amsterdam Clinic currently "recommend[s] that young children not yet make a complete social transition (different clothing, a different given name, referring to a boy as "her" instead of "him") before the very early stages of puberty" (de Vries & Cohen-Kettenis, this issue, p. 307–308).

3. This strong consensus is based in part on a near-universal recognition that "gender dysphoria rarely changes or desists in adolescents who had been gender dysphoric since childhood and remained so after puberty" (de Vries & Cohen-Kettenis, this issue, p. 306). See also Zucker et al. (this issue): "there is much less evidence that GID can remit in adolescents than in children" (p. 392).

4. See, for example, Edwards-Leeper and Spack (this issue) noting the prevalence of "gender fluidity even in our clinic of severely gender dysphoric individuals in terms of the extent which patients feel it necessary to alter their physical bodies in order to feel comfortable in their affirmed gender" (p. 334).

5. See Zucker et al. (this issue) arguing that treatments designed to reduce cross-gender behavior and identification in children are justified in part by avoiding "the attendant social ostracism that can ensue from GID persistence" (p. 390).

6. In addition to this empirical research, there is growing anecdotal evidence that many of the young people touted as success stories by clinicians who claimed to successfully treat GID in children were in fact harmed by those treatments. See, for example, Burroway, 2011.

REFERENCES

All things considered: Two-part series on transgender children. (2008, May 7–8). National Public Radio [Radio broadcast]. Retrieved from http://www.npr.org/ 2008/05/07/90247842/two-families-grapple-with-sons-gender-preferences)

Brill, S. & Pepper, R. (2008). *The transgender child: A handbook for families and professionals*. San Francisco, CA: Cleis Press Inc.

Burroway, J. (2001, June 7). What are little boys made of? *Box Turtle Bulletin*. Retrieved from http://www.boxturtlebulletin.com/what-are-little-boys-made-of-main

The Conversation: Transgendered people and the gender odyssey conference. (2007, August 27). NPR-AFFILIATE KUOW, 94.9FM [Radio broadcast]. Retrieved from http://www.kuow.org/program.php?id=13369

Crockett, L. J., Brown, J., Russell, S. T., & Shen, Y-L. (2007). The meaning of good parent-child relationships for Mexican American adolescents. *Journal of Research on Adolescence, 17*, 639–668.

de Vries, A. L. C., & Cohen-Kettenis, P. T. (this issue). Clinical management of gender dysphoria in children and adolescents: The Dutch approach. *Journal of Homosexuality*, 59, 301–320.

Doe ex rel. Doe v. Yunits, 001060A, 2000 WL 33162199 (Mass. Super. Oct. 11, 2000) aff'd sub nom. Doe v. Brockton Sch. Comm., 2000-J-638, 2000 WL 33342399 (Mass. App. Ct. Nov. 30, 2000).

Edwards-Leeper, L. & Spack, N.P. (this issue). Psychological evaluation and medical treatment of transgender youth in an interdisciplinary "gender management service" (GeMS) in a major pediatric center. *Journal of Homosexuality*, 59, 321–336.

Ehrensaft, D. (2011).*Gender born, gender made: Raising healthy gender non-conforming children*. New York, NY: The Experiment

Ehrensaft, D. (this issue). From gender identity to gender identity creativity: True gender self child therapy. *Journal of Homosexuality*, 59, 337–356.

Jancelewicz, C. (2011, February 11). Jordon Todosey on *Degrassi* and playing a transgender character [Web log post]. Retrieved from http://www.aoltv.com/ 2011/02/11/jordan-todosey-degrassi-adam-transgender-interview/

L.A. Unified School District. (2011). L.A. Unified School District Reference Guide No. REF-155, Transgender and Gender Nonconforming Students—Ensuring Equity and Nondiscrimination. Retrieved from http://www.lausd.net/lausd/ offices/eec/pdfs/TransgGuide.pdf

Menvielle, E. (this issue). A comprehensive program for children with gender variant behaviors and gender identity disorders. *Journal of Homosexuality*, 59, 357–368.

Melloy, K. (2010, September 29). Michigan high school students fight for a transgender prom king. Retrieved from http://www.edgeboston.com/index. php?ch=news&sc=&sc3=&id=110909

NCAA adopts new policy to embrace transgender student athletes, keep competitive equity. (2011, September 13). *Associated Press*.

On the team: Equal opportunities for transgender athletes. 2010. National Center for Lesbian Rights. Retrieved from http://www.nclrights.org/site/DocServer/ TransgenderStudentAthleteReport.pdf?docID=7901

Orton, K. (2010, November 2). Transgender GW basketball player Kye Allums says reaction has been "really positive." *Washington Post*. Retrieved from http://www.washingtonpost.com/wpdyn/content/article/2010/11/02/AR2010110205602.html

Ryan, C. (2009). *Supportive families, healthy children: Helping families with lesbian, gay, bisexual & transgender children*. San Francisco, CA: Marian Wright Edelman Institute, San Francisco State University.

Ryan, C., Huebner, D., Diaz, R.M. & Sanchez, J. (2009). Family rejection as a predictor of negative health outcomes in white and Latino lesbian, gay, and bisexual young adults. *Pediatrics*, *123*(1), 346–352.

Ryan, C., Russell, S. T., Huebner, D. M., Diaz, R., & Sanchez, J. (2010). Family acceptance in adolescence and the health of LGBT young adults. *Journal of Child and Adolescent Psychiatric Nursing*, *23*(4), 205–213;

San Francisco Unified School District. (2004). San Francisco Unified School District Policy, Art. 5, Non-Discrimination for Students and Employees. Retrieved from http://www.transgenderlaw.org/college/sfusdpolicy.htm

Transgender Law and Policy Institute. (2009). *Guidelines for creating polices for transgender children in recreational sports*. Retrieved from http://www.transgenderlaw.org/resources/TLPI_GuidlinesforCreatingPoliciesforTransChildreninRecSports.pdf

Zucker, K. J., Wood, H., Singh, D., & Bradley, S. J. (this issue). A developmental, biopsychosocial model for the treatment of children with gender identity disorder. *Journal of Homosexuality*, 59, 369–397.

Thoughts on the Nature of Identity: How Disorders of Sex Development Inform Clinical Research about Gender Identity Disorders

WILLIAM G. REINER, MD

Department of Urology, Pediatric Urology, and Department of Psychiatry, Division of Child and Adolescent Psychiatry, University of Oklahoma Health Sciences Center, Oklahoma City, Oklahoma, USA

D. TOWNSEND REINER, MA

Department of Psychiatry, University of Oklahoma Health Sciences Center, Oklahoma City, Oklahoma, USA

Disorders of sex development (DSD), like gender dysphoria, are conditions with major effects on child sexuality and identity, as well as sexual orientation. Each may in some cases lead to change of gender from that assigned neonatally. These similarities—and the conditions' differences—provide a context for reviewing the articles in this issue about clinical approaches to children with gender dysphoria, in relation to assessment, intervention, and ethics.

The essence of psychiatry might be in the perspectives it provides on behavioral phenotypes, albeit from the attribution of disordered behaviors. Still, the view that behaviors may be normal or abnormal begs the questions: What is normal, and what is pathological? Is normality defined by what is typical in a statistical sense or by what is adaptive? The converse is also important: What is abnormal— that which is merely atypical or that which is maladaptive? This issue of the *Journal of Homosexuality* focuses on the nature of clinical approaches to gender dysphoria, primarily in children and adolescents, and provides reviews of clinical approaches from a variety of theoretical and heuristic viewpoints. One important question repeatedly surfaces: Is gender dysphoria a psychopathology, that is, an abnormality? Certainly, gender dysphoric children present as patients to the healthcare system. How, then, does this system provide for the wellbeing of these children? And can other disorders of childhood sexuality—in particular, disorders of sex development (DSD)—inform our understanding or treatment approaches for gender dysphoric children?

Let us begin by reviewing the clinical articles in this issue in terms of the assessment and treatment protocols offered. First, the Toronto group, as discussed by Zucker, Wood, Singh, and Bradley (this issue), has contributed much of clinical value to the literature on gender dysphoria in children since the 1970s. This is the clinic that developed the Gender Identity Questionnaire for Children (Zucker et al., 1993), a useful screen for primary health care providers. Here, they present a balanced clinical approach to the children as well as to the parents and family more broadly, with a fairly extensive evaluation and follow up as well as a psychological testing protocol. Their assessment protocol, thoroughly explained with a patient example, screens for general psychiatric signs and symptoms in the children. They interview the parents and the child over several visits. Treatment approaches are similarly well considered in terms of psychosocial development and comorbid psychopathology. Assessment and intervention are based on a somewhat loosely coherent "developmental, biopsychosocial model informed by a variety of theoretical and empirical advances" (p. 374). Of particular note is that they are very sensitive to the potential long-term implications of treatment interventions both for the child and for the parents.

Unfortunately, despite their extensive experience, their primary etiological work has been with screening, in individual cross-sectional evaluations. Here, their "developmental, biopsychosocial model" raises its apparently eclectic head, like Medusa, but, or perhaps because of it, informs little of etiology. Some of their evaluative and treatment measures have strong psychoanalytic foundations but with low-level evidence in applications for children. Indeed, the authors provide a somewhat murky description of a multifactorial gender dysphoria model without clear focus. Their eclecticism seems, in some sense, a sort of review of the literature on gender development (see, e.g., Ruble, Martin, & Berenbaum, 2006), but more psychodynamically oriented than broad based.

Additionally, and perhaps more to the point, the lack of more longitudinal data from this group, separate from outcomes for gender dysphoria generally and sexual orientation specifically, underscores the common problem in this clinical research area: focusing on atypical sexuality as a condition. This is common to other areas of childhood sexual research, also, as in the literature on DSD in children. Longitudinal studies can follow specific behavioral patterns as well as more general nosological outcomes. In other words, cohorts, as well as individuals within each cohort, would be followed over time, tracking changes across groups and, more nearly specifically, cross-over from one behavioral or contextual cohort to another. Longitudinal studies can help dissect causal mechanisms at work in the early development of these children from mere coincidental associations, and may direct researchers toward more likely etiological factors, specific vulnerabilities, and clinical risks. Genetics and gene-variant commonalities (e.g., polymorphisms) might be explored, or prenatal conditions, complex gene by environment (G × E) interactions, and postnatal variations as well. Their patient population is rather large, allowing for longitudinal studies with enough power to suggest future research directions.

Next, the Washington, DC, Children's Hospital experience, as discussed by Menvielle (this issue), is a structured, clinically appropriate approach to gender dysphoric children very much like the Toronto group. Their sensitivity and their singular internal clinic response to the overall mental health needs of referred families and children are somewhat unique. This clinic places emphasis on particularly stressful developmental periods—entering school and entering adolescence—during which gender dysphoric children experience heightened difficulties in social dynamics. Menvielle describes sensitivity to the emotional impact on the parents, supporting an approach to help the parents to affirm their caring for their children. Like the Toronto clinic, peer relationship issues and problems are evaluated and appropriate psychoeducational approaches and parent effectiveness training are provided.

Although Menvielle does not address well the possibilities that the social difficulties and gender dysphoria might arise from a similar, earlier developmental etiology, he recognizes that some of these children are so rigid in their cognitive view that their gender identity issues cannot be ignored clinically. This cognitive rigidity, apparently somewhat common across gender dysphoric children (at least those who come to clinical attention), will be compared to children with DSD (discussed later). But this rigidity begs for research. There is, perhaps, too much emphasis here on a somewhat nebulous modern social notion of "diversity," although Menvielle does admit that gender dysphoria in children as a representation of a normal developmental variation is his assumption. As with the Toronto clinic, there is a team approach to these families, with separate child and parent support groups.

The Dutch approach, articulated by de Vries and Cohen-Kettenis (this issue), reflects a careful approach, like the Toronto group. It includes a reasonable assessment of vulnerability in the children and parents but appears to utilize more of a watchful waiting approach. However, only in gender dysphoric adolescents (i.e., persisters) are puberty suppression or other interventions suggested. Indeed, this group has efficacy studies demonstrating at least short-term positive outcomes with this approach. Again like the Toronto clinic, they emphasize a multifactorial etiology with psychosocial and biological aspects playing some kind of unclear role. They stress internalizing psychopathology in the children, although its exact role in etiology is unclear and not discussed. They recognize a plausible, if complex, interaction between biological predispositions in combination with intra- and interpersonal factors contributing to gender dysphoria in children and adolescents. This could explain the varying forms and intensities of expressed phenotype, perhaps a more plausible speculation than from the other clinics. Of note, as they emphasize, is that cross-gender behavior that persists into adolescence rarely changes.

When describing criteria for Gender Identity Disorder, de Vries and Cohen-Kettenis discussion (this issue) sounds very much like a discussion of any human variation; indeed, they call for greater consideration of gender dysphoria as a variation in the *Diagnostic and Statistical Manual of Mental Disorders* (5th ed.; *DSM-5*; American Psychiatric Association, in production). They do not address the fact that this variation, apparently rather unique to humans, is more likely to lead to clinical referral and intervention than other unique human variations (consider, e.g., early and profound prowess in music, drama or comedy, or school achievement, and their possible developmental implications).

de Vries and Cohen-Kettenis (this issue) also evaluate cognitive, psychosocial, and scholastic performance. In addition they evaluate children for psychiatric comorbidity and recognize a possible association with autism spectrum disorders. Their treatment approach is careful to address peer problems, psychiatric comorbidity, and family problems. Interestingly, they recognize that some adolescents in their clinic may have confusion about homosexuality or transvestitic fetishism rather than true gender dysphoria. Like the Toronto clinic, even if "younger," the Dutch clinic has not reported longitudinal developmental studies.

Next, Edwards-Leeper and Spack's (this issue) Boston Children's experience is somewhat unique in this group. This clinic refers all possibly-affected prepubertal children to other agents and accepts only appropriate gender dysphoric adolescents for clinic treatment. Mental health services are also referred out for their adolescents who have comorbid psychiatric disorders. Precisely what is deemed appropriate is not entirely clear. Additionally, the definition of adolescence is apparently postpuberty, although the presence and level of puberty is ascertained by telephone triage through the parents (who are notoriously poor at recognizing early to midpuberty). Nonetheless, their description of their five acceptance criteria appear to select for those mid-to-late pubescent children who are already clearly aiming for a transsexual social status; in fact, the authors describe a clinic in which their evaluation is primarily designed for adolescents who are ready for active intervention at the time of their first clinic visit. They embrace medical puberty suppression for Tanner stages 2–3, or early to mid puberty, basically following the Endocrine Society Guidelines in this regard and generally in agreement with the Toronto and the Dutch groups. Although puberty suppression may well be a psychologically positive intervention for many, what factors are crucial—patient age, Tanner stage, comorbid diagnoses—is really as yet unclear.

The Boston clinic's interpretation of psychological comorbidities (do they mean psychiatric diagnoses?) is based largely on their view that social and psychological aberrations are outcomes of gender dysphoria, a view that may often be clinically relevant, although specific evidence is difficult to find. They do not seem to consider much the possibility that the psychological aberrations and the gender dysphoria could both be phenotypes of the same primary brain condition, whether of genetic or environmental etiology or a complex interaction of both. Their stated clinic selection bias has a strong potential for relatively close followup of a narrowed population sample, although they do not report longitudinal outcomes.

Their team shares a philosophical belief with many in the transgender community that gender dysphoric children do not experience a gender change but rather possess a brain that has always been his or her affirmed gender. While trans-friendly, and, in general, patient-friendly, evidence for such a statement is generally lacking. Indeed, it may be possible to be too patient friendly; that is, their faith in following "the child's lead [as] paramount" could lead to misguided outcomes particularly if generalists treating such children are guided by their approach (p. 330). Few clinicians are likely to have their experience, expertise, or knowledge of the literature—or to recognize that this clinic chooses a very select population sample. Nevertheless, their discussion—both in terms of the children's native brains and of following the child's lead (clinically) can be restated as a clinical conundrum for many children with DSD (see discussion below).

Finally, they discuss possible comorbid, related diagnostic categories, such as Asperger's syndrome, although they omit specific discussions of the phenomenology in such adolescents that might interrelate to their gender dysphoria. They see a societal shift as necessary to protect gender dysphoric individuals from psychological distress, although greater social education might provide nearly as much protection without the need for such a difficult outcome as a societal shift.

Last, Ehrensaft's (this issue) approach appears to be an outlier among these clinics. Utilizing inventive terminology, the author provides almost poetic discussions with ethereal references to somewhat nebulous constructs. What is clear, however, is that Ehrensaft is celebrating these children with their gender nonconformity. She speaks that "they become enlivened and engaged" when allowed to live as the other sex; they become dysphoric when their desires are rejected (p. 338). This may often be true. On the other hand, typical children can become dysphoric when their desires are rejected. Seemingly absent from this approach is any sense of the broader theoretical and empirical advances that highlight the Toronto, Washington, Dutch, or Boston clinic approaches, as well as the overt sensitivity those clinics display to risks inherent to interventions in general. After all, clinicians do things to patients, intervene in their lives (and bodies)—and these patients are children.

Denying a dichotomy of gender the author affirms a belief in a wide range of gender identities (is it infinite?). Looking at the dichotomous conception of male and female with its nearly universal acceptance for at least thousands of years (as long as we have written records), this view would seem a bit suspect. Indeed, whenever a clinician or researcher has been deeply influenced by the work of any single theorist (here, D. W. Winnicott), especially without providing high levels of evidence, one must worry about perspective and bias.

Ehrensaft indeed firmly admits a bias that is in contrast to the other clinics. But a vision of reframing an individual's identity in a celebration of one aspect of identity, albeit an important aspect, as the embodiment of the sense of self—and it is an almost singularity of identity that comes across as being celebrated, in her article—seems in sharp contrast to the empirical, theoretical, and philosophical views discussed by the other authors. Each of us *is* different, of course. Still, we recognize multiple crucial variations to our own individual humanness. There is insufficient space here—or need, for that matter—to discuss those things that make us, peculiarly enough, human and diverse. But we recognize ourselves as male or female. (Do the children themselves not state that they want to be the other sex? Do they claim an undefined gender, or rather do they claim a male or female gender?). Finally, the author's dividing of the brain from the mind from the psyche is at least a break from "dualism"—but certainly not a theoretical or clinical advance.

WHAT IS SEX DEVELOPMENT AND WHAT ARE DISORDERS OF SEX DEVELOPMENT?

Before we can more broadly explore clinical realities of gender variance, a brief review of sexual differentiation will be helpful—that is, what is normal sex development? First, it is important to state that prenatal sexual differentiation in humans is largely a set of virilizing effects. In other words, because the embryological phenotype of the female is the "default" sexual picture, sexual differentiation is a change from that state. Differentiation begins when the Y chromosome gene, *Sry*, leads to the development of a testis. The testis produces testosterone, a male hormone that leads to virilization of the external genitalia through conversion to a more potent androgen, dihydrotestosterone (DHT), but virilizes the internal genitalia, some somatic structures, and (somewhat inextricably) the brain, as well. Brain virilization is demonstrated in part by observed postnatal male-typical as opposed to female-typical behaviors and interests.

Second, DSD are characterized as those embryological errors in which anomalous genitalia are present at birth.[1] However, anomalous—or atypical (for the affected child's karyotype)—brain differentiation may have occurred as well. That many children with DSD have not only atypical genitalia but some gender-atypical behaviors is well known. On the other hand, children with Gender Identity Disorder who do not have a somatic DSD have no known underlying hormonal, karyotypic, or embryological abnormalities. That gender dysphoria might reflect a DSD of the brain is speculative, but such ideas argue against gender dysphoria as a psychopathology.

An overview of clinical experience with children with DSD can provide insights into gender variance because some children (and adults) with DSD change their gender from their neonatally assigned sex. Clinical experience of this article's first author includes our own DSD clinic at the University of Oklahoma Health Sciences Center (called the SUCCEED Clinic, an acronym used to avoid negative attribution), a growing, multidisciplinary clinic for assessment and treatment of individuals with disorders of sex development. The clinic currently is following about 100 children, roughly half with XX and half with XY disorders of sex development (Schaeffer et al., 2010). Additional experience of the primary author includes clinical involvement with about 200 children and adults with major urogenital anomalies, mostly bladder or cloacal exstrophy (W. Reiner, 2004; W. Reiner, Gearhart, & Jeffs, 1999), and about 100 additional children who would formerly have been termed intersex children (W. G. Reiner, 2005). These 300–400 children all have some sex development disorder. Their growth and development have occurred within a variety of socioeconomic backgrounds, clinical settings, and places of residence. Let us first explore gender variance through this experience with DSD and then compare observations with gender dysphoric children.

Disorders of sex development, as implied above, can be divided between XX and XY disorders. First, XX DSD nearly always arise from congenital adrenal hyperplasia (CAH). This is a set of genetic errors in adrenal cortical metabolism affecting biosynthesis of glucocorticoid and mineralcorticoid, the vital end products of adrenal function. Absence of these endpoint adrenal hormones leads to a prenatal buildup of molecular precursors, which then are catalyzed to several accessory molecules but many through pathways leading to androgen production. These accessory hormones are all expressed in the normal fetus in small amounts. Adrenal errors can lead to global (if variable) prenatal androgen exposure, ceasing after birth when diagnosis and adrenal treatment are instituted. Such androgen exposure can be mild, moderate, or high, depending on the specific inborn error of metabolism. While the male fetus is already fully virilized by prenatal testicular androgens, affected XX fetuses experience mild, moderate, or high virilization of the external genitalia. Additionally, androgen imprinting of the brain, during sensitive or critical prenatal periods, is likely present in humans, if poorly understood (Auchus et al., 2010). This is of developmental importance to XX children with CAH because their brains experience inappropriate prenatal androgen exposure. Indeed, although these newborns are nearly always assigned female sex-of-rearing (due to their sex chromosomes and potential fertility as female), up to 30% are bisexual or homosexual and about 5% have gender dysphoria (Dessens, Slijper, & Drop, 2005).

Second, <u>XY</u> DSD arise from a number of etiologies, about 50% of which are never clinically determined. XY DSD can themselves be conveniently divided into two groups. In Group A, complete androgen insensitivity syndrome (cAIS), genetic males despite the presence of (undescended) testes have no responsiveness to androgen because they lack the receptor molecule. They are female in identity (Mazur, 2005) and also express the female default phenotype of female-typical external genitalia, behaviors, and interests. They have no internal female reproductive structures, however—these structures have atrophied under the prenatal influence of a second testicular hormone, anti-müllerian hormone, which is active in these individuals. In Group B, a variety of disorders create mild, moderate, or high androgen effects but that are, nevertheless, inappropriately low for a normal male fetus. They have ambiguous genitalia and are usually assigned female sex-of-rearing. Their behavioral phenotypes—and gender identity—can vary from more male typical to more female typical. More to the point, they sometimes desire to or do change gender from their neonatally assigned-sex—that is, are gender dysphoric. These XX and XY DSD individuals provide insight into complex interactions between variable prenatal androgen exposures and other environmental and genetic factors. Individual and diagnostic-group outcomes of gender and sexual orientation are known for a few diagnoses.

We have discussed phenotypes in XX DSD and in cAIS, a Group A XY DSD. Let us look further at individuals with Group B DSD, with variable prenatal testosterone effects but in the presence of a Y chromosome.

Aphallia (Congenital Absence of the Penis). These very rare XY individuals have normal testes, normal prenatal androgen effects, but absence of the penis due to embryological aberrations of pelvic development. Because we lacked surgical techniques until recently to construct a functional penis, these children have traditionally been castrated at birth and surgically—and socially—converted to female. Studies of 60 such individuals raised female revealed that 36 (60%) have transitioned from female sex-of-rearing to male gender between ages 4 and 26 years, without prior knowledge of their genetic or neonatal gonadal status. All 36 express sexual orientation (that is, attraction) to females. The remaining 24 (40%) have been unwilling to discuss orientation.

High Androgen Exposure (5α-Reductase Deficiency). These rare XY individuals are born with a female external phenotype due to absence of the enzyme converting testosterone to the (locally) more potent DHT, which is required to virilize external genitalia—they are raised female. However, because testosterone has some ability to attach to the androgen receptor, these individuals virilize after the massive testosterone produced physiologically beginning at puberty. According to the literature, about 60% have transitioned to male after puberty (sexual orientation, when reported, being towards females). In other words, they express gender dysphoria during pubescence.

Mild-to-Moderate Androgen Effects. A number of conditions leave XY newborns with variable but inadequate male genitalia and are typically raised female. The literature is sparse, but there is a real, if probably low, incidence of transitioning to male during childhood or adulthood. Sexual orientation has typically not been reported.

Clearly, then, recent DSD studies have included gender identity outcomes:

a. In genetic females with CAH, a recent review found that 5% expressed gender dysphoria, a much higher rate than typically quoted; a few women transitioned from female to male gender (H. F. L. Meyer-Bahlberg et al., 1996).

b. In cAIS, gender change from assigned-female to male is nil (Mazur, 2005): The brain in individuals with cAIS appears to be female.

c. In XY DSD individuals who have been assigned female at birth as their sex-of-rearing but with normal prenatal testosterone effects, gender change from female to male occurred in about 60% (Cohen-Kettenis, 2005; W. Reiner, 2004).

d. In XY DSD individuals with low prenatal testosterone effects, almost all of whom are assigned female at birth as their sex-of-rearing, gender change from female to male occasionally occurs.

PSYCHOPATHOLOGY AND GENDER DYSPHORIA

It appears that children with DSD, as noted in Table 1, have differences from but similarities to those with gender dysphoria. First, newborns with DSD present with a wide variation in genital phenotype, while gender dysphoria, when present, manifests over time. Second, children with gender dysphoria (as discussed in the clinical articles in this issue) and those with DSD

TABLE 1 Androgen effects in DSD and gender dysphoric children

	Androgen exposure	Gender dysphoria	Genital virilization	Brain virilization
XX gender dysphoria	None	Yes	None	Atypical (more male typical)
XY gender dysphoria	Normal	Yes	Normal	Atypical
XX DSD (CAH)	Abnormal but high	Rare	Mixed	Atypical (more male typical)
XY DSD (cAIS)	None	No	None	Female typical
XY DSD (aphallia)	Normal (prenatal)	Frequent, if raised female	Absence of penis	Male typical
XY DSD (mixed T effects)	Abnormal but low for males	Sometimes, if raised female	Mixed	Atypical (more male typical)

XX = female karyotype; XY = male karyotype; DSD = disorders of sex development; CAH = congenital adrenal hyperplasia; cAIS = complete androgen insensitivity syndrome; T = testosterone.

(Ebert, Scheuering, Schott, & Roesch, 2005; W. Reiner & Gearhart, 2006) have developmental vulnerabilities. Third, androgen appears to be at least a probabilistic factor in DSD children who actually identify as male, while being raised female, and in terms of their sexual orientation towards females. It is unlikely that androgen is deterministic, however. First, gender dysphoria in otherwise normal males occurs apparently despite their androgen exposures; second, male homosexuals have high and perhaps normal androgen exposure pre- and postnatally; third, following children clinically who have gender dysphoria, whatever the underlying diagnosis may be, reveals that not all who have experienced elevated prenatal androgen exposures are gender dysphoric when raised or converted to females, or have sexual orientation towards females. Androgen is likely important; presence of a Y chromosome may be important. But they are not sufficient as an etiology.

What, then, about this question of gender dysphoria as a psychopathology? The question has been posed, even if indirectly, within the gender dysphoria workgroup of the *DSM-5* (Zucker, 2010). Similar questions have arisen about gender dysphoria associated with DSD (H. F. L. Meyer-Bahlburg, 2005). Therefore, whether childhood gender dysphoria is similar in etiology, whatever the underlying diagnoses, is important to the question. But first, the issue begs a more fundamental question: what is the essence of a mental disorder (T. R. Insel & Wang, 2010)? This matter is controversial and relevant, even if not yet answerable, as it deals with the clinical foundation of psychiatry, of diagnosis and, therefore, of the entire *DSM* enterprise. It is notable, for example, that diagnostic categories in the *DSM* often fail to match clinical neuroscience and genetic findings (T. Insel et al., 2010; T. R. Insel & Wang, 2010).

A useful illustration for this discussion involves autism spectrum disorders (ASD), first, because a number of recent reports relate comorbidity of ASD with atypical gender representations (de Vries, Noens, Cohen-Kettenis, van Berckelaer-Onnes, & Doreleijers, 2010; Kraemer, Delsignore, Gundelfinger, Schnyder, & Hepp, 2005) and, second, because of the implications of recent etiological studies of autism itself. Now, if autism can be comorbid with gender dysphoria—both being rare conditions—then studies of etiological factors might be relevant to both. Indeed, autism appears to be a set of polygenic disorders likely interacting with multiple prenatal and postnatal environmental factors in complex $G \times E$ interactions—that is, genes and environmental factors interacting in more than simply additive forms (Sebat et al., 2007). The presence of a series of specific DNA errors in individuals with autism varies between individuals with variants of the disorder, suggesting that some of the social, communication, and emotional phenotypic expressions seen in full autism may be expressed only in part in some individuals—that is, if only a few of the DNA errors are present an individual may be prone to less-severe phenotypical expressions.

In fact, such variability in genetic and environmental factors between affected individuals likely explains at least some of the variability in many complex behaviors, including gender dysphoria; that is, not only can ASD and gender dysphoria sometimes be comorbid, but also complex etiological factors may sometimes be present in both—some factors may be shared in some individuals. This might explain the occasional comorbidity of ASD and gender dysphoria. It might be added here that the question of inherent psychopathology is rendered moot because children with gender dysphoria experience unique psychosocial difficulties. Parents take them to the doctor and chief complaints are given, a differential diagnosis is considered, a working diagnosis is chosen. Whether gender dysphoria is pathological by itself, its behavioral manifestations become clinical complaints. These children will be seen.

To further explore the question of gender dysphoria as a psychopathology, we next interject the idea of developmental psychopathology. This somewhat new attribution lends itself to a multidisciplinary field looking at psychopathology developing over the course of childhood. It is, like child development itself, hierarchical in nature; that is, psychopathology develops within a complex set of processes and patterns through constantly interacting genes and environment acting through whatever development—or psychopathology—has already occurred. While further elaboration of this field is beyond the scope of this manuscript, developmental psychopathology is central to this special issue of the *Journal of Homosexuality*.

Let us briefly examine psychopathology in children with DSD. Developmental psychopathology in these children occurs within a rather unusual set of circumstances: anomalous genitalia, parental reactions to the phenotype, surgical experiences, and assignment of sex-of-rearing based on somewhat nebulous criteria with sparse outcome data. Early experiences are quite unique for these children and include body image and genital image issues arising during development. Precisely which experiences initiate psychopathology, and how they interact with precisely which constitutional vulnerabilities, are not clear. Suffice it to say that internalizing disorders, especially depression and anxiety, are quite common in DSD (Ebert et al., 2005; W. Reiner & Gearhart, 2006; W. Reiner, et al., 1999; W. G. Reiner & Gearhart, 2004), but they can be common in gender dysphoria as well. Similarly, body image, genital image, and other psychosexual developmental factors play important roles in both sets of conditions.

CAN DISORDERS OF SEX DEVELOPMENT INFORM OUR UNDERSTANDING OF GENDER DYSPHORIA?

Clearly, some children with XY and a few with XX disorders of sex development are unhappy with their neonatal assigned sex and ultimately change gender. This is true of children with gender dysphoria as well. Nearly all of these gender dysphoric children and the DSD children who change gender appear to experience what was expressed by Edwards-Leeper and Spack (this issue): an experience that may not be a gender change but a recognition of the affirmed gender—that is, an affirmation of a brain that is at odds with the assigned sex-of-rearing. This similarity appears despite profoundly different early life experiences of children in the two groups. What does this mean for the poor, frail clinician, standing alone in his or her clinic with the child patient—and patients these children shall be—but in the face of sparse outcome data for decision making? How can appropriate interventions be determined for that specific child at that specific time?

Certainly, both theoretical and empirical considerations of gender dysphoria in children demand research, at the least because of clinical implications of intervening. Individual and diagnostic group variations can best be explored if clinics pool their population samples, because the diagnoses involved are so rare. Longitudinal studies of such pooled populations, observing individual changes and whether categories of individuals change with time, could inform broad-based neuroscience, genetic, and behavioral research approaches. Qualitative studies of clinical outcomes might provide valuable insights directing later, more technologically sophisticated, quantitative studies.

With such clinic collaboration diagnostic cohorts might be identified etiologically and followed over time. Crossover outcomes within and among groups—such as gender-dysphoria persisters versus desisters, the unfolding of the awareness or recognition of sexual orientation, and how these variables relate—might then be explicable. Developmental considerations of cognitive, personality, psychosexual, and psychosocial development might be correlated to clinical findings including: evidence of prenatal androgen exposure and imprinting of the brain; genomic aberrations; gender identity or sexual orientation; autism spectrum disorders, especially in gender dysphoria persisters versus desisters; other psychiatric comorbidity; patterns of quality of life; and family outcomes. Data mining for appropriate clinical relevance would be a bonus. Finally, educational materials could be developed to accentuate parental understanding of predicted developmental trajectories, along with risks of developmental psychopathology, for a given child.

CONCLUSION

Gender dysphoria has been well defined in the five clinical manuscripts in this special issue of the *Journal of Homosexuality*. Etiological factors have not. Their separate clinical enterprises have been discussed in terms of clinical philosophy, patient assessments, and clinical interventions. But the controversy over gender dysphoria as a developmental psychopathology itself remains. This controversy has many sources: clinicians; patients who have grown up through these clinics; parent support groups; and a variety of transgender adult support groups. There are clinically significant emotional overtones, political overtones, medicalization overtones, and, therefore, ethical overtones.

The first author's experience with a large cohort of children and adults with DSD as well as data from the literature appears to show that children with gender dysphoria and those with DSD experience wildly different early life experiences. Nevertheless, gender dysphoria can appear remarkably similar, at least clinically; that is, in both sets of conditions there appears to be a fundamental recognition of self in contradistinction to the assigned sex of rearing, an affirmation of the sensed, internal gender. Children in both sets of conditions experience developmentally important vulnerabilities for psychopathology, especially in terms of internalizing disorders (depression and anxiety). Just how similar these vulnerabilities are remains to be seen. That gender dysphoria is a psychopathology a priori appears to be challenged by these myriad outcome studies.

The early experiences of the two groups of children are radically different. Additionally, there may be some comorbidity with autism spectrum disorder in the children with gender dysphoria but not those with DSD. Still, despite the differences, the similarities in gender dysphoria as clinical complaints between the two groups is striking. Clearly research into such rare conditions would benefit by pooling resources—the patients themselves. Further, a longitudinal developmental approach—and a developmental psychopathology approach—might prove invaluable: directing research, determining appropriate interventions. Finally, while the similarities in gender phenotype will be useful, the dissimilarities can prove useful for directing research as well, including dissimilarities between XX and XY children with disorders of sex development and between XX and XY children with gender dysphoria.

NOTE

1. A much older, and narrower, term than disorders of sex development, *intersex*, is a set of developmental anomalies primarily indicating neonatal ambiguous genitalia, typically due to inadequate (in the XY fetus) or inappropriate (in the XX fetus) prenatal androgen exposure. The newer nosology is much broader, utilizing the term *disorders of sex development* as the family heading primarily for XX disorders of development and XY disorders of development; this broader conceptualization includes cellular and tissue growth-factor errors, cell migration errors, tissue migration errors, and pelvic field defects, each of them often leading to genital abnormalities but in the absence of hormonal or sex chromosomal anomalies.

Disorders of sex development, then, is a global term that was chosen by an international consensus committee of involved and highly interested experts mostly in the areas of intersex (Hughes, Houk, Ahmed, & Lee, 2006). This committee recognized that expertise itself was generally lacking, especially in terms of global outcomes for individuals or for their diagnostic categories. For several decades, overall clinical or social definitions of intersex were typically inconsistent, nosology was inadequate, and assessments and clinical interventions varied sometimes dramatically from clinic to clinic—not unlike gender dysphoria as a clinical entity over a similar time course. This consensus report, then, was established as a baseline to stimulate more nearly coherent clinical research as well as clinical approaches to these children.

REFERENCES

American Psychiatric Association. (in production). *Diagnostic and statistical manual of mental disorders* (5th ed.). Washington, DC: Author.

Auchus, R. J., Witchel, S. F., Leight, K. R., Aisenberg, J., Azziz, R., Bachega, T. A., et al. (2010). Guidelines for the development of comprehensive care centers for congenital adrenal hyperplasia: Guidance from the CARES Foundation Initiative. *International Journal of Pediatric Endocrinology*, 275213.

Cohen-Kettenis, P. T. (2005). Gender change in 46,XY persons with 5alpha-reductase-2 deficiency and 17beta-hydroxysteroid dehydrogenase-3 deficiency. *Archives of Sexual Behavior, 34*, 399–410.

de Vries, A. L. C., & Cohen-Kettenis, P. T. (this issue). Clinical management of gender dysphoria in children and adolescents: The Dutch approach. *Journal of Homosexuality, 59*, 301–320.

de Vries, A. L., Noens, I. L., Cohen-Kettenis, P. T., van Berckelaer-Onnes, I. A., & Doreleijers, T. A. (2010). Autism spectrum disorders in gender dysphoric children and adolescents. *Journal of Autism Developement & Disorders, 40*, 930–936.

Dessens, A. B., Slijper, F. M., & Drop, S. L. (2005). Gender dysphoria and gender change in chromosomal females with congenital adrenal hyperplasia. *Archives of Sexual Behavior, 34*, 389–397.

Ebert, A., Scheuering, S., Schott, G., & Roesch, W. H. (2005). Psychosocial and psychosexual development in childhood and adolescence within the exstrophy-epispadias complex. *Journal of Urology, 174*, 1094–1098.

Edwards-Leeper, L., & Spack, N. (this issue). Psychological evaluation and medical treatment of transgender youth in an interdisciplinary "gender management service" (GeMS) in a major pediatric center. *Journal of Homosexuality*, *59*, 321–336.

Ehrensaft, D. (this issue). From gender identity disorder to gender identity creativity: True gender self child therapy. *Journal of Homosexuality*, *59*, 337–356.

Hughes, I. A., Houk, C., Ahmed, S. F., & Lee, P. A. (2006). Consensus statement on management of intersex disorders. *Archives of Disease in Childhood*, *91*, 554–563.

Insel, T., Cuthbert, B., Garvey, M., Heinssen, R., Pine, D. S., Quinn, K., et al. (2010). Research domain criteria (RDoC): toward a new classification framework for research on mental disorders. *American Journal of Psychiatry*, *167*, 748–751.

Insel, T. R., & Wang, P. S. (2010). Rethinking mental illness. *Journal of the American Medical Association*, *303*, 1970–1971.

Kraemer, B., Delsignore, A., Gundelfinger, R., Schnyder, U., & Hepp, U. (2005). Comorbidity of Asperger syndrome and gender identity disorder. *European Child & Adolescent Psychiatry*, *14*, 292–296.

Mazur, T. (2005). Gender dysphoria and gender change in androgen insensitivity or micropenis. *Archives of Sexual Behavior*, *34*, 411–421.

Menvielle, E. (this issue). A comprehensive program for children with gender variant behaviors and gender identity disorders. *Journal of Homosexuality*, *59*, 357–368.

Meyer-Bahlberg, H. F. L., Gruen, R. S., New, M. I., Bell, J. J., Morishima, A., Shimshi, M., et al. (1996). Gender change from female to male in classical conginital adrenal hyperplasia. *Hormones and Behavior*, *30*, 319–332.

Meyer-Bahlburg, H. F. (2005). Introduction: gender dysphoria and gender change in persons with intersexuality. *Archives of Sexual Behavior*, *34*, 371–373.

Reiner, W. (2004). Psychosexual development in genetic males assigned female: the cloacal exstrophy experience. *Child and Adolescent Psychiatric Clinics of North America*, *13*, 657–674.

Reiner, W., & Gearhart, J. (2006). Anxiety disorders in children with epispadias-exstrophy. *Urology*, *68*, 172–174.

Reiner, W., Gearhart, J., & Jeffs, R. (1999). Psychosexual dysfunction in males with genital anomalies: Late adolescence, tanner stages IV to VI. *Journal of the American Academy of Child and Adolescent Psychology*, *38*, 865–872.

Reiner, W. G. (2005). Gender identity and sex-of-rearing in children with disorders of sexual differentiation. *Journal of Pediatric Endocrinology*, *18*, 549–553.

Reiner, W. G., & Gearhart, J. P. (2004). Discordant sexual identity in some genetic males with cloacal exstrophy assigned to female sex at birth. *New England Journal of Medicine*, *35*, 333–341.

Ruble, D. N., Martin, C.L., Berenbaum S.A. (2006). Gender development. In N. Eisenberg (Ed.), *Handbook of child psychology* (6th ed., Vol. 3, pp. 858–932). Hoboken, NJ: John Wiley and Sons.

Schaeffer, T. L., Tryggestad, J. B., Mallappa, A., Hanna, A. E., Krishnan, S., Chernausek, S. D., et al. (2010). An evidence-based model of multidisciplinary care for patients and families affected by classical congenital adrenal hyperplasia due to 21-hydroxylase deficiency. *International Journal of Pediatric Endocrinology*, 692439.

Sebat, J., Lakshmi, B., Malhotra, D., Troge, J., Lese-Martin, C., Walsh, T., et al. (2007). Strong association of de novo copy number mutations with autism. *Science*, *316*, 445–449.

Zucker, K. J. (2010). Reports from the DSM-V Work Group on sexual and gender identity disorders. *Archives of Sexual Behavior*, *39*, 217–220.

Zucker, K. J., Bradley, S. J., Sullivan, C. B., Kuksis, M., Birkenfeld-Adams, A., & Mitchell, J. N. (1993). A gender identity interview for children. *Journal of Personality Assessment*, *61*, 443–456.

Apples to Committee Consensus: The Challenge of Gender Identity Classification

DAVID C. RETTEW, MD

*University of Vermont, College of Medicine,
Department of Psychiatry, Burlington, Vermont, USA*

The debate surrounding the inclusion of gender dysphoria/gender variant behavior (GD/GV) as a psychiatric diagnosis exposes many of the fundamental shortcomings and inconsistencies of our current diagnostic classification system. Proposals raised by the authors of this special issue, including basing diagnosis on cause rather than overt behavior, reclassifying GD/GV behavior as a physical rather than mental condition, and basing diagnosis on impairment or distress, offer some solutions but have limitations themselves given the available database. In contrast to most accepted psychiatric conditions where emphasis is placed on ultimately changing internal thoughts, feelings, and behaviors, consensus treatment for most GD/GV individuals, at least from adolescence onward, focuses on modifying the external body and external environment to maximize positive outcomes. This series of articles illustrating the diversity of opinions on when and if gender incongruence should be considered pathological reflects the relative lack of scientific indicators of disease in this area, similar to many other domains of mental functioning.

This special issue of the *Journal of Homosexuality*, devoted to the conceptualization of gender dysphoric/gender variant (GD/GV) behavior in children, is a bold and productive effort to understand and help those who perceive a fundamental mismatch between the sex of their external body and their mind. The articles that form the basis of this discussion come from noted experts across the world who work with GD/GV individuals in a number of different capacities and approach the question from different perspectives. The following discussion will be influenced not from overwhelming expertise or experience in working extensively with GD/GV individuals but from my research and interest in child temperament and personality and related questions pertaining to the boundaries between what is categorized as normal versus pathological (Rettew, 2009).

The current debate regarding if or when GD/GV behavior should be considered disordered exquisitely exposes many of the fundamental flaws in our diagnostic system based on the *Diagnostic and Statistical Manual of Mental Disorders* (*DSM-IV-TR*; American Psychiatric Association, 2000). This statement is not meant as an assault on the hardworking scholars who are trying their best to bring order and definition to the broad array of emotional and behavioral problems, but more as an acknowledgment that our field's understanding of the precise neurobiological mechanisms of thoughts, emotions, and behavior and the natural boundaries between variation and illness remain in its infancy (Althoff & Waterman, 2011). The challenge of judging whether or not GD/GV behavior should be considered a disorder is, thus, rendered very difficult by the lack of definitive markers or even principles that define mental illness.

According to *DSM-IV-TR* (APA, 2000), a mental disorder is conceptualized as a clinically "significant behavioral or psychological syndrome or pattern that occurs in an individual and is associated with present distress (e.g., a painful symptom) or disability (i.e. impairment in one or more important areas of functioning) or with a significantly increased risk of suffering death, pain, disability, or an important loss of freedom." The text further explains that the behavior "must not be merely an expectable and culturally sanctioned response to a particular event" and must be considered to be "a manifestation of a behavioral, psychological, or biological dysfunction (p. xxxi)." Contained in this definition are a number of key words such as distress and dsyfunction that are open to a great deal of interpretation. Distress caused by the inherent properties of the behavior or due to a lack of acceptance by a rigid society? Dsyfunction as defined by the presence of something detectible and qualitatively different that does not belong or from crossing some arbitrarily defined threshold along a general continuum?

The vacuum created by the absence of solid scientific benchmarks for mental illness allows other factors to move in, including aspects of society, convention, precedent, and even economics. One unique aspect of the controversy regarding retention of adult gender identity disorder (GID) in the *DSM* (presently proposed to be renamed as *Gender Dysphoria*) as well as the forthcoming eleventh edition of the International Classification of Disease (ICD-11) is that medical care would often be more intensive and more expensive for many people in the absence of a defined disease. Indeed, a common concern for removing the diagnosis of GID and related constructs would be that hormonal and surgical procedures used to realign one's assigned and affirmed gender might no longer be covered by medical insurance (Drescher, 2010). While a valid worry in its own right, the fact that this aspect can carry such weight in what should be a scientific investigation illustrates the degree to which the community is unable to base the discussion on purely empirical grounds.

The articles that this issue brings together deserve attention. It is interesting to note that the vast majority of them express more nuanced viewpoints on the central question of whether or not GD/GV behavior should be considered a disorder rather than a blanket opinion for all instances. Each article also brings out different points for discussion that will be considered in turn.

DIAGNOSIS BASED ON PERCEIVED CAUSE

Ehrensaft (this issue) describes her practice of utilizing True Gender Self Therapy (TGST) techniques as part of a facilitative process that encourages each child to find their authentic gender that exists along a natural continuum. Ehrensaft contends that there is nothing at all inherently disordered in gender nonconforming youth and that, for most individuals, maximal mental health is achieved when the child is encouraged by others to express their gender as they feel it. At the same time, however, Ehrensaft acknowledges cases in which gender incongruence is an outcome of a more problematic process and proposes the diagnosis of gender dysphoria in these instances.

In so many ways, diagnosis based on cause and not just outward behavior makes extraordinary sense. Yet, as reasonable and important as this distinction may be between youth whose gender incongruence is an authentic expression of self versus a reaction to other developmental struggles, such an effort would likely prove extremely difficult and subjective given the field's lack of understanding regarding the specific processes involved in the development of gender identity. In addition, the requirement of a specific cause to qualify for a *DSM* diagnosis would represent a significant departure from the current system that has attempted to base diagnoses on overt or reported symptoms and not on what determined them (with exception to the "due to a medical condition" clause). Further, a gender dysphoria diagnosis keeps the diagnosis in a gender identity category, suggesting that what is disordered is the gender incongruence itself rather than using something like *adjustment disorder with disturbance in gender identity*. As a comparison, there are likely some individuals (both heterosexual and homosexual) whose sexual orientation is a source of anguish and is, at least in part, the result of more negative developmental processes. This point was the rationale for including a diagnosis of Ego-Dystonic Homosexuality in the *DSM-III*. Lack of support for its empirical basis led to its removal from the *DSM-III-R* in 1987 (Drescher, 2010), and there seems to be little momentum scientifically to bring that diagnosis back. Of note, however, the diagnostic category still persists in the ICD-10 as Ego-Dystonic Sexual Orientation.

Thus, the current convention of basing diagnoses on symptoms rather than cause is certainly unsatisfying to many. In other areas of medicine, classification of disease is frequently made on the basis of cause such as inflammation or infection. Such a system in mental health is a laudable goal but seems unrealistic at this point given the current state of knowledge. As such, there seems no shortcut around the need to make a judgment of whether or not GD/GV thoughts and behaviors qualify, in and of themselves, as symptoms.

DISORDERS AS EXTREMES OF A CONTINUUM

The previous statement arguing for a need to make a decision about the place of gender incongruence as a legitimate symptom in no way, however, compels the authors of the *DSM-5* to make a judgment about all GD/GV behavior. Menvielle's (this issue) article describes his belief, shared by many other authors in this issue, that while gender variance is not pathological per se, there is a need both in assessments and interventions to take into account fully the broad spectrum of gender identity when making recommendations to children and families.

Research into the quantitative nature of behavior has shown conclusively that, despite the *DSM*'s binary yes-or-no classification structure of disease versus no disease, nearly every type of core behavior that is encountered in the *DSM* exists along a continuum (Rettew, 2009). Symptoms of Attention Deficit Hyperactivity Disorder (ADHD), anxiety, mood, and even more medical sounding entities such as autism exist in the population along a wide range (Constantino & Todd, 2003). Indeed, many of the most common nonpsychiatric diagnoses such as hypertension and hyperlipidemia exist that way as well. In all of these cases, what is being described as a disorder is not the behavior or emotion itself but having excessively high levels of it. Anxiety, for example, is extremely adaptive and is likely responsible for keeping our species alive. The diagnosis of Generalized Anxiety Disorder comes into play only when the level of anxiety is sufficiently high enough as to cause significant problems.

A vital piece of information that remains unknown for most of these spectra is whether or not the biological mechanisms that underlie one person having a moderate or trait amount of that dimension are shared, but amplified, with those who have a clinical levels of that dimension. Intelligence, for example, clearly works along a continuum, but that fact does not negate the existence of discrete etiological factors, such as trisomy 21, that underlie some people who are at the extreme end of that spectrum. Such discrete causal factors have been hard to find among most individuals who exhibit even more extreme levels of anxiety, inattention, and mood, yet a lack of such evidence is not used to discount the validity of these diagnoses.

A similar system seems to be proposed for *DSM-5* Gender Dysphoria (www.dsm5.org) in that the underlying trait of gender identity is not viewed as inherently pathological but can be so in more extreme form. Indeed there appears to be an effort in the criteria to raise the bar somewhat to allow for greater levels of GD/GV to be assessed as nonpathological. Such a model challenges clinicians with then trying to find the appropriate boundary between what is considered a trait and what is considered a disorder. As is true for many other definitions of psychopathology, the principle distinction proposed here between disorder and nondisorder has to do with distress and impairment. Along these lines, someone could be aware of feelings of gender incongruence, but in the absence of clinically significant distress or impairment, there is no disorder. As tidy as the impairment distinction sounds, however, evidence has shown that impairment itself is dimensional in nature. Studies in mood disorders, for example, have shown that while individuals who meet criteria for full Major Depressive Disorder indeed have substantial life impairment, those who have subthreshold symptoms suffer real impairment as well (Judd et al., 2003). Further, the issue of distress with regard to children and adolescents is complicated further by the question of impairment to whom? Many behaviors manifested by children do not bother them a bit but certainly are viewed as impairing to other individuals such as parents or teachers. This situation certainly appears to be true with many GD/GV children.

MEDICAL VERSUS MENTAL DISORDERS

Arguably one of the crowning achievements of the modern age of mental health is the slow progress that is finally being made in getting the public to understand psychiatric illnesses as brain-based conditions that are fundamentally no different than other types of nonpsychiatric illnesses. Nonetheless, the archaic mind versus body debates have proven to be remarkably tenacious in the face of overwhelming scientific evidence and are a major source of the significant stigma that persists against people who struggle with emotional and behavioral problems. From this perspective, it seems an understandable but misguided effort to advocate that GID or gender dysphoria be understood as some kind of physical disorder separate from other brain functions. A potentially more scientifically valid concep-tualization may emphasize the mismatch between the brain-based gender identity and one's bodily characteristics. Such a view would preserve the logical desire to bring one's body into alignment with one's affirmed gender without diminishing brain function as being "nonphysical."

Edwards-Leeper and Spack (this issue) discuss the assessment and care of transgender youth from the perspective of large pediatric hospital based clinic. Perhaps due to the perspective of coming from a large tertiary hos-pital, terms such as *patient* or *diagnosis* or *treatment* are used freely and divorced from some of the negative connotations that others may associate with them. The authors describe in detail the comprehensive and compas-sionate process that goes into the decision of beginning hormonal treatment in adolescence. The authors appear quite comfortable with the notion of GID as a diagnosis apart from their statement that it should be seen as a physical rather than mental condition and despite their finding that many youth are cured of depression and other disorders once medical intervention for their gender dysphoria is completed.

This article features the interesting juxtaposition of a clinic that is one of the few places willing to follow the wishes of gender dysphoric adolescents and use hormonal treatment while at the same time doing so in a more con-ventional medical model of GID as a true diagnosis. The combination may rest on the previously mentioned economic concern that procedures such as hormonal treatment might be seen in the same light as cosmetic surgery if there were no diagnosis behind the intervention. This concern seems quite legitimate and realistic although there are certainly other areas of medicine such as obstetrics where nonpathological medical care is covered (Drescher 2010). The solution, however, should lie in further efforts to educate and oversee the insurance industry rather than retreating back into old notions of mind body dualism.

DOES IMPROVEMENT IMPLY DIAGNOSIS?

The article by de Vries and Cohen-Kettenis (this issue) describes their pio-neering clinic in the Netherlands and their work that includes younger children. The authors carefully articulate their goals of a balanced approach to younger children with gender dysphoria that includes both acceptance of the thoughts and behaviors but also hesitation in some cases to embrace the full gender transition that some children want. The authors state that for adolescents to be eligible for hormonal treatment, they must be diag-nosed with GID but at the same time be free of "psychological problems *other* [italics added] than the gender dysphoria" (p. 312). The authors report their experience that individuals who have completed gender reassignment under these conditions generally are functioning well and have experienced a decrease in depressive and other psychological symptoms, an observation noted by other special issue's authors as well.

The question then is, what, if anything, do these positive outcomes with hormonal treatment and gender reassignment imply about the overall debate? On the one hand, it could be argued that the improved adaptation that occurs in the absence of changing the core belief about one's assigned gender reaffirms the contention that there was no intrinsic psychological disorder in the first place. Such reasoning, however, could be applied elsewhere. The source of psychological pain and decreased self-worth of many children with poor attention skills could likely be significantly improved by changing the school and home environment so that the children are not made to feel inferior about their differences. Indeed, the need for care that focuses more broadly on the entire environment of children (parenting behavior and attitudes, media habits, school policies, sibling and peer behavior) has been argued quite convincingly in general (Hudziak, 2008; Rettew et al., 2011). In these contexts, however, the necessity for these types of interventions is rarely used as evidence to refute the validity of a diagnosis any more than normal glucose levels are used to refute the diagnosis of diabetes in an individual with good dietary habits.

GENDER IDENTITY AND TEMPERAMENT

There are some important parallels between the issues being examined in this special issue and temperament. Temperament is not in and of itself considered to be pathological, yet, it can be associated with significant emotional distress particularly when paired with unsupportive environments. Even in the absence of an overtly hostile environment, individuals may or may not want to change their behavior, such as a shy child uncomfortable in many social situations.

Zucker and colleagues (this issue) diligently try to answer each of the editors' challenging questions in discussing their approach to families with gender variant youth. In outlining the origins of gender identity, the authors explicitly describe investigations in temperament that have shown differences between GD/GV and non-GD/GV children such as activity levels that tend to be more similar to the affirmed rather than assigned gender. Gender dysphoria is then described as a phenomenon resulting from a sort of cognitive dissonance in which a child builds an explanation on their developmental level to explain the feelings and behaviors they see in themselves. This process could be accentuated in children who tend to think more concretely such as those with autistic spectrum disorders. In contrast to some of the other authors, there is greater emphasis paid to genetic and psychodynamic factors possibly underlying GID relative to individuals who arrive at their gender dysphoria through a more healthy self-actualization process as described by, for example, Ehrensaft (this issue). The authors also seem to be more comfortable with actively trying to reduce gender incongruent behavior in younger children if that is according to the parent's desires. This position may be based on their assessment of the psychosocial outcome of many GID children being less rosy than what is described by some of the other researchers. It is tempting to speculate here that many of the case examples noted in the Zucker et al. article would likely not have passed the screenings from other centers to be eligible for hormonal treatment and surgical reassignment due to the presence of significant individual and family turmoil. These individuals may consequently not be included in other centers' follow-up studies.

The authors explicitly point out that they do not view homosexuality as a disorder, and do not see the prevention of homosexuality as a treatment goal. While these points are important, it would then certainly be of interest to hear the authors' perspective regarding the essential features that lead them to conceptualize gender identity as a valid subject for a diagnosis while sexual orientation is not.

CONCLUSIONS

The articles contained in this special issue compile a tremendous amount of experience and expertise on how to understand gender identity and how to facilitate individuals with GD/GV behavior to lead happy and productive lives. There appears to be strong consensus that efforts to maximize outcomes should be devoted not only to the individual but also to an environment that can be confused, stigmatizing, and, at times, overtly hostile. There is general agreement that gender identity is formed from many different factors ranging from more abnormal internal conflicts to healthy developmental journeys. Finally, there is an increasing appreciation that from adolescence onward gender identity remains a relatively fixed part of one's self perception.

What seems most unresolved and most avoided in these scientific discussions is whether gender incongruence, in its persistent and pervasive form, should qualify as a psychiatric diagnosis. As a relative outsider to this area, it seems apparent at least from this group of articles that the conceptualization of GID or Gender Dysphoria as a diagnosis, especially among those whose feelings are intense and stable enough to drive the desire for hormonal suppression and gender reassignment, is not particularly objectionable to many of the professionals working with these youth and their families. The bulk of the diagnosis removal energy, rather, comes from the LGBT community itself in a desire to be accepted rather than treated. As "treatment" for adolescents and adults is currently defined as changing the body to fit the brain in contrast to other mental health treatments in which the targets of treatment are the thoughts, emotions, and behaviors themselves, the scientific argument outlining the rationale for the inherent pathology of gender incongruence, particularly in the context of homosexuality being "settled law" with regards to being a variant of normal human functioning, has yet to be made. The problem is that it has not been made that well for many other diagnoses either. Neuroscience in 2012 has progressed impressively over the past decades, and, yet, questions regarding what constitutes normal and pathological brain functioning remain unanswered at some of the most basic levels. As clinicians and scientists, we owe it to our patients and clients not to be satisfied with diagnostic labels that lack substance or meaning and to remember that suffering, whatever it is officially called, still hurts.

REFERENCES

Althoff, R. R., & Waterman, G. S. Psychiatric training for physicians: A call to modernize. (2011). *Academic Medicine, 86*, 285–287.

American Psychiatric Association. (2000). *Diagnostic and statistical manual of mental disorders* (4th ed., text rev.). Washington, DC: Author.

Constantino, J. N., & Todd, R. D. (2003). Autistic traits in the general population: A twin study. *Archives of General Psychiatry, 60*, 524–530.

de Vries, A. L. C., & Cohen-Kettenis, P.T. (this issue). Clinical management of gender dysphoria in children and adolescents: the Dutch approach. *Journal of Homosexuality, 59*, 301–320.

Drescher J. (2010). Queer diagnoses: parallels and contrasts in the history of homosexuality, gender variance, and the diagnostic and statistical manual. *Archives of Sexual Behavior, 39*, 427–460.

Edwards-Leeper, L., & Spack, N.P. (this issue). Psychological evaluation and medical treatment of transgender youth in an interdisciplinary "gender management service" (GeMS) in a major pediatric center. *Journal of Homosexuality, 59*, 321–336.

Ehrensaft, D. (this issue). From gender identity disorder to gender identity creativity: True gender self child therapy. *Journal of Homosexuality, 59*, 337–356.

Hudziak, J. J. (2008). Genetic and environmental influences on wellness, resilience, and psychopathology: A family-based approach for promotion, prevention, and intervention. In J. J. Hudziak (Ed.), *Developmental psychopathology and wellness: Genetic and environmental influences* (pp. 267–286). Washington DC: American Psychiatric Publishing.

Judd, L. L., Schettler, P. J., & Akiskal H. S. (2002). The prevalence, clinical relevance, and public health significance of subthreshold depression. *Psychiatric Clinics of North America, 4*, 685–698.

Menvielle, E. (this issue). A comprehensive program for children with gender variant and gender identity disorders. *Journal of Homosexuality, 59*, 357–368.

Rettew, D. C. (2009). Temperament: Risk and protective factors for child psychiatric disorders. In B. J. Sadock, V.A. Sadock, & P. Ruiz (Eds.), *Kaplan and Sadock's comprehensive textbook of psychiatry* (9th ed., pp. 3432–3443). Philadelphia, PA: Lippincott Williams & Wilkins.

Rettew, D. C., DiRuocco L., Ivanova, M., & Hudziak J. (2011). *The Vermont family based approach: A new teaching model for child psychiatry assessments.* Poster presented in March at the annual meeting of the American Association of Directors in Residency Training, Austin, TX.

Zucker, K. J., Wood, H., Singh, D., & Bradley, S.J. (this issue). A developmental, biopsychosocial model for the treatment of children with gender identity disorder. *Journal of Homosexuality, 59,* 369–397.

Listening to Children Imagining Gender: Observing the Inflation of an Idea

DAVID SCHWARTZ, PhD

Private Practice, Westchester and New York,
New York, USA

Using three of the clinical articles in this special issue of the Journal of Homosexuality *as examples, the author attempts to show how their views of gender may influence clinicians' conceptualizations and treatment choices in response to children diagnosed with gender identity disorder (GID), or gender dysphoria. In particular the author argues that the belief that gender is a psychophysiological entity that is organismic and transhistorical, that is, the view known lately as essentialism, promotes more invasive interventions (e.g., endocrinological and surgical) and mistakenly deemphasizes psychological therapies as a clinical response to the suffering of trans children. He tries to show that the drawbacks of essentialism and its correlated treatment approaches are twofold, that a) they promote treatments with insufficient attention to our limited knowledge regarding their safety and efficacy, and b) they advance a reified differentiation of the genders that is politically problematic. The author suggests that a better response to trans children would be one that emphasizes the child's broadly subjective role in his or her construction of transgressive, gender-related psychological and interpersonal phenomena (both painful and not), thus, offering a deeper validation for trans children's challenges to our gender system.*

I am disquieted and stimulated by my mediated encounter with the children, parents, and clinicians represented in these clinical articles.

The children have a deeply felt complaint, expressed explicitly or indirectly through the disruptions they inevitably provoke. They say they are unhappy with being named, classified, and treated in accord with the match between their visible genitalia and the prevalent set of conventions regarding those genitalia. For them, gender has become preoccupying. They are pained within this preoccupation and have formulated a solution to their pain about which they are surprisingly unambivalent, considering the almost universal antipathy with which it (their solution) tends to be greeted. They seem oddly unaware of the outlandishness of their defiant desires, even beyond the unselfconsciousness that might be expected for their ages: they offer their improbable and impossible self-perceptions and wishes boldly.

The parents seem to be trying to catch up with terribly surprising news, with varying degrees of success. They are frightened, frustrated, freaked out, and, finally, defeated, as they are forced to relinquish a cherished perception. Their particular defensive configurations vary (guilt, despair, anger, embrace), but all face extreme intrapsychic disruption and pain.

The clinicians try to make this child/parent/symptom matrix fit into a model of liberal psychiatric treatment. As is common in the medical sciences, most push against ambiguity, preferring to emphasize speculative generalizations ("genetics is likely a factor") instead of highlighting the lack of data from controlled studies. All seem acutely aware that they are in difficult waters, politically and scientifically. They try hard to accommodate the many conflicting pressures under which they labor: the child's suffering, the parents' suffering, cultural imperatives, political forces, and their own training, formal and informal.

I, privileged to be an outside the fray (though not disinterested) observer, hear something unsaid or at least not clearly articulated, that is sporadically discernible among the three groups of subjects. Each, in different ways, gives signs of trouble—psychological, political, and epistemological. Listening with the ears of a deviant psychoanalyst, admittedly eager to see gender troubled, I think I hear echoing themes representing unarticulated desires and conflicts. I hopefully imagine that these themes may prove pertinent to understanding trans children,[1] and as important to me, to understanding better what may be involved in the pursuit of sexual equality (in the broadest sense), since these children seem to me to be involved in that pursuit. Before I try to articulate these themes and point to their particular manifestations, I offer a word on methodology.

Clinical articles are usually designed to tell the reader something about an encounter between an agent of medicine and a seeker of help. In particular, they are written to show the reader something about the methods of the clinician, usually to support those methods and the theorizations on which they are based. Only secondarily, if at all, do they attempt to render the patient as person. The articles which my colleagues and I are discussing are about people—children and parents—and, yet, they are more than usually remote from a phenomenology of the patients and families whose treatments are described. This is because, as per the instructions of the editors, they principally give us protocols, that is, approaches to diagnosis and treatment planning, only supplemented by abbreviated case material. Paradoxically, this is a situation where a felt sense of the patients (and their parents)—their personalities and idiosyncratic styles—is more than usually important (really crucial) to achieving a grasp of this particular psychosocial situation. After all, trans children purport to be representing something about their very state of being; they do not see themselves as troubled by a transient condition, like a depressed mood or an obsessional habit. Their parents tend ultimately to concur that their children's problems are truly existential, even though they may wish it were not so, and seek help in the offices of medical practitioners, not of clerics or even of psychoanalysts, where the soul and mind are addressed, respectively. Their therapists, as represented in the present articles, vary in their degree of concurrence with the existential claim.

Regardless of whether we discussants finally agree to the trans child's claim of existential difference, should we not at least include experiential dimensions—both of the subject and of the observer—in our effort to apprehend them? It is not surprising that the clinical articles are largely without phenomenological data about the children, since the editors' requests did not explicitly ask for that sort of material. But surely something will be missed if no attention is given to the expressive and qualitative aspects of these children. Imagine how they might react years from today upon reading these articles. Beyond the likelihood that they would take offense at their objectification, many might also feel that their efforts to communicate had been missed. So, as I began to compose my thoughts for my own article, it became apparent to me that without some less mediated contact with these children and their parents, my apprehension of all this was going to be handicapped, if not systematically distorted. By way of remedy, I did the obvious: I googled. I was, thus, able to view several videos of trans children. They were taken from television news shows, such as those featuring Barbara Walters and Lisa Ling. They featured interviews and candid filming of trans children, their parents, siblings, and, occasionally, their clinicians. It is worth noting here that the methodological sequence I describe is literal: I did not seek films of trans kids until I had read the clinical articles. The internal gap I experienced motivated me to want to see them.

Of course, I do not imagine that I now have objective data, or am equipped to contest controlled research findings. But I have, if only to some limited degree, heard a bit of the children's point of view, seen them represent themselves, watched some parents react and offer their own understandings, and glimpsed the clinicians at work, all albeit, through the literal lens of mainstream journalism, but at least enacted by all three groups of subjects themselves. These perceptions, in turn, have mingled with my personal schemata of gender and authority and with my psycho-analytic imagination. In addition, I have had brief clinical contact with three trans adolescents and have heard some descriptions by other psychoanalytic clinicians.

THE CHILDREN

The two characteristics of the trans girls that were most striking to me through the videos and the articles were 1) their expressed certainty and determination about their true gender, and 2) the stereotypy of their gender performances.

The pointed representation of certainty on the part of the trans girls shows itself directly, expressed by the children themselves, and indirectly, channeled through the parents and clinicians. When asked by television interviewers if they had any doubt about truly being a girl, rapidly and seem-ingly without thought, came the emphatic reply: "No." Parents frequently sought medical help after their efforts and some degree of social ostracism failed to dissuade a child from active pursuit of cross-gender behavior and identity. "This child would not give up," and "life was a daily battle [over clothing and hair]" were some of the phrases heard on the videos. Parents expressed anxiety about an implicit danger of suicide, and expressed with resignation that they were "lucky it was only this." Did the trans girls know of the degree of their impact on their parents, that is, did they receive any enhanced sense of power? I cannot know this, but my impression was yes. Children listen and learn.

The trans girls' gender performances themselves had a stereotypy that left me feeling that they were not representing themselves as actual female children, but rather as arch and whimsical hyperboles of adult women's styles, or even urgent efforts to persuade the other of their femaleness. They are frequently shown expressing a stereotypical preference for pink. Images of flamboyant, narcissistically toned dancing were frequent in the videos— chosen by the filmmaker, no doubt, but enthusiastically executed by the children with parental cooperation. Scenes of trans girls excitedly selecting girl's clothing or getting their hair styled had an eerie feeling of being made to persuade. Of course it is possible that this is chiefly an artifact of film making, but the collaboratively expressed enthusiasm of parent and child seemed to belie that possibility.

In more general phenomenological terms, the trans girls seemed to me to be struggling, to be internally busy. Their insistent demand that adults accept and materially aid their non-conforming self-portrayals felt like plead-ing for authoritative ratifications of solutions they themselves doubted. The intensity of the demands—they tended to literally strike fear in the hearts of parents—left me imagining a terrible sense of weakness, or even impotence, on the part of the children, but an impotence that these children were refusing to accept.

The phenomenology of the trans boys was different. They felt to me more purposeful and reflective, less expressive, and interpersonally active. At times they seemed sheepish, as if modest about an achievement. It could be said that these are merely some culturally consistent attributes of newly acquired masculinity. It did not feel that way. Their message seemed more sober and they seemed more content. Their performances seemed smoother.

THE PARENTS

The most poignant emotion the mothers of trans children left me with was grief. Something cherished had been lost, and it was a loss that it behooved a mother to accept and transcend. These mothers wept with pointed bravery, which is to say with no hint of self-pity. They would not be daunted in their love for their "new" child, but neither would they forget the first child, now seemingly lost. Interestingly none seemed especially aware that their "first" child would likely return, since most trans kids ultimately desist in their gender nonconformity. Indeed, it was surprising to me how little this fact was highlighted (with the exception of Zucker, Wood, Singh, & Bradley, this issue). No filmed parent mentioned it. Surely an emphasis on that probability might have ameliorated their pain and grief, and the necessity for such manifest courage.

The fathers seemed gripped by barely concealed anxiety. Their frozen smiles were in contrast to the mothers' open distress. They seemed to say that the tragedy belonged to their wives, whom they would support unflinchingly.

THE CLINICAL ARTICLES (OR, REALLY, THE CLINICIANS)

For me, the most important task with respect to the articles is to illuminate the unarticulated assumptions and unconscious communications that they make to patients, parents and readers. In other words, embedded in the assessment and treatment protocols, and evident in the specific recommendations made to parents, are theoretical beliefs that are taken-for-granted, and woven into the very language of the clinicians. It is this unspoken material, differing subtly from article to article—in effect a set of varying theoretical assumptions (truisms, really) about human nature—that is most significant to understanding the psychocultural matrix that is here represented.

The superordinate and most significant unstated assumption is that gender, as an organismic condition, not only as a social psychological interpretation of a genital configuration, is real. In its strongest form this assumption states that gender is not only a subjectivity, but is an objective condition of every human, the observable nature of which is independent of external situations. Furthermore, while the subjective experience of gender and its representations may be influenced by culture, its underlying nature is not. It then follows that, even if it is granted that gender's development in a given individual is affected by environmental conditions, including culture, its operation in any given moment is a function of some interplay between the individual's physiology and psychology, not his or her external situation. Thus, gender comes from within the body and is discoverable. From this point of view, the modification of gender often entails surgical or endocrinological intervention, not mere behavioral change. It is only secondarily a performance.

The reply might be that of course the reality, stability, and unity of gender is assumed in these articles; it is assumed most everywhere in human discourse, be it colloquial, medical, or scholarly, and, therefore, this is unremarkable. But among the people about whom these articles speak, gender is at issue: Its existential nature, including its source, modifiability, and location, are under scrutiny and contested, albeit, by children. These children, through their complaints and insistences, are making claims about gender that push, however ambivalently, against the assumption of real gender as articulated above. Consider this: Some of them are saying, in words or deeds, that their gender can be modified through an act of the will, or, that despite the absence of any pertinent physical change, their gender has changed, observably to them if not to their doctors and parents. Most deny any correspondence between their anatomy and physiology (of course, most particularly their natal genitalia) on the one hand and their self-affirmed genders on the other. This assumed mutability of gender, of which they propose to avail themselves, is way out of line with stable gender as written about in most of these articles.

By contrast, the superficial logic of the trans children's claims often comports well with the conventional discourse of essential gender, which, for the most part is present in most of the clinical articles. For example, they proclaim which gender they really are, purporting to describe intransigent inner conditions, and pressing for accommodation by their social environment in the strongest terms possible. At least in form this self-narration is very much in line with an acceptance of essential gender as described above—a material condition that requires a material response. Yet, this is a significantly limited acceptance of conventional gender. The words the children use to talk about their genders sound as if it is a psychophysiological reality, but their actions—impassioned demands for the other to recognize them in accordance with their own rules—and hopefully expressed desires to be something they are not, make of gender a plaything controllable by its owner, a psychic toy whose operation is entirely up to the child, but for the requested batteries (principally parental and institutional recognition).

It is possible to respond to children in a manner that is either organized around their literal narratives, or around psychological interpretations of those narratives, which themselves take into account such inner contradictions and perplexities as described above. Toward which path the clinician leans may be strongly influenced by the degree to which he or she shares the child's apparent view of gender, that is, holds the assumptions of essential gender, or not. Simply put, if you believe gender is an internal reality, you will likely be guided or motivated to accept a literal hearing of the child's narrative, since it matches that view. The child's self-presentation may then seem straightforwardly comprehensible enough to guide you in clinical decision making. On the other hand, if your prejudice is to hear any claims about real, inner gender as necessarily—necessarily because you do not believe gender is real in the sense described above—composed of symbolic or metaphoric representations, then the child's story instigates an active interpretive process, and clinical decision making proceeds differently. Contrasting scenarios of clinical responses differentially related to the clinicians' gender assumptions are well illustrated in the five clinical articles. A close look at three of these articles[2] from this perspective will additionally show how assumptions about gender on the part of clinicians is systematically correlated with preferences for some treatment approaches and avoidance of others.

Edwards-Leeper and Spack's article (this issue) shows how a strong commitment to gender as inner reality affects clinical theory and practice. There are in their article numerous subtle examples of that commitment, but the following is fairly unambiguous: " . . . we perceive . . . severe gender dysphoria, cross-gender behavior, and strong identification with the other gender . . . to be a *primary physical rather than psychological condition* [italics added]" (p. 333). While the authors qualify this statement to indicate that they are talking about the more extreme cases of gender dysphoria, they do not deny the implication that normal gender is also physiological, an objective reality of the person's body. Moreover, they object to "insurance denial . . . based on the premise that GID is a mental disorder, rather than a physical one" (p. 323).

Two interrelated aspects of Edwards-Leeper and Spack's article (this issue) stand out for my purposes: a) their advocacy of the alleged advantages of intervention over nonintervention, either in the form of supporting social transitioning or of offering pharmacological puberty suppression, and b) their principally anecdotal defense of this advocacy.

With respect to the advocacy of intervention, Edwards-Leeper and Spack (this issue) say that they "have learned that delaying proper diagnosis can lead to significant psychological consequences" (p. 322). This warning implies that the reliability of diagnosis and associated prognosis in this area has been established, which is the case only for diagnosis, that is, we cannot say reliably what the course will be for a given child with GID or gender dysphoria. In particular, we cannot reliably say whether he or she will persist with an expressed need to be affirmed in his/her non-natal gender, or not. In fact, the majority do not sustain the diagnosis, that is, they *desist*. Given this uncertainty of prognosis, it is significant that Edwards-Leeper and Spack's presentation of the pros and cons of pubertal suppression, a primary intervention in their protocol and their frequent recommendation following diagnosis, is imbalanced. They offer seven physiological benefits to pubertal suppression (for the most part just a list of the physical effects) and no disadvantages. Likewise they tout the psychological advantages, but note no potential disadvantages. Their conclusion is: "Therefore, it is our clinical impression that preventing these unwanted secondary sex characteristics with puberty blocking medical intervention allows for better long-term quality of life for transgender youth than what they would experience without this intervention" (pp. 329–330). The claim of offering "better *long-term* [italics added] quality of life" based on clinical impression only, and absent significant longitudinal experience or controlled data collection, is questionable. Considering that Edwards-Leeper and Spack are advocating a pharmacological intervention aimed at prepubertal children and adolescents, a number of whom are likely to desist, it is surprising and of interest that they so minimize the importance and value of alternative interventions, ones that might have fewer unknown consequences, both physiological and psychological. An alternative sort of intervention would of course be some variety of psychological therapy. Most typically this might include support, reality testing, empathic interpretation and psychoeducation offered to both parents and children. Psychotherapeutic responses to individuals displaying gender (and sexual) nonconformity may have become associated in the minds of some with the right-wing, Christian agenda of so-called reparative therapy. But this latter practice, or any practice[3] that uses an apparently psychotherapeutic situation to foster self-suppression, or aims to replace a child's transgressive psychology with a normative one, is of course, not what I have in mind. In fact, assiduous attention to the danger of inadvertently promoting conformity and suppressing agency when responding psychotherapeutically to a trans child is necessary for by now obvious reasons. One can easily imagine how a conflict among parent, child, and therapist about limiting a particular gendered behavior might be resolved prejudicially in favor of conformity, given the differential power of the parties involved and the adults' natural propensity to want some conformity given the amount of nonconformity with which they have probably been coping.

The intransigent style (cognitive and behavioral) of trans children may deter some clinicians from considering that some of their suffering might be helped without rhetorically opposing their desires or trying to persuade them to relinquish their assertions. I will have more to say about this later, but briefly: The goal of psychotherapy in this situation would be to help the child feel better and offer reality-based guidance for social situations, as well as the prevention of self-harm, in the rare cases where that is an issue. In general, psychotherapy should entail increasing (parents' and children's) self-understanding, not coaxing or pressuring them to change their minds. The disturbing demands and claims of trans children, as well as reports of self-harm (untabulated, to my knowledge) may shock and scare both parents and clinicians into expecting less frustration tolerance from them than is realistic. Such an underestimate of the trans family's resilience may be abetted by the availability of puberty suppressing drugs. Frightened of the onset of puberty, and intimidated by the at times ominous articulations of the children, parents and clinicians are relieved to imagine even a temporary solution.

Edwards-Leeper and Spack's (this issue) usage of anecdotal data concerns me. To counter what they describe as the leeriness of parents with respect to the taking on of transgender identities on the part of adolescents with no prior history of gender dysphoria, they say: "However, many of these adolescents report that their friends are not surprised by their declaration of their affirmed gender, often responding that they had suspected it for some time" (p. 332). We must assume that Edwards-Leeper and Spack are aware that an adolescent's report of other adolescents' validation of a gender identity claim is not credible evidence of more than the first adolescent's desire to persuade. How then are we to understand their inclusion of this anecdotal information? It would seem that natural skepticism has been suspended in favor of literality. Are they trying to highlight the alleged power of essential gender by pointing to its observability by others even before the subject himself or herself has self-awareness? If so, the weakness of an anecdote such as this gives the appearance of a lack of appropriate scientific and psychological skepticism, and inattention to methodology.

Of course the problematic aspects of Edwards-Leeper and Spack's (this issue) article, detailed above, are not necessarily caused by their commitment to essential gender. But they are consistent with it and support it. It is real gender that demands treatment urgently and speaks for itself. When children claim to feel its powerful inner message, they are to be believed with less than the usual scientific skepticism.

Zucker et al.'s (this issue) article contrasts with that of Edwards-Leeper and Spack. Zucker et al. do not express an unambiguous view on the existential status of gender. Instead they offer thinking about particular patients, aspects of gender identity disorder and some theoretical questions, in that order, thus, implicitly leaving the epistemological status of gender as an open, and likely unanswerable question. Their way of addressing theory is well illustrated in the following, in which they respond to the question of whether or not gender identity is fixed in childhood: "For most children, no one tries to alter their gender identity after it is first expressed, for a host of psychological and social reasons. To formally answer the question of whether or not a young child's gender identity is fixed and unalterable, one would have to conduct a randomized psychosocial trial in which, for half the children, some type of intervention was attempted to alter the child's gender identity. It is unlikely that such an "experiment of nurture" would attract many volunteer parent participants" (p. 375). Zucker et al. wittily remind us of a fundamental epistemological fact that is present in all discussions of gender, but which some tend to forget: The research that would be necessary to answer most questions about the origins and nature of gender with any degree of scientific certainty, cannot be done for ethical and technological reasons. Thus, they officially demur on the existential status of gender, which amounts to not making the reifying assumption that Edwards-Leeper and Spack (this issue) (and most others) make.

Three aspects of Zucker et al.'s (this issue) article stand out: 1) their portrayal of the children, 2) their theoretical notion of gender as a "phenotype," emerging out of "biological factors, psychosocial factors, social cognition, associated psychopathology, and psychodynamic mechanisms" (p. 375), and 3) their underlining of one of the few replicated findings about trans children, that a large majority desist in their trans claims and identities during adolescence.

Zucker et al.'s (this issue) descriptions of the children are notable for being phenomenological and psychological. They describe the emotional tone and style of the children's reports. They ask the parents for their own understanding of their child's behavior, and use that information in formulating a psychological understanding of the child's gender peculiarities, which often points them to psychological dimensions besides gender, such as obsessionality and power seeking. In particular, their discussion of symptomatic overlaps between children diagnosed with Asperger's syndrome and children diagnosed with gender identity disorder, questions how frequently gender disturbance is inferred as primary, when cognitive or social pathology may be playing an equal, stronger, or interactive role.

Zucker et al.'s (this issue) conceptualization of gender as a phenotype, quietly, but effectively, dispenses with gender as a separate entity altogether. They carefully discuss each factor that they see as contributory to the epiphenomenon of gender, illustrating each with clinical material. But at the end of this compelling analysis they make no summary conclusion about the existential status of gender. This is either a stroke of rhetorical genius in which they avoid participation in a politically incendiary situation, or admirable modesty. In either case, as we shall see, Zucker et al.'s view of gender is associated with a treatment approach that is quite different from the one associated with the gender-as-physiology view articulated elsewhere.

"The majority of children followed longitudinally appear to 'lose' the diagnosis of GID when seen in late adolescence or young adulthood, and appear to have differentiated a gender identity that matches their natal sex" (Zucker et al., this issue, p. 375). Thus, Zucker et al. remind us of a fact (supported by five research articles going back to1987)[4] that every clinician and parent of a child who is gender dysphoric needs to keep firmly in mind. This fact is mentioned only once in Edwards-Leeper and Spack's (this issue) article. Perhaps this is because their clinic limits its patient population to those on the cusp of puberty and older, a subgroup of trans children many of whom are less likely than the majority of trans children to desist in rejecting their natal gender with time alone. However their description of the recommendations they make to the parents of young trans children, whom they refer out, likewise fails to emphasize the usually short natural life of GID. Their clear emphasis, instead, is on "acceptance of the child's budding gender development," not on considering the simultaneously multiple potential sources of trans children's behavior and experience, and the correlated possibility that the least intervention may be the best. Moreover, Edwards-Leeper and Spack take pride in what they see as their avoidance of the mistakes prior generations of mental health professionals made, in particular when the latter refused to accept gay and lesbian people at their word, sans diagnosis. Indeed, the analogy is tempting, but I would argue, deeply flawed, itself an aspect of the conflation of gender and sexual orientation.

Zucker et al.'s (this issue) treatment approach is quite simple: psychotherapy for the children, counseling and psychotherapy for the parents, medication for any observed psychiatric conditions for which medication is indicated. It is an approach to treatment that need not even mention the term gender. Again, Zucker et al. do not make much of the significance of this. Instead they have quietly diminished the function of real gender in their practice and theory.

At the beginning of this article, I referred to a repetitive unconscious theme that I heard variously represented by the children, parents and clinicians. Of course, the theme I have in mind is about essential gender. Let me try to narrow that down, using the observations offered so far, and material from a third clinical article.

CLINICIANS AGAIN

The two articles I've used for illustration thus far suggest that when clinicians integrate the notion of essential gender into their efforts to respond to trans children, their therapeutic efforts change significantly. With essential gender in mind they are likely to be less psychologically minded and less thorough in their consideration of the cost–benefit ratio of invasive interventions and of research that might militate against their impulses to intervene. To be sure, they are trying to be respectful of and responsive to children's stated wishes. But it seems that beyond that, when child patients talk about their gender, their belief in its reality seems to distract the clinician from the fact that we cannot listen to children in the same way that we listen to adults. Patients' communications always need some degree of interpretation; that is especially true for children, who, necessitated by their cognitive limitations, speak more symbolically. This is why we offer them play therapy. I assume Zucker et al.'s (this issue) inclination to respond to trans children with therapeutic restraint was in part spawned by their recognition of gender as epiphenomenon, but no doubt listening to patients with interpretive ears also helped them to rethink gender. The contrast between Zucker et al. and Edwards-Leeper and Spack (this issue) tells us something important about the risks entailed in the use of the term *gender*. Perhaps aware of the danger of allowing an epiphenomenon, a shorthand term for a convergence of variables, not a thing itself, to guide practice, Zucker et al. are careful to listen, question and prescribe quite apart from it, emphasizing the convergent variables for which it is a shorthand—temperament, cognitive style, behavioral style, and so on. Edwards-Leeper and Spack do something different from Zucker et al.. They assume that gender is a primary physical condition and organize their observation and prescription around what they believe to be the effects of variations in it. Edwards-Leeper and Spack might reply that they have only specified primary physicality for the gender dysphoria syndrome, not for gender in general. But if the pathology of a system is seen as primarily physical, and its recommended treatment is likewise physical, then the system, the disturbance of which constitutes the pathology, is at least significantly, if not predominantly physical. Certainly Edwards-Leeper and Spack do not address or preclude this inference. Reading the articles with these differing stances one gets the dizzying impression of some writers carefully negotiating the dangerously misleading attributions that gender calls forth, while others eagerly deploy them. It would seem that the idea of gender is potent and troublesome. When it is significantly present, choices are made.

Ehrensaft's (this issue) clinical approach is informative here, because she combines aspects of Zucker et al.'s (this issue) psychological approach with aspects of Edwards-Leeper and Spack's essentialism. Ehrensaft's explicit technique, to both help the child with emotional distress and to make recommendations to parents, is empathic listening. But what she is listening for—"the true gender self"—pulls her back toward essentialism and literal listening. The ontological status of "the true gender self" is unclear, since it seems to be both externally real and subjective: it is "the *kernel of gender identity that is there from birth* [italics added], residing within us in a complex of chromosomes, gonads, hormones, hormone receptors, genitalia, secondary sex characteristics, but most importantly *in our brain* [italics added] and mind . . . .its center always remains our own *personal possession* [italics added], driven from within rather than from without" (p. 341). But if the kernel of gender identity is there from birth, it cannot be created. Ehrensaft finds herself accepting without interpretation the child's claim of a real inner structure that must be accommodated externally. It is then no surprise when the clinical process she describes largely lacks a consideration of the psychodynamics of her patient. Ehrensaft tells us that throughout a session to which Brady/Sophie arrived fully dressed as a girl, "[she] kept sucking in her tummy, in an attempt to make herself more girl on top" (p. 351). This child is less than 5 years old. Sucking in her tummy will not make her more girl on top, since little boys and girls are the same on top, which Brady/Sophie surely knows: It will make her more woman, a very different thing. One possible interpretive direction in light of this slip would be that this child is more interested in a ticket to adulthood than a gender change, but for some reason sees being female as a necessary first step. But Ehrensaft makes no mention of the slip to the reader or to the patient, so I assume it eluded her. I wondered if Ehrensaft had not been briefly distracted by a countertransferential process in which the concept of the true gender self promoted an inadvertent collusion with this very bright child's defenses. To be specific, did the prospect of relief from the anxiety of intense inner (and interpersonal) conflict, unconsciously broadcast by the child and received by the therapist make the notion of an anxiolytic true gender self (and anything that goes with it, like wanting breasts) more appealing? If so, was the consequent interpretive process then limited in its imaginative range? Indeed, it seemed to me that the rich and dark constructions of Ehrensaft's patient Brady/Sophie were understated or neutralized in her account. At a point when Brady is given more permission to enact a female persona, the material in the therapy session is strongly inflected with aggression, including the image of Brady's mother feeding Brady's dead male self to the family dog. Ehrensaft sees this as a "creative, albeit gruesome whimsical solution for consolidating a transgender identity" (p. 351). Maybe. Another, I think more parsimonious possibility, would be that there are unarticulated aggressive processes in the family unconsciously perceived by Brady. Seeming empathic acceptance can function to diminish experiences of unconscious conflict and, thus, limit knowledge of a difficult part of the self. This is of course speculation in this case, but with no less foundation than hypothesizing the consolidation of a transgender identity.

Ehrensaft (this issue) does not see the true gender self as speculation. Instead she believes that its therapeutic value is shown in this treatment, as follows. At the conclusion of this patient's treatment, parents and therapist decide that it is best to permit Brady/Sophie to present as a girl at all times.

Sophie (still not 5 years old) proclaims: "I'm the happiest I've ever felt in my life." Ehrensaft furnishes a putative expert statement to the parents, which says in part: "To promote her wellbeing and emotional health, it is imperative that Sophie be seen and treated as a female by her parents, her educational settings, and the community surrounding her" (p. 353). Such certainty in matters so fraught with unforeseeable possibilities including the welfare of a child surprises me. The certainty of the child about her gender is matched by the clinician's certainty about the outcome, both of whom, I suggest, are encouraged by the notion of a true gender found at last. Moreover, I wonder if Ehrensaft has not imagined the inner life of this child, who is rather adult-like in her speech (do 4 year olds commonly speak of "in my life?"), as more adult than it is. This could be for many reasons including, of course, the personality of the child. However, I believe it is easier to be distracted from the childishness of a patient's claims when the terms they use conceptually match the clinician's ideas. Ehrensaft and Sophie agree on Sophie's gender problem: There is a little girl inside, effectively begging the very difficult question of what it *means* to a child to be a boy or a girl, on the inside. Indeed, children of Brady/Sophie's age typically conceptualize most abstractions concretely. In therapy with a child, we must not question this concreteness aloud if we are to be of help. But we must be guided by our knowledge that the adult abstraction gender, likely refers to something very different from the child's idea, and of which the child has as yet, little knowledge.

CHILDREN AGAIN

Perhaps because trans children are so much trouble—they freely embarrass and threaten their parents, provoke their therapists with creativity, unreasonableness and impracticality, and make it hard for their political defenders with essentialist rhetoric—we may lose sight of how potentially enlightening they may be. Children as a group, of course, present special problems to the mental health profession. They have limited means to express their interior lives, so we must listen and observe much more intensively, considering alternative interpretations, imagining their experience, and testing our hypotheses as we go, there and then. As I mentioned above, it was to address this very problem that play therapy was invented. It was, therefore, striking how some of the clinical articles entirely avoided interpretation of the children's behavior (including their verbal behavior), and instead took them literally. If the boy says he feels like a girl inside, then something about his boyness is acting up, instead of the more parsimonious assumption that as with all children's at first puzzling complaints, something in their experience, dynamic and as yet unknown, is being symbolized, and not that we need to consider the malfunction or influence of any particular

psychophysiological system. But the latter practice, unparsimoniously inject-
ing the role of theorized psychophysiological gender per se, is what many
clinicians tilt toward when an aspect of gendered psychology is present.
Why is this? Well that is the subject of another and much longer article, but
we should consider that the peculiar rhetorical and structuring power of the
concept *gender* is here operating, in parents, children, and clinicians alike.
Others (notably Rubin, 1975), have evolved theorizations of the compelling
and intransigent presence of gendering across cultures, without positing
essential gender, in effect accounting for our infatuation with it without
succumbing to its claims.

It seems to me that trans children, in response to great psychic pain
(and adaptively or not) have engaged the rhetoric of gender and, thus,
stumbled upon a communication of such potency that their parents and
therapists are detoured from listening to them as children, instead crediting
them with adult-like cognition. When we infer that the trans child has a
disturbance in an unobservable gender system, based on a claim of gender transformation, we are granting the truth of a child's self-analysis and
proposed self-construction. I doubt that the receipt of such a gratifying abun-
dance of respect from the clinician is consciously intended by the child. It is
more likely that the child longs inchoately for an emotional experience like
respect and rapidly gains unconscious awareness of the power of gender
complaints to bring such gratification. When the longing is unwittingly satisfied by the parent or clinician who, thinking they understand the child's
problem, validates the terms of the discussion as the child has set them, the
child is likely to reiterate the complaint in those terms. For that child, a psychological structure, more or less transient, begins to develop. For the adult,
the illusion of understanding begins to perpetuate itself. The most immediate lesson that the trans child has learned, and then enacts, encouraged by
these interactions, is that the idea of gender is very powerful, and if you
want to get a rise out of people, play with it daringly. The lesson for the
parent or clinician should be: Stop talking about gender. Zucker et al. (this
issue) seem to appreciate this.

It would be folly to expect any parent to look upon their young child
without experientially centralizing its perceived gender as real. All the details
of our cultural practices surrounding the bearing and raising of children,
including language itself, militate in favor of experiencing the gender of
the child not only as real, but as central in parental consciousness. The
assumed validity of essential gender is both challenged and affirmed by
trans children, and its simultaneous weakness and potency in the face of that
challenge deals their parents a terrible blow, for their children are playing
with gender in a way that traumatizes them. First, because gender is so
central to parents' experience of their children, their very sense of reality
is shaken. Second, the children have placed the parents in a classic double
bind: They insist on the flexibility to choose their gender, that is, flout genital

rule, but then act as though the new gender is essential, inflexible. Even the rare parent, caught in this cross-fire but still trying to adopt a constructivist attitude, cannot win for losing. The child demands infinite latitude and the parent gets none. We, who would help both, are much reduced in our psychological armamentarium because of the special position of gender in the culture of parenting. But we are not empty handed. We have knowledge that if emphasized can help parents, if not to listen psychoanalytically, at least to feel calmer and do less. We know that their children's preoccupation with gender is very likely to wane. We cannot persuade most parents to become constructivists, but we are obliged to be frank with them about a full range of possible outcomes, including the often short and benign course of gender dysphoria.

SELF-HARM, TRANS CHILDREN, AND OUR DISCUSSION

The specter of harm to children—any harm to any children—is surely a powerful influence in all discussions about children, and no doubt it is playing a role, spoken or not, in this one. In reality, our society does not devote appropriately disproportionate resources to the welfare of children. But symbolically, and in particular contexts, we become obsessed with the possibility of harm to them, especially physical injury, but psychological harm as well. Aid to poor mothers and education are slashed, but you can quickly get your neighbor in deep trouble with a simple anonymous phone call to a usually underfunded child protective services agency. Protecting children from the imagined depredations of lesbians and gay men is a central trope in the right wing attack on sexual minorities, while the abuse of children in a variety of institutional settings eludes appropriate scrutiny. Many more illustrations of our culture's ambivalence toward the welfare of children could be cited, but my point for the present is that latent or manifest images of harm to the innocent bodies and minds of children, and, perhaps worst of all, of child suicides, change the tenor of any discussion. Has it changed this discussion, however subtly? Has it changed the imaginings of clinicians and parents when they consider responses to trans children's articulations of pain? These questions are not readily answerable, but, before I write my conclusions, I would offer some observations that are less debatable and, perhaps, pertinent to these questions.

I am aware of no controlled data to indicate that the incidence of self-harm among trans children is any greater than somewhere between very infrequent and rare. I am aware of no data to suggest that pubertal suppression, cross-sex hormone administration, or genital surgery diminishes the probability of self-harm in trans children. Moreover, there is no reason to believe that the three above-mentioned physical interventions are any better for the welfare of trans children than supportive psychotherapy and psychoeducation for parents. There are anecdotal reports of threats by children and of children dramatizing the possibility of self-mutilation. There are psychiatric protocols for addressing the patient who seems to pose a risk of self-harm that are minimally intrusive and unquestionably reversible. The long-term psychological and physiological consequences of chemogenic pubertal suppression, cross-sex hormone administration, and genital surgery are unknown, and, as is the case with all self-selected populations, very difficult to assess owing to problems of control and limited sample numbers. The palpable misery of an articulate child may distract the empathic clinician or parent from the venerable admonition: First, do no harm.

CONCLUSION

I believe the disquiet and stimulation I initially experienced after reading these articles and watching some videos, was a reaction to my perception of children and adults struggling in the thrall of an artificially vitalized concept that subjugates and empowers each in complementary ways, a phenomenon both intriguing and worrisome. Most of these adults—parents and clinicians—have been persuaded that gender is biologically real, with specific rules for healthy functioning. The children, having unconsciously learned of the adults' imbuing of gender with particular potencies, that is, with reification, medicalization, and transgressive possibility, try to put it to use in the course of their own self-development. It proves to be a high-risk and high-gain tool. It has the power to command adult attention, to affect adult emotions and thus to alter the position in the family of the child who chooses to deploy it. As well, in the unconsciously operating hands of the child it can also bring enormous pain, which in its compelling resemblance to physical pain further misleads the adults toward the reification of gender. Painful and continuing maladaptation is usually the result of unconsciously instigating a noxious mechanism that is initially subjectively adaptive, but then via feedback mechanisms develops a life of its own that cannot easily be halted, despite its now problematic consequences. I would classify the disturbances of gender described in these articles as special cases of such maladaptation, novel in their content, but not in their interpersonal and intrapsychic structure.

It is disquieting to observe clinicians unconsciously colluding with troubled parents in the inflation of concepts that are inherently psychologically constricting. But there is another, perhaps deeper, reason that the observation of this particular image provokes me. None would dispute that, while the reasons for the hatred of same-sex eroticism and same-sex pairing are multiple, it is the transgression of gender norms by gay men and lesbians, especially the perceived elevation of the feminine by gay men, and of the female body, by lesbians, that most disturbs the ruling culture. Whatever psychological mechanisms are behind it, it is the intrusion of men who are willing to be feminine—erotically submissive and openly adoring of other men—and women preferring dominance and insisting on power that threatens the social order enough to license violence against lesbians and gay men and to legislate their inequality. The intellectual scaffolding for the dread and persecution of gender transgressors is primarily the belief that the organization of society around reproductive roles correlated with particular (and unequal) social roles is the reflection of a natural biological situation, that gender is a real structure of the human nervous system, prior to culture and history, and necessary. Just as racism requires belief in natural races, sexism and homophobia require belief in natural genders. If we organize our responses to children who play or become preoccupied with gendered behavior around the idea that there are natural genders from which they are deviating or toward which they can aspire with medical help (transitioning), then, however indirectly, we are buttressing the very structures upon which the hatred of gay men and lesbians stands. Or put differently: As clinicians responding to trans children, we are responding to a subjectivity, not to the results of a biopsy or blood test. We and parents must choose whether we respond to that subjectivity as the upshot of a hypothesized psychophysiological gender system, on the one hand, or choose to go no further than regarding it as a mutable psychological situation on the other. Choosing the former, the more elaborately and speculatively theorized framework of essential gender, accepts a theoretical structure that has been used to rationalize sexism and homophobia and, therefore, tends to promote them despite good intentions.

As should be clear by now, for me, abjuring the assumption of essential gender in responding to children, is in fact the venerable practice of making fewer assumptions, that is, theoretical parsimony, not an added politicization of clinical responding. This is important because my argument against a literal hearing of trans children's claims about their genders may be mistakenly read as a high-handed, quasi-diagnostic denigration of anyone who chooses to centralize gender and genitals in their self-conception. For example, some might think it inferable from my clinical and theoretical rejection of essentialism, that male-to-female transsexuals who see themselves as having women's brains encumbered by male bodies, are inherently politically retrograde. That is not my view. It would be deeply contrary to my purpose to use my analysis to disparage any experience or to obstruct the efforts of any adult to determine any aspect of their own bodies or minds. I restrict my political critique to those with power—clinicians, theorists, and parents. While an individual's subjectivity may ultimately have political consequences, I take it for granted that political change is first of all the prerogative of institutional authority, in this case, institutionalized medicine.

It may appear to be a failure of respect for the child's subjectivity to refuse to take their desires literally, and to refuse to be guided by the terms they have set. However, to accept their terms without interpretation, and even embellish and inflate them with scientific-sounding speculation, does them no service and is pseudo-respect if not outright condescension. A psychological treatment is respectful of the individual's subjectivity insofar as it assumes the individual's freedom and agency, not when it halts its analytic function to accept the individual's disavowal of agency in favor of the imagined power of gender. That principle, central to the insight-oriented psychotherapies—always strive to return disavowed or stolen agency to the patient—might be helpfully emphasized, especially for the trans child who seeks treatment, for that child, perhaps more than others, is contending with the terrible conflict that all humans experience between acknowledging freedom, and wishing they did not have to.

There is much more to children than what they say. We owe to them a deeper listening than a literal one. We will then likely find that their engagement with gender, especially when it is transgressive or countercultural, may reveal a creativity and even a politics that can contribute to the erosion (if not destabilization) of the gender system as it presently operates. If we listen to them literally, interpret their communications and performances through the categories we adults have grown up with, and of course have ourselves failed to transcend, we will miss whatever new story they are telling or protest they are making. If we listen and respond to what they are saying in the mirror of the old system, they will seem to buy it, because it comes with the feeling, although not the reality, of being understood, which they no doubt crave. Thus, stasis is guaranteed for the child and for our culture. I am not naïve enough to imagine an intellectual transcendence of essential gender. But, in the name of equality—of gender and of sexuality—we must avoid promoting its continued entrenchment.

NOTES

1. I will use the adjective *trans* to describe the children. I am deliberately avoiding any pathologizing or reifying terminology. But I do not mean to imply by this term that I accept literally or completely all trans children's narrations of themselves. The term trans seems to me general enough to encompass transgression, transcendence, and related concepts without necessarily precluding a range of interpretive formulations.

2. I have limited myself to these three articles in order to contain the length of my commentary and for the range of viewpoints they represented.

3. Some nonreligious, but no less ideologically committed, clinicians have also contributed to the impression that psychotherapeutic or psychoanalytic responses to trans children necessarily promote conformity in disregard of health.

4. These are Green, 1987; Drummond, Bradley, Badali-Peterson, & Zucker, 2008; Singh, Bradley, & Zucker, 2010; Wallien & Cohen-Kettenis, 2008; Zucker, 2008.

REFERENCES

Drummond, K. D., Bradley, S. J., Badali-Peterson, M., & Zucker, K. J. (2008). A follow-up study of girls with gender identity disorder. *Developmental Psychology*, *44*, 34–45.

Edwards-Leeper, L., & Spack, N.P. (this issue). Psychological evaluation and medical treatment of transgender youth in an interdisciplinary "gender management service (GeMS)" in a major pediatric center. *Journal of Homosexuality*, *59*, 321–336.

Ehrensaft, D. (this issue). From gender identity disorder to gender identity creativity: True gender self child therapy. *Journal of Homosexuality*, *59*, 337–356.

Green, R. (1987). *The "sissy boy syndrome" and the development of homosexuality*. New Haven, CT: Yale University Press.

Rubin, G. (1975). The traffic in women: Notes on the political economy of sex. In R. Reiter (Ed.), *Toward an Anthropology of Women* (pp. 157–211). New York, NY: Monthly Review Press.

Singh, D., Bradley, S. J., & Zucker, K. J. (2010, June). A follow-up study of boys with gender identity disorder. Poster presented at the University of Lethbridge Workshop, The Puzzle of Sexual Orientation: What Is It and How Does It Work?, Lethbridge, Alberta, Canada.

Wallien, M. S. C., & Cohen-Kettenis, P. T. (2008). Psychosexual outcome of gender dysphoric children. *Journal of the American Academy of Child and Adolescent Psychiatry*, *47*, 1413–1423.

Zucker, K. J. (2008). On the "natural history" of gender identity disorder in children [Editorial]. *Journal of the American Academy of Child and Adolescent Psychiatry*, *47*, 1361–1363.

Zucker, K. J., Wood, H., Singh, D., & Bradley, S. J. (this issue). A developmental, biopsychosocial model for the treatment of children with gender identity disorder. *Journal of Homosexuality*, *59*, 369–397.

Commentary on the Treatment of Gender Variant and Gender Dysphoric Children and Adolescents: Common Themes and Ethical Reflections

EDWARD STEIN, JD, PhD

Benjamin N. Cardozo School of Law, New York, New York, USA

This commentary offers preliminary ethical reflections on the range of treatments for gender variant and gender dysphoric children, adolescents, and young adults described in the preceding five clinical articles. After clarifying the terminology used to discuss these issues, this commentary reviews several common themes of the clinical articles. Focusing on ethical values of informed consent, full disclosure, the minimization or avoidance of harm, and the maximization of life options, the commentary expresses concerns about various treatment options endorsed by some of the articles. In particular, this commentary focuses on how these practices problematically reproduce social prejudices and stereotypes and how they fail to acknowledge and embrace the multiple pathways for expressing one's gender. It also compares and contrasts the ethical issues related to gender variant and gender dysphoric youths and youths who identify as lesbian, gay, bisexual, or queer.

The five preceding clinical articles—Edwards-Leeper and Spack (this issue), Menvielle (this issue), de Vries and Cohen-Kettenis (this issue), Zucker et al. (this issue), and Ehrensaft (this issue)—describe practices used in the treatment of children and adolescents whose gender identities are to varying degrees discordant with the gender roles and behaviors typically associated with individuals of their natal sex,[1] with particular focus on those who are experiencing distress as a result of this discordance and meet the criteria for Gender Identity Disorder of Childhood set out in the *Diagnostic and Statistical Manual of Mental Disorders* (4th ed., text rev; *DSM-IV-TR*; American Psychiatric Association, 2000).

This commentary offers preliminary ethical reflections on strategies for and theories underlying the psychological and medical treatment of gender variant and gender dysphoric children, adolescents, and young adults discussed in the clinical articles. Among the ethical issues that I address are informed consent, full disclosure, maximizing life options, avoidance of harm, not blindly reproducing social prejudices and stereotypes, and acknowledging and embracing the multiple pathways for the expression of various gender identities. I also compare and contrast the ethical issues related to gender variant and gender dysphoric children, adolescents, and young adults with ethical issues related to children, adolescents, and young adults who identify as lesbian, gay, bisexual, and queer (LGBQ) or who identify as such at a later stage of development. While the clinical articles do not, for the most part, discuss LGBQ children directly, comparing these conceptually distinct groups highlights interesting and important ethical issues and leads to conceptual clarity about such issues.

I begin with the conceptual framework that undergirds my thinking about gender identity generally. This framework informs my ethical reflections and it may be in tension with some of the assumptions made by certain clinical articles. Laying out this conceptual framework should also bring to the foreground implicit assumptions of the clinical articles, especially as they relate to the ethical issues that flow from the clinical articles.

SEX, GENDER, GENDER IDENTITY, GENDER VARIANCE, AND GENDER DYSPHORIA

Sex

It is surprisingly difficult to give a precise account of the concept *sex* and how it differs from the concept *gender*. (The discussion in this section is loosely based on Stein, 1999, pp. 23–38.) Intuitively, sex is bodily, while gender is cultural as it involves the social expectations and assumptions associated with sex; sex is between the legs, under the shirt, and in the genes, while gender is between the ears and emerges from culture. (For a discussion of this way of distinguishing sex and gender, see Ehrensaft, this issue.) On this view, gender involves the cultural characteristics and assumptions socially associated with physical sex characteristics that are not socially determined and that in some sense transcend cultural differences. There are two significant characteristics typically viewed as part of sex that I reject: that sex is binary and that sex is discrete. Sex is often seen as binary, that is, a person is either male or female. Sex is also often seen as discrete—as opposed to continuous—because the line between the sexes is supposed to be a clear one and every male (and every female) is as much a male (or female) as any and every other male (or female). Sex is a continuous category if there is no clear line between different sexes but rather if there is a continuum on which different sexes exist.

There are various difficulties facing the picture of sex as binary and discrete. First, in humans, sex can be defined and understood in multifarious ways that do not necessarily sort people in the same manner. Among the different lenses for defining and understanding sex are chromosomal sex, gondal sex, external genitalia, internal genitalia, and secondary sex characteristics (such as facial hair and breast shape and size). Even the simplest of these categories, chromosomal sex, does not support the traditional view of sex as binary and discrete. One of the 23 pairs of chromosomes that humans typically have consists of the sex chromosomes. Typically, the egg from which a human develops contributes an X sex chromosome while the sperm from which a human develops contributes either an X chromosome (in which case the person is female) or a Y chromosome (in which case the person is male). But not everyone has two sex chromosomes—some people have three sex chromosomes that are all X or include a combination of X and Y, while some have only one sex chromosome. Although people with such sex chromosomal configurations are relatively uncommon, their existence shows that sex, even looked at in a simple fashion, is neither binary nor discrete since some humans are neither XX nor XY.

Expanding this analysis beyond just chromosomal sex, applied to some people, not all the ways of understanding sex point in the same direction. For example, a person with a genetic condition known as *complete androgen insensitivity syndrome* (CAIS) has male-typical sex chromosomes, gonads, and internal genitalia, but female-typical external genitalia and secondary sex characteristics. In all reported cases of CAIS, these individuals have been considered by themselves and others as female, that is, belonging to the social category that includes girls and women. Nevertheless, some have suggested that, because they have a Y chromosome, they could be considered males (Bell et al. 1981). Focusing on one way of understanding or defining sex, such a person would be classified female, while adopting another way this person would be classified male.

People who are in some ways male-typical in terms of their bodies and in some way female-typical in terms of their bodies were once called *hermaphrodites* or *pseudohermaphrodites*, then called *intersexed*, and are now starting to be called people with *disorders of sex development* (DSDs). Some people with DSDs are not clearly one sex or another under a particular understanding of sex. For example, some people with DSDs have ambiguous external genitalia (e.g., a phallus that according to some medical guidelines would be considered too large to be a clitoris but too small to be considered a penis; Fausto-Sterling, 2000), while some have atypical gonads (e.g., a mixture of ovarian and testicular tissue (ovotestes) rather than either testes or ovaries). The existence of DSDs undermines the simple picture of sex as binary and discrete and straightforwardly determined by the bodies of humans.

Matters are further complicated because humans experience developmental changes with respect to sex characteristics. While chromosomal sex is constant, various sex characteristics (e.g., the emergence of secondary sex characteristics with puberty) change between conception and birth and between birth and adulthood as a result of hormone levels, the functioning of hormone receptors, and various environmental factors. In some DSDs, however, the changes may be more dramatic. As one example, consider children with another genetic condition, 5-alpha reductase deficiency, the condition that affected the main character in the celebrated novel *Middlesex* (Eugenides, 2002). Such children develop looking for the most part like girls in terms of their visible characteristics, including their external genitalia and secondary sex characteristics. They have testes and male-typical internal genitalia and, at puberty, the testes descend into the labia, the phallus enlarges, and male-typical secondary sex characteristics emerge. At birth, such children have external genitalia that are discordant with their gonads, internal genitalia, and genetic sex (XY), but as they develop, some of this discordance is reduced, especially with respect to their external genitalia.

The above discussion shows the problems with the term *biological sex* (as used, e.g., by Edwards-Leeper & Spack, this issue). One can look at a person's sex through various biological lenses, and what sex a person seems to be or is determined to be can differ depending on which lens is used. In other words, biological sex purports to mean one thing but, in fact, on close examination or on application to a variety of contexts and people, the explanatory value of this term dissolves. If, however, we give up on the idea that sex is a discrete category, the concept of biological sex may have some use in social or legal parlance (in contrast to scientific contexts), even though its definition is contested.[2] If sex is indexed to the presence or absence of a Y chromosome, then sex would be a discrete category, but this account does not capture many of our intuitions about what sex many people are (e.g., it would count as female many people who seem to be male). Most of the other possible biological accounts of sex (e.g., those indexed to external genitalia, internal genitalia, or hormonal sex) are continuous categories. This reveals a tension regarding the concept of sex;

while our intuitive notion is that sex is discrete and binary, especially in the face of the existence of people with disorders of sex development, sex is revealed as complicated, largely because it is multifactorial and some of its component factors are continuous to varying degrees and, in some individuals, may be discordant (Fausto-Sterling, 2000). Further, because many of the component factors of sex may change through development, in the context of the clinical articles, a more appropriate way of talking about sex is in terms of natal sex rather than biological sex. In what follows, I use the term *natal sex* to mean a person's assigned sex at birth, acknowledging that this concept does not really apply to people with DSDs. Among the problems with the term *biological sex* is that it may imply that the body in which a person is born is his or her true sex in virtue of chromosomes or genitalia and, thus, if this person has a gender identity that diverges from bodily sex, this is a psychological problem. In contrast, some *trans* people[3] say that their gender identity reflects the biological configuration of their brains and that they have a physical disorder (not a psychological one) because the sex of their genitalia does not match the sex of their brain.[4]

Gender

According to the intuitive account of the difference between sex and gender discussed above, gender is the social overlay to sex. This usage of the terms *sex* and *gender* emphasizes that gender roles differ from society to society and that, while a person's gender generally tracks a person's sex, for some people, their gender presentations are atypical for their natal sex. Consider, for example, that in some agricultural societies the farming is primarily done by men, in some it is primarily done by women, while in others, it is shared between the sexes. In these societies, gender roles include whether or not one will be engaging in farming, but in those various societies, gender roles differ significantly: farming will be female-typical behavior in some and male-typical behavior in others.

In some societies, a natal male who adopts the gender roles typically associated with females, and who is treated by members of his society as female, is considered to be either a woman or a male living as woman. (The parallel point is true for natal females who adopt roles and behaviors typical of males in a particular society.) In some Native American cultures, for example, natal males who play the roles that females in those cultures typically play are known as *berdache*. These individuals marry men, do chores typically done by women, and otherwise play the roles typical of natal females in that society, even though they are known to be natal males (Williams, 1986). Some have argued that such a society has more than two genders; since these males adopt women's roles while still being recognized as males, they constitute a third gender. A society that also allowed for natal females to play roles typically associated with men, to marry women, and so on, might be said to have four genders.

Societies that recognize more than two genders demonstrate that natal sex and subsequent gender presentation do not necessarily accord. The idea that one's natal sex must match one's gender is thus merely a social construct. Even though in most cultures most natal males present themselves in the roles of men and most natal females present themselves as women, and the majority of people behave in accordance with their culture's gender norms, not everyone fits this standard configuration; in fact, some cultures have distinct gender categories for people whose gender presentations are atypical for their natal sex and more typical for a different sex.

Gender Identity, Gender Variance, and Gender Dysphoria

A person's gender identity is one's psychological sense of one's sex. As discussed in the clinical articles, some people who have XY chromosomes and male-typical internal and external genitalia have a strong sense that they are not male, but really female, and vice versa. Gender identity is, thus, a cognitively mediated characteristic. In contrast, eye color is an example of a characteristic that is not cognitively mediated, but rather is a straightforward physical fact about a person.

Some of the clinical articles discuss what causes people to have the gender identities that they do (de Vries & Cohen-Kettenis, this issue; Zucker et al., this issue). Addressing this etiological issue is not necessary to engage the clinical or ethical issues relating to gender variant and gender dysphoric children, adolescents, and young adults. *Gender variant* people have gender presentations and related behaviors that do not conform to expected social roles for males and females. So, for example, a person with male-typical genitalia and male-typical sex chromosomes who behaves in a female-typical manner and/or self-identifies or self-conceptualizes as a woman (or as not a man) is gender variant. According to the *DSM-IV-TR* (American Psychiatric Association, 2000), *gender dysphoric* people are those who experience serious distress from being gender variant or from societal attitudes toward their gender variance. *Gender identity disorder* (GID) is the formal psychiatric diagnosis for individuals who experience significant gender dysphoria and clinically significant distress or impairment as a result (Drescher, 2010). Further, the etiological discussions in the clinical articles are of little help with the clinical and ethical issues since there is no settled scientifically supported theory of the genetic, biological, and environmental factors that shape a person's gender identity. Gender identity can change over time, especially in children—namely, one may think of oneself as a boy for a period of time and then think of oneself as a girl.

SOME COMMON THEMES OF THE CLINICAL ARTICLES

Several common themes emerge from the clinical articles, despite differences in the terminology and approaches that their authors use for thinking about and treating gender variant individuals and the distress that some of these individuals experience. First, although there is some disagreement about the precise percentages (Zucker et al., this issue), the clinical articles agree that the vast majority of children who experience gender variance and gender dysphoria do not continue to do so as adolescents or young adults.[5] Those whose gender variance and gender dysphoria do not continue through adolescence are known as *desisters*, while those whose gender variance and gender dysphoria continue are called *persisters*. None of the clinical articles offer any explanation of why some individuals persist and others desist and the only suggestion in this series of articles for predicting which gender variant or gender dysphoric youth will be persisters and which will be desisters is the "intensity of gender dysphoria, with more intense dysphoria predicting higher likelihood of persistence" (Menvielle, this issue, p. 362). A majority of children with GID turn out to be desisters. As adults, a majority will turn out to identify as gay men, lesbians, or bisexuals, with a significant portion of the rest becoming heterosexuals without gender dysphoria. In only a small proportion of children with GID does the condition persist from childhood and into adulthood.[6] As a result, the recommended clinical response to gender variance and dysphoria in children is to provide appropriate support and counseling to these individuals and their parents rather than to begin medical treatment in childhood. There is, however, disagreement regarding what is appropriate support and counseling.

Second, the clinical articles in this special issue support the practice of using puberty suppression drugs for persisting gender variant adolescents, although they seem to have different thresholds for recommending or offering this course of treatment. Ehrensaft (this issue), for example, says that "children who are approaching puberty and are faced with a sudden trauma that forces to consciousness the horror that they are living in a body that is totally at odds with the gender they know themselves to be ... are in gender crisis and need to be attended to immediately with an evaluation for puberty blockers ... " (p. 345). De Vries and Cohen-Kettenis (this issue) consider adolescents "eligible for puberty suppression when they are [i] diagnosed with GID [specifically "very early onset gender dysphoria that has increased around puberty"], [ii] live in a supportive environment and [iii] have no serious psychosocial problems interfering with the diagnostic assessment or treatment." (pp. 310–311). Edwards-Leeper and Spack (this issue) consider an individual in "early or mid puberty" to be a candidate for puberty suppression when i) a clinical evaluation "indicates strong and persistent gender dysphoria and a desire [for] medical intervention," ii) there is "no evidence of severe, untreated psychiatric conditions," iii) his or her parents support use of puberty suppression, and iv) the individual will continue mental health counseling during treatment (p. 325). (For related discussion, see Menvielle, this issue, p. 365, and Zucker et al. this issue.) It is difficult to assess how such thresholds are utilized in clinical practice, but it seems to this reader that Ehrensaft's test for puberty suppression is more easily satisfied than the conditions required by either de Vries and Cohen-Kettenis or Edwards-Leeper and Spack.

Despite the seemingly varied tests described by the clinical articles for when puberty suppression is appropriate, they seem to share the same rationale for this treatment regimen, namely to allow for a wait-and-see approach, giving gender dysphoric individuals time to experience additional emotional and cognitive maturation before they decide how they wish to deal with their gender variance. The onset of puberty seems to be a critical phase for gender dysphoric adolescents. At that stage in their physical development, some of them experience increasing distress about the development of secondary sex characteristics typically associated with their natal sex (e.g., natal males may experience distress about getting spontaneous erections and deeper voices and natal females may experience distress about developing larger breasts and the start of menstruation). Puberty suppression drugs will halt such physical developments, often relieving the distress that apparently comes from the emergence of undesired secondary sex characteristics. In addition, because some pubertal changes are difficult or impossible to fully reverse (e.g., those involving skeletal changes and the development of an Adam's apple; Edwards-Leeper & Speck, this issue), puberty suppression sets the stage for a more physically convincing gender transition down the road if such a course of treatment is chosen. The idea is that more mature youths will be better able to make a thoughtful and informed decision about how to respond to their gender variance, specifically, what treatment options, if any, to undertake. Although the psychological and physical effects of puberty suppression have not been well studied, the clinical articles endorse this practice in light of "a patchwork of empirical evidence about natural history" (Zucker et al., this issue, p. 392) and indications that to date suggest suppression has no lasting side effects, whether or not such individuals decide to undergo hormone treatments or surgery to harmonize their gender identity and their bodily sex.

Third, although not all of their clinics provide such procedures, most of the clinicians are supportive of cross-hormone treatment regimens and sex reassignment surgery (SRS) for gender dysphoric young adults who desire such procedures when clinically indicated[7] in light of the observation that most individuals who get to puberty still experiencing significant gender dysphoria will opt for medical or other types of sex-reassignment procedures. Their stance is supported by recent studies that show such procedures reduce gender dysphoria, produce a subjective sense of psychological improvement in individuals, and are typically successful insofar as rarely will individuals who have undergone such procedures report major regrets about having done so (de Vries & Cohen-Kettenis, this issue; Ehrensaft, this issue, who supports this proposition with a citation to a National Public Radio interview with Spack).

ETHICAL REFLECTIONS

The ethical discussion that follows draws on some of the common themes of the clinical articles, but also diverges from some of the implicit assumptions these articles make.

Informed Consent

Informed consent is an important ethical value and legal principle for medical and mental health professionals. Before a health care provider treats a patient, she must make sure that her patient understands his condition, the prognosis, the treatment the health care provider is recommending, the benefits and risks of this treatment, and the treatment alternatives and their comparative benefits and risks. Having provided this information to the patient, the provider needs to determine that the patient, with this information in mind, consents to the treatment. The primary exception to this rule is that a health care provider may provide treatment in the case of an emergency when a patient is not able to consent.

The standard of informed consent is different when the patient is a child. The general legal approach in the United States—which roughly tracks the standard ethical approach—is that children and adolescents do not have the capacity to consent to medical treatment; instead, their parents (or guardians) have the authority to provide (or withhold) such consent. There is, however, a sliding scale related to informed consent that applies to children in recognition of the developmental changes they go through that affect the extent to which they can understand and assent to medical treatments. Very young children and infants simply cannot understand any medical or mental health procedures, their risks, and the alternatives to them. In such cases, a very young child's parent or legal guardian can provide informed consent in his place. For older children who are perhaps too young to fully appreciate the costs and benefits and to evaluate the alternatives and make long-term decisions, but old enough to understand the general situation and to appreciate some of the tradeoffs involved, age-appropriate information about the condition, the recommended treatment, and alternatives should be given and their consent—or at least their assent— should be obtained along with parental consent. This framework is based on legal tradition that has been, for the most part, buttressed over the decades by scientific research, most recently contemporary cognitive psychology and neuroscience.

Against this ethical background, the so-called "mature minor doctrine"[8] allows health care providers to treat mature minors in accordance with their wishes without parental consent or even if parents oppose such treatment.[9] Accepting the mature minor doctrine, which not all jurisdictions in the United States or Europe do,[10] is, in effect, accepting a more robust sliding scale related to the significance of a child's opinion about medical treatment: the older a child or adolescent is, the more autonomous, the more mature, and the more reflective he or she is, the more important his or her opinion is about what should be done, and the more likely it is that he or she can consent in an ethically relevant manner.

The clinical articles at least implicitly seem to accept the ethical principles of informed consent and the idea of the mature minor doctrine, as evidenced in particular by the endorsement of puberty suppression as a technique for gender dysphoric adolescents. Puberty suppression fits with a general bioethical principle for the treatment of minors that unless there is some urgency to make a decision about treatment, it is better not to allow parents to make decisions for children because sometimes parents do not or cannot know what is best or appropriate for their children and even children do not know what they want. It also fits with the well-supported claim from psychology that an individual will tend to be happier with a result if he or she plays a role in the decision to seek that result. This observation may, however, be more applicable to adults than to children and adolescents, especially with respect to profound decisions. (Note, also, that there is support for the claim that people who are not satisfied with an outcome tend to be happier if they can hold someone else accountable for the decisions that led to it.) Despite this apparent fit between the ethical principle of informed consent and the justifications for puberty suppression, I have some related ethical concerns about the use of puberty suppression, which are addressed in the section that follows.

Maximizing Life Options

Many of the clinical articles follow, at least approximately, the Standards of Care of the World Professional Association for Transgender Heath (WPATH). De Vries and Cohen-Kettenis (this issue) distinguish among completely reversible interventions, partially reversible interventions, and completely irreversible interventions. Among the claimed virtues of reversible interventions such as puberty suppression are that they facilitate the maximization of life options for children and adolescents. In general, it is an ethical strategy to leave options for young people. This empowers them and gives them time to come to a better understanding of their preferred mode of gender presentation and to decide whether additional medical interventions would be helpful in facilitating it.

I have, however, a cluster of related concerns about puberty suppression. It seems possible that the decision to make use of puberty suppression drugs may unintentionally and, in various ways, push adolescents toward cross-sex hormone therapy and sex reassignment surgery (SRS). The clinical articles claim that most adolescents who undergo puberty suppression proceed to transition away from their natal sex, but this claim is consistent with various explanations, no one of which is strongly justified. It might be a reasonable hypothesis—in contrast to the assumptions that the clinical articles seem to make—that temporarily stopping puberty in and of itself has the effect of increasing the likelihood of persistence. If that is the case, parents who opt for the use of puberty suppression drugs on their gender variant offspring are not truly adopting a wait-and-see approach, but rather may be unintentionally pushing their offspring toward hormone treatment and SRS. Further, given that there are almost no data on the longer-term effects of puberty suppression on those adolescents who ultimately do not choose to transition or on possible long-term harms of puberty suppression, and given the absence of well-established and accepted ethical treatment guidelines for puberty suppression,[11] the basis for this course of treatment is at least weak—both from the ethical and the medical perspectives. Given that we do not know how puberty suppression affects gender variant adolescent persistence or desistence, and given the lack of data about its effects, the use of puberty suppression may not necessarily maximize life options—it may close off some options by keeping others open. For these reasons, puberty suppression does not neatly fit with the idea of allowing gender variant and gender dysphoric individuals the option to give informed consent. However, for some gender dysphoric adolescents, the distress they experience with the onset of puberty is so extreme that puberty suppression seems to be the most ethical and compassionate course of treatment and would be justified under a similar rationale to the emergency exception to the standard of informed consent.

Full Disclosure

What sort of information should be provided to gender variant and gender dysphoric children and adolescents and their parents as part of obtaining informed consent? What we tell parents as compared to children will differ for at least two reasons. First, the information provided to children and adolescents should be age appropriate. Second, often the recommendation for gender variant children is to do nothing to the children and instead to provide support, counseling, and advice to the parents. Parents may want a professional's opinion (or perhaps the opinions of several professionals) about the likelihood that SRS will be an appropriate treatment for their gender variant child in a few years. Children, in contrast, may not ask about this, although if they do, the ethical principle of full disclosure would suggest that an age-appropriate answer should be given.

It is especially important to explore various alternative clinical approaches with parents and adolescents. There is surprisingly little information comparing available treatment approaches for gender variant and gender dysphoric children and adolescents, which is partly why this special issue is so important; providing descriptive accounts of five clinical approaches to treatment in a side-by-side fashion is unprecedented (although the approaches described in the various clinical articles are more similar than what one might have expected from superficial online research about the respective clinics). For parents with the wherewithal to read scholarly articles, this will hopefully prove to be a terrific resource. Also, these articles will assist clinicians doing work in this area by enabling them to place their clinical practices in the context of the work of others in the field. This will allow clinicians to provide their patients and their patients' parents with a comparative account of the type of clinical work they are doing; one can say, for example, that her clinical approach is much more like Ehrensaft's than like Zucker's. More importantly, from my perspective, pairing the clinical articles with ethical reflections allows parents, clinicians, and others to not only compare the treatment options but to consider their possible risks, their social costs, and some of their problematic assumptions.

Part of full disclosure involves telling parents things that they may not want to hear. Ethically, a clinician has to admit ignorance or uncertainty where it exists. That is something parents do not like to hear (and many clinicians may not like to admit): They may want to know, for example, exactly what is going to happen to their child or what the best course of action is for her. It is unethical to provide a definitive answer when in fact there is none. Given the state of knowledge about the different clinical methods and the effectiveness of each, an honest clinician cannot say that objective evidence shows his or her approach to be the best. Various ethical challenges are likely to emerge. A parent who is greatly distressed by his 7-year old son's gender variant behavior may not want to hear that there is a significant chance that his child will grow up to be gay. One might think it is better to tell this parent the truth about his son's likely development, but what if the parent says he would rather his son be dead than gay? Or, what if a parent of a gender dysphoric child repeatedly punishes the child for gender variant behaviors and refuses to consent to puberty suppression even though a clinician recommends it? These are among the types of questions for which clinicians need to be prepared even though there are no agreed-upon ethical guidelines that presently exist. The clinical articles cannot be expected to have solutions to all these ethical challenges, but to my lights, they do need to be more cognizant of them.

Acknowledging Gender Fluidity and the Multiple Healthy Manifestations of Gender

Another important part of full disclosure is to truthfully convey what we know about sex and gender. For me, as for some of the clinical authors—especially Ehrensaft (this issue) and Menvielle (this issue)—a crucial part of this disclosure involves acknowledging that, for some people, gender identity can be fluid and, more generally and importantly, that there is no single way to conduct one's life as male or female with regard to gendered behaviors or presentation. For example, not all natal males or men have penises, not all like to play with trucks or toy guns as boys, not all are sexually attracted to women, not all want to work in traditionally male professions, and not all behave in a male-typical fashion in social contexts. It is important to convey to gender variant and gender dysphoric children and adolescents the nearly infinite ways of being a person of a particular gender or, to use a different turn of phrase, the nearly infinite ways of performing gender. Ehrensaft's clinical approach, more so than the other clinical articles, seems to embrace the fluidity of gender and suggest to children and adolescents the multiply varied modes of gender presentation available to individuals regardless of their natal sex.

As a simple example, consider a treatment plan for a natal female with a male gender identity that includes masculinizing hormones and breast removal surgery but that does not involve genital surgery, leaving both internal and external genitalia untouched. Although more extensive surgery might result in an individual who looks more like a typical man, that alone is neither a medically or ethically strong reason to prefer the more extensive treatment plan.[12] An ethical approach to gender dysphoria should seriously consider the less extensive treatment plan and inform individuals of this treatment option even though it will less fully harmonize the individual's biological sex and gender identity. An individual might not embrace this treatment plan if it would not address the individual's gender dysphoria. However, failure to at least consider the less extreme treatment plan simply because of social mores or personal prejudice would be unethical.

Avoiding Harm

There is a further reason to favor the treatment plan that involves less extensive surgery or even none at all. All surgery involves risk and the more extensive the surgery, the greater the risk. At a minimum, surgery involves a risk of infection, risk of negative reaction to anesthetic, and risk of surgical error.[13] Additionally, some SRS may result in the need for life-long hormone therapy, which in turn has uncertain long-term consequences. With SRS, there is also the risk that the patient will be unhappy with the results and will want to undo the sex reassignment (although, as several of the clinical articles mention, this is relatively rare in cases where clinicians follow the guidelines of the WPATH Standards of Care). Of the clinical articles that discuss surgery, only Zucker et al. (this issue) mention associated risks as a relevant consideration. Because of the risks of surgery and because some aspects of SRS (e.g., gonadectomy) are not reversible at all, the WPATH guidelines call for a gradual and step-wise gender transition beginning with fully reversible steps, followed by partially reversible steps, with irreversible surgery as the last step of treatment for gender dysphoria in young adults. Zucker et al. (this issue) seem to infer from this conclusion that "the prevention of transexualism [is] a [reasonable] treatment goal for children with GID [gender identity disorder]" (p. 392). Preventing gender variant and gender dysphoric children from embracing a gender different from the one associated with their natal sex is, as I have suggested above, not the only way to avoid SRS. The desire for surgery might be minimized by helping youths to appreciate that there are multiple ways of having a particular gender, some of which involve non-surgical intervention. Sometimes, however, as discussed above, nothing short of full SRS will relieve a gender dysphoric individual of the distress associated with having a body that does not feel right because it does not match one's gender identity. It is unfortunate that someone is born with a body that causes them distress. Based on the above arguments, if there were ways to help people become comfortable with the bodies they have, regardless of their outward presentation of gender, that would be preferable to having surgery.

Appropriately Distinguishing Gender Dysphoria and Gender Variance

Although the clinical articles typically distinguish between gender variant children and adolescents and gender dysphoric children and adolescents, sometimes they elide these two concepts. This elision is problematic because some treatments that seem warranted for gender dysphoric individuals are not appropriate for gender variant individuals. If an adolescent is not distressed by his or her gender variance, neither medical nor psychological intervention seems necessary except to the extent that such adolescents should be provided counseling and other support to help them deal with the social disapprobation, discrimination, and bullying that they are likely to encounter (this sort of counseling is discussed, e.g., by Menvielle, this issue; Ehrensaft, this issue; Richardson, 1996). As an example of how this elision leads to problems, consider the report by Zucker et al. (this issue) that their clinic almost never gets a referral that is a false positive; that is, they never encounter someone who was referred for gender identity issues who turns out not to have them. Focusing on the *DSM* criteria, Zucker et al. report that 70% of the children evaluated by their clinic have gender identity disorder and that very few of the remaining 30% who do not have gender identity disorder were free from "clinically significant gender identity issues" (p. 389).

Zucker's analysis—both in the clinical article he coauthored and in other articles he has written over the years (e.g., see the discussion of gender-problem children in Zucker, Finegan, Doering, & Bradley, 1984)—seems to inadequately appreciate the ethical difference between gender dysphoria and gender variance. As a result, Zucker and his various coauthors seem to lose sight of the fact that a gender variant child or adolescent can be happy, healthy, and "comfortable in one's skin" (a turn of phrase used by Zucker et al., this issue). Even if such an individual is experiencing social disapprobation and ostracism, he or she may not have a gender identity issue. Insofar as there is an issue when a gender variant child or adolescent is healthy and happy, it may be society, the youth's parents, or the youth's peers that have the gender identity issue, not the particular youth in question. Certainly more than a few of the referrals to Zucker's clinic are healthy gender variant children or adolescents who should in fact be counted as false positives. Classifying such individuals as having gender identity issues is a mischaracterization, one that may result in unethically treating healthy youths as if they are disordered (Richardson, 1996, 1999). This critique of Zucker et al. dovetails with Ehrensaft's (this issue) warning not to "pathologize perfectly healthy children who are simply expressing their authentic gender identity" (p. 339).

Avoiding the Reproduction of Social Stereotypes

Clinicians should avoid reproducing social stereotypes in counseling and treating gender variant and gender discordant children and adolescents. By creating an assembly line for the treatment of gender variant and gender dysphoric youths that starts with puberty suppression and ends with SRS, clinicians are in effect implying that there is one way to be a man and one way to be a woman, that gender identity and bodily sex need to be brought into accord, and that achieving this concordance is the path to good mental health. This is especially the case if, as suggested above, the use of puberty suppression has the effect of increasing the likelihood of hormone treatment and SRS. Of the clinical articles, Ehrensaft (this issue) and Menievelle (this issue) do the best job of avoiding this assembly line approach. Insofar as the three other clinical articles justify puberty suppression and less reversible medical interventions for gender variant and gender dysphoric adolescents for the purpose of reducing ostracism and other negative social reactions to gender non-conformity (Zucker et al., this issue), they are reproducing social stereotypes.

Langer and Martin (2004) argue that attempting to change a youth's gender identity "seems as ethically repellant as bleaching black children's skin" in order to improve their social interaction with white children (p. 14).

Zucker's (2008) response is that if a black child expresses the desire to be white, the recommended treatment "would not be to endorse the [b]lack child's wish to be [w]hite, but rather to treat the underlying factors that have led the child to believe that his life would be better as a [w]hite person" (p. 359). Zucker's response continues, saying "it is as legitimate to want to make youngsters comfortable with their gender identity (to make it correspond to the physical reality of their biological sex) as it is to make youngsters comfortable with their ethnic identity (to make it correspond to the physical reality of the color of their skin)." Part of the dispute between Langer and Martin and Zucker has to do with what is fixed and what can be changed. Both start with the idea that it would be ethically problematic to change a youth's skin color. Zucker suggests that the ethical course of action when presented with black youths who want to be white is to make them comfortable with the physical reality of their skin color. Similarly, he suggests that gender variant and gender dysphoric children should be made comfortable with the physical reality of their biological sex. But, especially given the problems with the notion of biological sex discussed above, it seems unjustified to prioritize biological sex over gender identity, which can also be seen as part of one's physical reality, insofar as gender identity is instantiated in the brain.

COMPARING AND CONTRASTING SEXUAL ORIENTATION AND GENDER VARIANCE/GENDER DYSPHORIA

The comparison of GID to "ethnic identity disorder" (Zucker, 2008) is less apt than the comparison of GID to homosexuality. In fact, it is useful to compare and contrast how most medical and psychological practitioners think about attempts to shape and change sexual orientation with how they think about attempts to shape and change sex or gender identity. If a parent presented himself or herself to a mainstream physician or mental health care provider with concerns that his or her child is gay or lesbian or likely to become gay or lesbian, the parent would not be offered therapeutic options for changing the sexual orientation of his or her child. Most mainstream researchers and commentators agree that there is no scientific basis to conclude that clinicians can change a person's sexual orientation (American Psychological Association, 2009) and the major medical and psychological organizations have made statements that explicitly oppose such conversion or reorientation procedures. Some religious conservatives, practitioners of reparative therapy, members of ex-gay religious groups, and a significant portion of the general public insist that at least some gay men and lesbians can become heterosexual. Even if a parent reported that his son or daughter was experiencing great distress about his or her sexual attractions to people of the same sex, a mainstream health care provider would, presumably, propose to help the child deal with his or her sexual orientation, not to change it, and try to help the parent to accept the child's sexual orientation.

Children and adolescents who say they are gay, lesbian, or bisexual, or who think they might be, especially those who are experiencing distress about their apparent sexual orientations, are encouraged to embrace being gay and told that, insofar as they are unhappy with their sexual orientation or how society reacts to it, things "will get better" (see, e.g., It Gets Better Project, www.itgetsbetter.org). One might think that there is a tension between how medical and mental health care providers respond to such youths, on the one hand, and what they say to gender dysphoric children and adolescents—namely, that they will have the option to have sex reassignment surgery to bring their bodies into accord with their gender identities. How do we explain this difference and is this difference justified?

The most significant difference is that cross-hormonal treatment and, when properly used, SRS actually work to address gender dysphoria. In contrast, the evidence suggests that changing one's sexual orientation is virtually impossible (American Psychological Association, 2009; Bohan, 1996; Drescher, 2002; Shidlo, Schroeder, & Drescher, 2002). Many LGBQ people have struggled with their attraction to people of the same sex and some have spent years of wrenching psychotherapy or gone through some other physically unpleasant procedures to try to change their sexual orientation. Although most psychologists and scientists with expertise in this area believe that sexual orientations are basically fixed by early adulthood at the latest and very difficult to change, there is some suggestive evidence that a small number of highly motivated individuals can, for at least some period of time, change their sexual behaviors and their sexual identities (Beckwith, 2001; Shidlo & Schroeder, 2002; Spitzer, 2003). While the American Psychiatric Association and other professional organizations are skeptical about such treatment (Commission on Psychotherapy by Psychiatrists, 2000), various conversion therapies—also called reparative therapies, reorientation programs, or ex-gay programs—have come into existence and attained some notoriety (Besen, 2003; Erzen, 2006; Nicolosi, 1991; Satinover, 1996; Wolkomir, 2006). However, much of the psychological evidence supporting success in "converting" LGBQ people into heterosexuals suffers from methodological or design problems (American Psychological Association, 2009; Bohan, 1996; Drescher & Zucker, 2006). The overwhelming evidence indicates that, for most people, sexual orientations are not consciously chosen and are very difficult or impossible to volitionally change. To put this point another way, sexual orientation is more like gender identity than it is like natal sex. Sexual orientation and gender identity are cognitively mediated, whereas natal sex is not. Ironically, physical characteristics like sex are easier to change than certain entrenched psychological characteristics. This explains why SRS is among the ethical options to offer gender dysphoric individuals while changing a person's sexual orientation is not among the ethical options for LGBQ individuals.

CONCLUSION

When children and adolescents experience distress about their gender, some sort of intervention is appropriate to relieve that distress. The clinical articles agree that medical intervention is not appropriate for such children. Some of these articles suggest that the only appropriate interventions are to provide counseling to parents and to children insofar as they are suffering from other psychological problems. The articles diverge about how to approach gender variance in children and adolescents and gender dysphoria in adolescents. This commentary has expressed some concerns about how social norms, prejudice, and stereotypes influence how clinicians advise, inform, and treat gender variant and gender dysphoric children and adolescents. Care needs to be taken not to push such youths toward treatments that reproduce, rather than broaden, social expectations about how to be a man or a woman.

NOTES

1. I adopt this term from de Vries and Cohen-Kettenis (this issue) who define *natal sex* as biological sex at birth. This term, while not without problems, is, I think, more appropriate than *biological sex* as used by other authors in this issue and elsewhere in a manner intended to be synonymous to natal sex, because biological sex could also mean bodily sex at times other than at birth. See below for further discussion of biological sex and natal sex. Given the problems I have with the term biological sex, I do not ultimately accept the definition of natal sex offered by de Vries and Cohen-Kettenis (this issue).

2. Compare Littleton v. Prange, 9 S.W.3d 223 (Tex. 1999), holding that sex—for purposes of access to marriage in a jurisdiction that only allows marriages between people of different sexes—is defined as genital or chromosomal sex at birth, with M.T. v J.T., 355 A.2d 204 (N.J. App. 1976), holding that sex—for purposes of access to marriage in a jurisdiction that only allows marriages between people of different sexes—is defined as the sex the person identifies and presents as at the time of marriage.

3. The term *transgender* (*trans*, for short) is an umbrella term for a person whose gender identity and natal sex differ. This is more of a social and gender identity term, in contrast to gender variant, which is more of a behavioral term. The term *cisgender* is used by members of the transgender community and Ehrensaft (this issue), for people whose gender assigned at birth, gender typically associated with the type of body they have, and their sense of what gender they are all match; in others words, a person who is not transgender is cisgender.

4. Note that despite my skepticism about biological sex as a scientific term, I do continue to use standard locutions such as "sex reassignment surgery" rather than the less standard put perhaps more appropriate "gender (or gender identity) affirming surgery."

5. Menvielle (this issue) says that "fewer than 20% of children who meet the diagnostic criteria for gender identity disorder of childhood before puberty will continue to experience gender dysphoria during and after puberty" (p. 362); Zucker et al. (this issue) found "a persistence rate of 12% for GID girls . . . and . . . 13.3% for GID boys" (p. 392); and de Vries and Cohen-Kettenis (this issue) report that recent studies show persistence rates between 12% and 27% (p. 305).

6. A person's *sexual orientation* concerns the sex of the people to whom a person is sexually attracted. One's sexual orientation is distinct from one's gender identity although some gender variant

individuals see themselves as attracted to people of the same sex. Lesbians, gay men, and bisexuals are not—simply by virtue of their sexual orientations—gender variant individuals.

7. None of the clinicians represented in this issue who offer SRS will offer such intervention for children younger than 18, although de Vries and Cohen-Kettenis (this issue) seem to favor making such treatment options available for even younger children. They say that "withholding [early physical medical] intervention is even more harmful for the adolescents' wellbeing during adolescence and in adulthood" (p. 315).

8. The American Academy of Pediatrics, Committee of Bioethics (1995) found that the mature minor doctrine was of limited application to the practice of pediatrics, saying that typically parents and guardians should provide "informed permission" for pediatric procedures while children should provide "assent," which is compliance with a medical procedure when the child is not of an age or does not have the maturity to make true consent possible. Assent requires an age-appropriate explanation of the child's condition and the treatment. The child, by assenting, agrees to the procedure and may feel empowered (in either the short or long term) by being able to play a role in the decision making, but does not provide true informed consent, which would be obtained from the parents or guardians.

9. Another exception that is invoked only in extreme instances allows the state, on a temporary or even a permanent basis, to replace the parent with a guardian for the child, or, through a judge, order life-saving medical treatment to be provided against a parent's wishes. This is only done when a parent acts in a manner inimical to a child's health and wellbeing. See, for example, Custody of a Minor, 393 N.E.2d 836 (Mass. 1979), in which the court gave the state agency the power to administer chemotherapy to a 3-year old child with leukemia whose parents wanted to give him alternative—and unproven—therapies.

10. In the case of O.G. v. Baum, 790 S.W.2d 839 (Tex. Ct. App. 1990), a 16-year-old Jehovah's Witness severely injured his arm and needed surgery to save it; the parents refused to consent to a blood transfusion that was likely to be needed during surgery. Rather than allowing the child to make a decision about the surgery by applying the mature minor doctrine, a Texas court appointed a temporary guardian for the child with the authority to consent to a transfusion if necessary.

11. Edwards-Leeper and Spack (this issue) cite the 2009 guidelines of the Endocrine Society (of which Cohen-Kettenis and Spack were among the authors). While these guidelines represent the consensus within an established subspecialty within the practice of medicine, these guidelines do not discuss the ethical issues raised herein.

12. Some jurisdictions require the more extensive surgery before they will amend a birth certificate to indicate a person's new assigned sex. New York City (but, oddly, not New York State) has such a law requiring genital surgery for a legal sex change. This law is currently being challenged in lawsuits by two trans people (Eligon, 2011).

13. Similar worries can be raised about hormone therapy. Hormone replacement treatment in post-menopausal women is controversial, partly because of a possible link to cancer and other complications. There might be such complications involved in the use of hormone therapy on gender variant and gender dysphoric individuals, although this is not discussed in the clinical articles.

REFERENCES

American Academy of Pediatrics, Committee on Bioethics. (1995). Informed consent, parental permission, and assent in pediatric practice. *Pediatrics 95*, 314–317.

American Psychiatric Association. (2000). *Diagnostic and statistical manual of mental disorders* (4th ed., text rev.). Washington, DC: Author.

American Psychological Association, Task Force on the Appropriate Therapeutic Response to Sexual Orientation. (2009). *Report of the Task Force on the Appropriate Therapeutic Response to Sexual Orientation*. Washington, DC: Author.

Beckwith, A. L. (2001). Cures versus choices: Agenda in sexual reorientation therapy. *Journal of Gay and Lesbian Psychotherapy* 5(3–4), 87–115.

Bell, A., Weinberg, M., & Hammersmith, S. (1981). *Sexual preference: Its development in men and women*. Bloomington, IN: Indiana University Press.

Besen, W. (2003). *Anything but straight: Unmasking the scandals and lies behind the ex-gay myth*. New York, NY: Routledge.

Bohan, J. (1996). *Psychology and sexual orientation: Coming to terms*. New York, NY: Routledge.

Commission on Psychotherapy by Psychiatrists, American Psychiatric Association. (2000). Position statement on therapies focused on attempts to change sexual orientation (reparative or conversion therapies). *American Journal of Psychiatry, 157*, 1719–1721.

Custody of a Minor, 393 N.E.2d 836 (Mass. 1979).

de Vries, A. L. C., & Cohen-Kettenis, P. T. (this issue), Clinical management of gender dysphoria in children and adolescents: The Dutch approach. *Journal of Homosexuality, 59*, 301–320.

Drescher, J. (2002). Sexual conversion ("reparative") therapies: History and update. In B. Jones & M. Hill (Eds.), *Mental Health issues in lesbian, gay, bisexual, and transgender communities* (pp. 71–92). Arlington, VA: American Psychiatric Publishing.

Drescher, J. (2010). Queer diagnoses: Parallels and contrasts in the history of homosexuality, gender variance, and the *Diagnostic and Statistical Manual*. *Archives of Sexual Behavior, 39*, 427–460.

Drescher, J., & Zucker, K. J. (Eds.). (2006). *Ex-gay research: Analyzing the Spitzer study and its relation to science, religion, politics, and culture*. Binghamton, NY: Harrington Park Press.

Edwards-Leeper, L., & Spack, N. (this issue). Psychological evaluation and medical treatment of transgender youth in an interdisciplinary "gender management service" (GeMS) in a major pediatric center. *Journal of Homosexuality, 59*, 321–336.

Ehrensaft, D. (this issue). From gender identity to gender identity creativity: True gender self child therapy. *Journal of Homosexuality, 59*, 337–356.

Eligon, J. (2011). Suits dispute city's rule on recording sex changes. *New York Times*, March 23, p. A24.

Erzen, T. (2006). *Straight to Jesus: Sexual and Christian conversions in the ex-gay movement*. Berkeley, CA: University of California Press.

Eugenides, J. (2002). *Middlesex*. New York, NY: Farrar, Straus and Giroux.

Fausto-Sterling, A. (2000). *Sexing the body: Gender politics and the construction of sexuality*. New York, NY: Basic Books.

Langer, S. J., & Martin, J. I. (2004). How dresses can make you mentally ill: Examining gender identity disorder in children. *Child and Adolescent Social Work Journal, 21*, 5–23.

Littleton v. Prange, 9 S.W.3d 223 (Tex. 1999).

M.T. v. J.T., 355 A.D.2d 204 (N.J. App. 1976).

Menvielle, E. (this issue). A comprehensive program for children with gender variant behaviors and gender identity disorders. *Journal of Homosexuality, 59*, 357–368.

Nicolosi, J. (1991). *Reparative therapy of male homosexuality: A new clinical approach*. Northvale, NJ: Jason Aronson.

O.G. v. Baum, 790 S.W.2d 839 (Tex. Ct. App. 1990).

Richardson, J. (1996). Setting limits on gender health. *Harvard Review of Psychiatry*, *4*, 49–53.

Richardson, J. (1999). Finding the disorder in gender identity disorder. *Harvard Review of Psychiatry*, *7*, 43–50.

Satinover, J. (1996). *Homosexuality and the politics of truth*. Grand Rapids, MI: Baker Publishing Group.

Shidlo, A., & Schroeder, M. (2002). Changing sexual orientation: A consumers' report. *Professional Psychology: Research & Practice*, *33*, 249–259.

Shidlo, A., Schroeder, M., & Drescher, J. (Eds.). (2002). *Sexual conversion therapy: Ethical, clinical, and research perspectives*. Binghamton, NY: Haworth Medical Press.

Spitzer, R. (2003). Can some gay men and lesbians change their sexual orientation? 200 participants reporting a change from homosexual to heterosexual orientation. *Archives of Sexual Behavior 32*, 403–417.

Stein, E. (1999). *The mismeasure of desire: The science, theory, and ethics of sexual orientation*. New York, NY: Oxford University Press.

Williams, W. (1986). *The spirit and the flesh: Sexual diversity in American Indian culture*. Boston, MA: Beacon Press.

Wolkomir, M. (2006). *Be not deceived: The sacred and sexual struggles of gay and ex-gay Christian men*. New Brunswick, NJ: Rutgers University Press.

Zucker, K. J. (2008). Children with gender identity disorder: Is there a best practice? *Neuropsychiatre de L'enfance et de L'adoscence 56*, 358–364.

Zucker, K. J., Finegan, J. K., Doering, R. W., & Bradley S. J. (1984). Two sub-groups of gender-problem children. *Archives of Sexual Behavior 13*, 27–39.

Zucker, K. J., Wood, H., Singh, D., & Bradley, S. J. (this issue). A developmental, biopsychosocial model for the treatment of children with gender identity disorder. *Journal of Homosexuality*, *59*, 369–397.

Gender Dysphoric/Gender Variant (GD/GV) Children and Adolescents: Summarizing What We Know and What We Have Yet to Learn

JACK DRESCHER, MD

New York Medical College, New York, New York, USA

WILLIAM BYNE, MD, PhD

Mount Sinai School of Medicine, New York, New York, New York, USA

The optimal approach to treating minors with gender dysphoria/ gender variance (GD/GV) is much more controversial than treating these phenomena in adults. This is because children have limited capacity to participate in decision making regarding their own treatment, and even adolescents have no legal ability to provide informed consent. Minors must, therefore, depend on parents or other caregivers to make treatment decisions on their behalf, including those that will influence the course of their lives in the long term. Presently, the highest level of evidence available for selecting among the various approaches to treatment is best characterized as "expert opinion." Yet, opinions vary widely among experts and are influenced by theoretical orientation and assumptions and beliefs regarding the origins of gender identity, as well as its perceived malleability at particular stages of development. This article outlines some of the more salient points raised by the clinicians who treat GD/GV and their discussants. This article summarizes what the editors believe is known and what has yet to be learned about minors with GD/GV, their families, their treatment, and their surrounding cultures.

adolescence, gender variance, pubertal suspension, transgender, transsexual, treatment

One goal of this issue is to assist parents and other primary caregivers who face the dilemma of treatment selection. We wished to provide both authoritative detailed descriptions of the various treatment goals and approaches to treatment of minors with gender dysphoria/gender variance (GD/GV) and scholarly comparative analyses of the various approaches. A second goal is to stimulate discussion among the stakeholders in this debate, including consumers of clinical services, clinicians, academics and gender activists. We are pleased to report that the contributors have done an admirable job and we believe this special issue fulfills both goals. We hope this contribution will facilitate the further thought, discussions, and research needed to optimize not only clinical approaches to gender variance but the quality of life and social acceptance of gender variant individuals.

The optimal approach to treating minors with GD/GV is much more controversial than treating these phenomena in adults. This is because children have limited capacity to participate in decision making regarding their own treatment, and even adolescents have no legal ability to provide informed consent. Minors must, therefore, depend on parents or other caregivers to make treatment decisions on their behalf, including those that will influence the course of their lives in the long term. One complication in the process of selecting among treatment options for minors is the lack of randomized controlled treatment outcome studies for any presentation of GV/GD. In the absence of such studies, the highest level of evidence available for selecting among the various approaches to treatment is best characterized as "expert opinion." Yet, opinions vary widely among experts, and are influenced by theoretical orientation, as well as assumptions and beliefs regarding the origins of gender identity as well as its perceived malleability at particular stages of development. Parents and other primary caregivers may be overwhelmed by the range of professional opinions and options and have difficulty making decisions for minors in their care. Alternatively, instead of weighing the evidence available regarding each treatment approach, they may seek out clinicians who mirror their own world views, believing that goals consistent with their views are in the best interest of their children.

As a service to our readers, below we outline some of the more salient points raised by the clinicians and their discussants (de Vries & Cohen-Kettenis, this issue; Dresher & Byne, this issue; Edwards-Leeper & Spack, this issue; Ehrensaft, this issue; Fausto-Sterling, this issue; Menvielle, this issue; Minter, this issue; Reiner& Reiner, this issue; Rettew, this issue; Schwartz, this issue; Stein, this issue; Zucker, Wood, Singh, & Bradley, this issue). It is a summary of what we believe is known and what has yet to be learned about minors with GD/GV, their families, their treatment, and their surrounding cultures. By delineating the best approximation of what we do and do not know, we hope to help parents and caregivers in their decision-making process, to help professionals thinking of making referrals for care, and to lay out some areas of future research in the treatment of minors with GD/GV.

ABOUT THE CHILDREN AND ADOLESCENTS WITH GD/GV

What We Know

- The children and adolescents (collectively referred to here as minors) who present for clinical evaluation and treatment are a heterogeneous group.
- For some of these minors, the major issue is cross-gender behaviors or identifications; for others, the gender issues seem to be epiphenomena of psychopathology, exposure to trauma, or attempts to resolve problems such as higher social status or other benefits they perceive to be associated with the other gender.
- In general, a minor's notions of gender and gender identity will vary with age.
- Until children master the capacity for operational thought (between the ages of 5–7 years), they tend to conflate sex and gender with surface expressions of gender role.
- Prior to developing the capacity for operational thought, a child may think that merely wearing the clothes associated with boys will make one a boy, while the clothes or hairstyles associated with girls will make one a girl.
- Minors with GD/GV challenge the conventional notions of gender of their parents, extended families, schools, and neighbors.
- Despite the attention they get in the popular media, the number of minors with GD/GV is low in the general population; while still relatively small, the number presenting to gender clinics in recent years is increasing.
- The gender dysphoria of the majority of children with GD/GV does not persist into adolescence, and when it does not the children are referred to as "desisters."
- Prospective studies indicate that the majority of those who desist by or during adolescence grow up to be gay, not transgender, and that a smaller proportion grow up to be heterosexual.
- There is at present no way to predict in which children GD/GV will or will not persist into adolescence or beyond.
- While in the case of disorders of sexual development (DSD or intersex conditions), the emergence of GD/GV relative to neonatally assigned gender is somewhat predictable based on biological factors (such as status of androgen receptors and fetal androgen production), this is not the case in minors with GD/GV when a DSD is not present.

- GD/GV that persists into adolescence is more likely to persist into adulthood.
- The presence of GD/GV does not necessarily indicate the presence of concomitant psychopathology.
- GD/GV may be mimicked by gender confusion that occurs as an epiphenomenon of other problems (e.g., gender confusion as the result of sexual trauma or delusions in the context of psychotic disorders).
- Severe concomitant psychopathology must be addressed prior to addressing gender issues in minors with GD/GV.
- Compared to the general population, children referred to a gender identity clinic have a higher incidence of autism spectrum disorders, an association that has only recently been reported and remains little studied and poorly understood.
- The presentations and needs of prepubertal children with GD/GV differ from those of adolescents, requiring different clinical approaches for the two age groups.
- Entering school and entering puberty are particularly stressful developmental periods for minors with GD/GV.
- Children entering puberty with persisting gender dysphoria (persisters) may become psychologically distressed as they develop the unwanted secondary sex characteristics of their natal gender. This may lead to onset of severe anxiety, depression, and perhaps even suicidal ideation and gestures.
- Minors seeking treatment for GD/GV are unable to obtain such treatment without consent from a parent or legal guardian.
- Empirical studies suggest that the majority of adolescent persisters do well when they receive family and professional support for early interventions that will eventually ease the way for an adult transition.
- Children and adolescents with GD/GV are often subject to teasing, harassment, bullying, and even violence, not only from strangers but sometimes even from their own families.

What We Have Yet to Learn

- The "causes" of GD/GV in minors.
- The relative contributions of biology and environmental factors to GD/GV.
- How gender identity develops in anyone.
- The extent to which gender identity in individuals with GD/GV does or does not develop along the same lines as gender identity in cisgender (non-transgender) individuals.
- The relative contributions of biology and psychosocial environmental factors in the development of gender identity, whether cisgender or transgender.

- The extent to which the stress experienced by minors with GD/GV should be attributed to GD/GV, per se, as opposed to society's nonacceptance of gender atypicality—or whether there is even just one answer to this question.
- Why the gender dysphoria of most children desists around puberty while it persists in others into adolescence and adulthood.

ABOUT THE FAMILES

What We Know

- There is no contemporary empirical research demonstrating that GD/GV results from any particular parenting style.
- Families vary in their reactions to their children with GD/GV, ranging from rejection and punitive responses to complete and early acceptance of social transition from the natal gender to other forms of gender expression.
- Treatment is usually initiated by families for children and adolescents with GD/GV.
- When families seek professional advice and treatment, they often do so after having failed in their own efforts to have a child with GD/GV conform to gender norms.
- Many families are deeply concerned about the present and future social implications for a child who has GD/GV.
- Families may themselves be stigmatized for having a child with GD/GV, both by nonrelatives (neighbors, school officials, strangers) and extended family members.
- Some families seek professional treatment hoping to prevent either adult homosexuality or transsexualism in their child or adolescent with GD/GV.
- Families have a role to play in whatever treatment option they, in collaboration with mental health professionals (and age-appropriate input from the minor), choose for their child or adolescent with GD/GV.
- Parents of minors with GD/GV who feel isolated appear to benefit from the social support provided by both mental health professionals and peer support groups; there also appears to be a growing online presence of family support groups, some of which offer oversight by child and adolescent mental health professionals.

What We Have Yet to Learn

- Whether increased cultural acceptance of diverse forms of gender expression will lead to fewer parents seeking psychological interventions for their minors with GD/GV.

ABOUT THE TREATMENTS MINORS WITH GD/GV RECEIVE

What We Know

- All the clinicians who contributed to this issue are highly committed to helping children and families cope with a complex situation with few easy solutions.
- Clinicians treating minors with GD/GV range from those who work with large interdisciplinary groups in academic centers and engage in empirical research to those doing no formal research and engaging in solo clinical practice.
- In contrast to the treatment of most diagnoses from the *Diagnostic and Statistical Manual of Mental Disorders* (4th ed., text rev; *DSM-IV-TR*; American Psychiatric Association, 2000) where emphasis is on changing thoughts, feelings, and behaviors, the consensus treatment of what *DSM-IV-TR* refers to as GID, at least from adolescence onward, often emphasizes modification of the body.
- There is a need for more research on the treatment of minors with GD/GV, particularly prospective longitudinal studies that employ standardized and validated assessment instruments.
- The randomized controlled trial is the form of study that provides the most convincing evidence favoring one treatment over another, but such studies are neither feasible nor clearly ethical for GD/GV (e.g., few parents would consent for their child's treatment to be assigned randomly).
- There are no reliable screening instruments that differentiate between young children in whom GD/GV will desist and those in whom it will persist.
- Some clinicians believe that facilitating childhood gender transition may increase the probability of persistence into adolescence and adulthood.
- Some clinicians view persistence as an undesirable outcome in light of the medical risks associated with hormonal and surgical gender transition and the chronic hormonal replacement therapy.
- The malleability of a child's gender identification is believed to decrease with age, and some clinicians believe that childhood interventions—compared to interventions in adolescence—have an increased likelihood of preventing persistence into adulthood.
- No clinician recommends medical (hormonal/surgical) treatment for GD/GV for prepubertal children.
- Clinicians have differing views on whether GD/GV in minors should be regarded as a purely medical condition, a psychiatric disorder, or a normal variation of human gender expression.
- Clinicians may use differing terminology that is either pathologizing (e.g., GIDC) or normalizing (e.g., GV) to describe the clinical populations they are treating.

- Adopting a nonpathologizing view of GV does not mean that it can never be a symptom of some other disorder or an attempt to solve an emotional problem rather than a healthy expression of self.
- Clinicians have strong and differing views on what constitutes appropriate forms of public cross-gender expression in minors with GD/GV.
- Clinicians aim their interventions in a manner that is age appropriate to a particular minor. As a minor's decision-making capacity increases, especially as they enter adolescence, they are allowed a greater role in clinical decision making regarding their own treatment.
- Clinical responses to prepubertal children with GD/GV vary. At one pole, clinicians discourage social transitions such as name changes and public gender role changes until a child reaches puberty and proves to be a persister. At the other pole, clinicians support not only cross-gender identifications but expressions of gender transition such as name change and public gender role change, even though it is not known whether the child's cross-gender behaviors and identifications will desist or persist.
- Based on evidence that GD/GV persisting into adolescence is more likely to persist into adulthood, some clinicians take a different approach with adolescents (more supportive of gender transition) than with children (neutral or discouraging of cross-gender manifestations) with GID.
- The treatment literature is lacking in terms of rigorous comparative evaluations of these differing approaches, thus, subjective factors and values play a role in a clinician's choice of approaches.
- The limited existing evidence suggests that medical suppression of puberty has minimal associated risks; however, long-term studies on a large number of subjects are lacking.
- Pubertal suspension both buys more time for the adolescent and health-care providers to more fully consider the desire for hormonal and surgical gender transition, and minimizes the development of undesired secondary sex characteristics that are not fully reversible by cross-sex hormones and gender reassignment surgery once they have developed.
- The legal age to give informed consent in most jurisdictions is 18 years. Although cross-sex hormones are sometimes administered earlier, in the absence of a disorder of sex development, gender reassignment surgery is not done prior to the age of 18 in the United States, Canada, or the Netherlands.
- The existing position statements of the American Psychiatric Association and the American Psychological Association regarding so-called reparative therapies deal primary with effort to change an individual's sexual orientation and do not directly address the ethics of trying to change an individual's gender identity.

What We Have Yet to Learn

- As it is a relatively recent approach to GD/GV adolescents, we cannot be certain of either the physical or psychological long-term effects of suppressing puberty through the use of hormone blockers.
- Whether outcomes will be as uniformly positive when such treatments are instituted outside specialty clinics in academic settings.
- Whether early acceptance of a child's expressed cross-gender identification, including allowing full childhood gender transition, encourages persistence of GD/GV into adolescence and adulthood.
- Whether early discouragement of a child's gender role transition prevents persistence of GD/GV into adolescence and adulthood.
- Whether clinical efforts to change a GD/GV minor's gender identity in order to prevent adult transsexualism should be considered ethical or unethical.

ABOUT CULTURAL ATTITUDES MINORS WITH GD/GV FACE

What We Know

- Compared to 30 years ago (when the diagnosis of GIDC first appeared in the *DSM*), in some communities, cultural change has been characterized by increased social acceptance of gender atypical children (and adults).
- Presentations in the popular media suggest that the culture is fascinated by GD/GV in children and adolescents.
- There is an increased, albeit gradual, acceptance of transgender people in many cultures around the world.
- Increasingly, states and localities are enacting legal protections from bullying and discrimination for transgender minors in schools.
- Increasingly, schools are permitting children with cross-gender identifications to express their affirmed gender identity.
- Stigma against minors and adults with GD/GV persists and is further exacerbated by the stigma associated with diagnoses of mental disorders, in this case Gender Identity Disorder of Childhood.
- Access to endocrinological interventions for adolescents (and adults) with GD/GV is often not covered by either private or public health insurance.
- The American Psychiatric Association' forthcoming *DSM-5* (in press) is likely to retain diagnoses for GD/GV individuals that will be renamed Gender Dysphoria in Children and Gender Dysphoria in Adolescents or Adults.
- GD/GV raises questions about what does and what does not constitute a diagnosable psychopathological condition versus a normal variant of human gender expression; and further, whether psychiatric diagnoses in the *DSM* necessarily require the presence of psychopathology.

- Economic concerns regarding access to treatment are frequently enmeshed with discussions of whether GID should be considered a physical or mental disorder and this enmeshment often infuses discussions of exactly what constitutes a mental disorder.
- The current legal systems in most countries do not have uniform mechanisms in place to accommodate gender transition of minors.

What We Have Yet to Learn

- Whether society will grow more or less accepting of transgender, transsexual, and other gender-nonconforming individuals.
- Whether it is professionally ethical, given the inability to distinguish between persisters and desisters, to affirm a child's gender role transition at an early age.
- Whether it is psychologically damaging and, therefore, professionally unethical to discourage a child's gender role transition at an early age.
- The future status of the diagnoses of Gender Identity Disorder of Childhood and Transsexualism in the forthcoming (2015) International Classification of Diseases, 11th Revision (ICD-11).
- Whether clinical responses to minors with GD/GV organized around the notion of a limited range of acceptable gender expressions—from which the minors are deviating and toward which they can aspire by transitioning to the other or opposite gender—reinforce binary gender stereotypes upon which intolerance of GV and homophobia are based.
- Whether the rate of hormonal and surgical gender transitions will increase or decrease as these services become more widely available at the same time social tolerance of a wider range of gender expressions, including gender queer, appears to be increasing.

REFERENCES

American Psychiatric Association. (2000). *Diagnostic and statistical manual of mental disorders* (4th ed., text rev.). Washington, DC: Author.

American Psychiatric Association. (in press). *Diagnostic and statistical manual of mental disorders* (5th ed.). Washington, DC: Author.

de Vries, A. L. C., & Cohen-Kettenis, P. T. (this issue). Clinical management of gender dysphoria in children and adolescents: The Dutch approach. *Journal of Homosexuality, 59*, 301–320.

Drescher, J., & Byne, W. (this issue). Introduction to the special issue on "The treatment of gender dysphoric/gender variant children and adolescents." *Journal of Homosexuality, 59*, 295–300.

Edwards-Leeper, L., & Spack, N. P. (this issue). Psychological evaluation and medical treatment of transgender youth in an interdisciplinary "gender management service" (GeMS) in a major pediatric center. *Journal of Homosexuality*, *59*, 321–336.

Ehrensaft, D. (this issue). From gender identity disorder to gender identity creativity: True gender self child therapy. *Journal of Homosexuality*, *59*, 337–356.

Fausto-Sterling, A. (this issue). The dynamic development of gender variability. *Journal of Homosexuality*, *59*, 398–421.

Menvielle, E. (this issue). A comprehensive program for children with gender variant behaviors and gender identity disorders. *Journal of Homosexuality*, *59*, 357–368.

Minter, S. P. (this issue). Supporting transgender children: New legal, social, and medical approaches. *Journal of Homosexuality*, *59*, 422–433.

Reiner, W. G., & Reiner, D. T. (this issue). Thoughts on the nature of identity: How disorders of sex development inform clinical research about gender identity disorders. *Journal of Homosexuality*, *59*, 434–449.

Rettew, D. (this issue). Apples to committee consensus: The challenge of gender identity classification. *Journal of Homosexuality*, *59*, 450–459.

Schwartz, D. (this issue). Listening to children imagining gender: Observing the inflation of an idea. *Journal of Homosexuality*, *59*, 460–479.

Stein, E. (this issue). Commentary on the treatment of gender variant and gender dysphoric children and adolescents: Common themes and ethical reflections. *Journal of Homosexuality*, *59*, 480–500.

Zucker, K. J., Wood, H., Singh, D., & Bradley, S. J. (this issue). A developmental, biopsychosocial model for the treatment of children with gender identity disorder. *Journal of Homosexuality*, *59*, 369–397.

Index

Page numbers in **bold** represent figures and tables